THE SOCIOLOGY OF SOCIAL PROBLEMS

Theoretical Perspectives and Methods of Intervention

ADAM JAMROZIK
and
LUISA NOCELLA

CAMBRIDGE
UNIVERSITY PRESS

PUBLISHED BY THE PRESS SYNDICATE OF THE UNIVERSITY OF CAMBRIDGE
The Pitt Building, Trumpington Street, Cambridge, United Kingdom

CAMBRIDGE UNIVERSITY PRESS
The Edinburgh Building, Cambridge CB2 2RU, UK   http://www.cup.cam.ac.uk
40 West 20th Street, New York, NY 10011–4211, USA   http://www.cup.org
10 Stamford Road, Oakleigh, Melbourne 3166, Australia

First published 1998

Printed in China by L. Rex Printing Company Ltd.

Typeset in New Baskerville 10/12 pt

A catalogue record for this book is available from the British Library

National Library of Australia Cataloguing in Publication data

Jamrozik, Adam.
The sociology of social problems: theoretical perspectives and
methods of intervention.
Bibliography.
Includes index.
ISBN 0 521 59932 6 (pbk.).
ISBN 0 521 59070 1.
1. Social problems. 2. Australia – Social conditions.
I. Nocella, Luisa D. II. Title.
361.1

ISBN 0 521 59070 1 hardback
ISBN 0 521 59932 6 paperback

THE SOCIOLOGY OF SOCIAL PROBLEMS
Theoretical Perspectives and Methods of Intervention

Social problems such as unemployment, poverty and drug addiction are a fact of life in industrialised societies. This book examines the sociology of social problems from new and challenging perspectives. It analyses how social problems emerge and are defined as such, who takes responsibility for them, who is threatened by them, and how they are managed, solved or ignored. The authors examine and critique existing theories of social problems before developing their own theoretical framework. Their theory of residualist conversion of social problems explains how certain social problems threaten legitimate power structures, so that problems of a social or political nature are transformed into personal problems, and the 'helping professions' are left to intervene. This book will become a key reference on class, inequality and social intervention, and an important text for students in sociology and social work courses.

Adam Jamrozik and Luisa Nocella both work in the School of Social Work and Social Policy at the University of South Australia. Jamrozik has previously held positions at the Social Policy Research Centre at the University of NSW and the Department of Sociology at Flinders University. He is the author of *Class, Inequality and the State, Children and Society* and co-author of *Social Change and Cultural Transformation*, published by Cambridge University Press in 1995. Nocella, a practising social worker, is currently a doctoral candidate.

Contents

Tables

Figures

Preface and Acknowledgements

Social problems are integral to our daily living. Some social problems emerge unexpectedly, and disappear equally fast from our concerns. Other problems acquire a perennial quality. Unemployment, poverty, urban traffic congestion are on our minds and on our television screens. Social problems are of concern to sociologists, social workers, politicians, and, at one time or another, to all of us. They are studied, remedied, sometimes even solved; often they are forgotten because they do not affect us personally. Nevertheless, social problems are always with us.

This book is about the sociology of social problems. It examines how social problems emerge, who is concerned about them, who is threatened by them, and how societies attempt to solve them, attenuate them or perhaps ignore them. This is a theoretical book. The text is based on a theoretical framework that we have developed to enable us to systematically analyse social problems as social phenomena that emerge in society as a form of threat to values and interests dominant in society at a given time and that lead to methods of intervention designed to attenuate, control or solve such problems. In our theoretical framework, a social problem is a form of a 'negative residue' that logically emerges from the everyday pursuit of dominant values and interests. We have defined our framework as a 'Theory of residualist conversion of social problems'.

The types of social problems we examine in this book are problems that often affect the whole community, but through certain methods of intervention are converted into individuals' problems (usually individuals and families in the lower social strata). Other problems remain in the public arena and are solved or controlled through political action such as legislation, allocation of funds or change in policy. Yet other problems become our constant companions.

This book has been written for sociologists and other professionals who are concerned with social problems – as researchers, administrators, and members of the 'helping professions' (such as social workers, psychologists, counsellors etc.) – who provide services to individuals and families experiencing social problems as their personal problems. It should also be of relevance to anyone who is interested in what happens in society. It is not a 'how to' book, but one that seeks to explain how social problems emerge and why. It looks at the social actors concerned with social problems. It is a theoretical book, but a readable one.

This book is the fruition of three years of research and teaching in sociology at Adelaide's Flinders University and in social work at the University of South Australia. It has been a joint effort, and although Adam Jamrozik did a bit more of the writing, Luisa Nocella contributed her share through writing, research, and especially the chapter on the family. Other people have also contributed to this effort. We wish to particularly acknowledge assistance from the Australian Research Council's Small Research Grants, which we received in the Department of Sociology at Flinders University, and some additional assistance from the Faculty Research Performance Fund at the School of Social Work and Social Policy, University of South Australia. For assistance with research we want to thank Gail Smith for her efforts in finding research material and contributing helpful comments. To Ruth Errey go our thanks for editing the manuscript. Jonathan Flynn also edited some work and provided useful suggestions. Finally, our sincere thanks and appreciation must go to Phillipa McGuinness, Commissioning Editor of the Cambridge University Press, and her associates Sharon Mullins, Rosemary Perkins and Jane Farago, as well as Glenys Osborne, the copy-editor.

ADAM JAMROZIK AND LUISA NOCELLA

CHAPTER 1

Introduction: Theoretical Perspectives on Social Problems

Social problems are an integral part of social life. The term 'social problem' applies to social conditions, processes, societal arrangements or attitudes that are commonly perceived to be undesirable, negative, and threatening certain values or interests such as social cohesion, maintenance of law and order, moral standards, stability of social institutions, economic prosperity or individual freedoms. A social problem may also be experienced as a feeling of collective guilt created through an awareness of collective neglect to remove or alleviate certain undesirable social conditions that negatively affect some sections of society.

In this definition of social problems therefore there is no presumed value- or attitudinal-neutrality in perception, interpretation or intervention. This particular attribute differentiates social phenomena that are perceived to be social problems from other social or physical phenomena or conditions that are regarded as problems *tout court*, and that are perceived perhaps as not quite desirable or pleasant but without an element of threat. Furthermore, a social problem is also a condition 'created' by society that is, potentially at least, feasibly alleviated or solved by society. On the other hand, some physical phenomena or 'natural disasters' such as earthquakes, droughts or floods occur beyond social control, although the knowledge of their probability enables societies to take preventive or remedial actions. With such physical phenomena, the knowledge of the ability to take preventive or remedial actions but the failure to do so would then be perceived as a social problem.

In common perceptions and usage, the term 'social problem' may be applied to phenomena or conditions of non-societal origins such as those mentioned above. While undesirable, unpleasant or in some way

1

threatening, these cannot legitimately be called 'social'. To be appropriately regarded as social problems, social phenomena or conditions must therefore have three identifiable minimum features: first, the condition must have an identifiable societal origin; second, the condition must constitute a threat or be perceived to constitute a threat to certain values or interests; and third, the condition must be amenable to removal or at least attenuation or solution. These three features may not always be immediately and clearly 'visible' in a condition, but can be revealed through appropriate sociological analysis.

Theories of Social Problems

There are a number of sociological theories of social problems. These range from the 'social pathology' perspective that originated in the 19th century from theories formulated by Francis Galton, Cesare Lombroso and others, to 'conflict theory' and 'critical theory' derived from the sociological insights of Karl Marx, and formulated and elaborated upon by the Frankfurt Institute of Social Research. In between, there are other theories and perspectives, such as the 'disorganisation theory' originated in the Chicago School of Sociology in the 1920s; the 'anomie theory' of Robert Merton; and a range of social deviance theories developed by Howard Becker, John Kitsuse, Aaron Cicourel and others. One of the more recent sociological theories is the 'constructionist theory', which focuses not on social problems *per se*, but on the processes through which social problems are identified and on the social actors who identify them (Rubington and Weinberg 1995). A number of constructionist theories were formulated by American sociologists in the 1960s and early 1970s, at a time when issues of social order and social cohesion in the United States became a matter of grave concern. Most theories of social problems at that time were concerned with problems more appropriately defined as problems of social deviance, and for this reason analyses of these phenomena tended to focus on populations whose characteristics departed in various degrees from the 'norm', although what the desired 'norm' was supposed to be is not always clear. The constructionist theorists, however, shifted the focus from the 'deviant population' and its 'problems' to the people who made claims about certain phenomena as 'problems', and to the activities these people engaged in to make their claims accepted by society (Spector and Kitsuse 1987).

Although more recent analyses of society from the perspective of the postmodern era, such as the studies by Zygmunt Bauman (1992, 1995), do not focus specifically on social problems as such, they identify sources of social problems in the structural and ideological fragmentation of society and in the resulting lack of a dominant social model or dominant social value to be followed. The great variety of postmodern perspectives on contemporary society presents a new problem in social analysis, as such a variety challenges the possibility of objective perceptions or even the existence of phenomena that may be appropriately referred to as social in nature.

A critical overview of sociological theories of social problems is presented in Chapter 2. With such a variety of theories and perspectives it is relevant to consider which aspects of society would constitute the field of study that might be legitimately called the sociology of social problems. Much sociological analysis is indeed concerned with aspects of society that are perceived to be in some degree 'problematic' and that are therefore the subject of concern and research interest. However, the problematic nature of certain social phenomena may simply mean either that the nature of a phenomenon is not clearly understood or that it is perceived and explained in such a variety of theories or perspectives that it creates confusion and uncertainty.

In contrast, a 'social problem', by definition, is a social condition that is regarded as in some ways 'undesirable' by society or by some sections of society, in that it represents a 'threat' of some kind – explicit, latent or potential. From a similar perspective, too, the term 'social problem' is commonly used and understood in everyday life. As Merton and Nisbet (1976) state, the term 'social problem' is applied to any social condition that is seen to differ from what people think it ought to be. The normative aspect present in studies of phenomena perceived in society or in some of its sections as 'social problems' is therefore important for the sociologist to consider, more so than in studies of phenomena where a 'threat' is not present in the problem. Nevertheless, because of the normative subjectivity in perceptions of what constitutes a social problem, it needs to be emphasised that studies of the sociology of social problems do not constitute an entirely discrete category of sociological studies.

Social problems, due to their very nature, can be adequately explained only in the context of the society in which they occur. Furthermore, although some social problems (e.g. violence in public places) may be experienced by the whole population of a society, others (e.g. unemployment among young people) may be experienced only by certain individuals or social groupings with similar characteristics. Most social problems do not occur in, or are not experienced in, the same frequency or intensity throughout the entire social structure. In Western industrialised societies, such problems as poverty, unemployment, violence, child abuse and so on are social phenomena that occur with greater or lesser frequency among certain population strata identified

⌐y social characteristics such as income, education, occupation and other attributes of social class. The nature and frequency of certain social problems also differ among population groupings identified by such attributes as age, ethnicity, religion, or geographic locality. Therefore, while the causes of social problems experienced by some population groupings rather than others can be explained by societal arrangements in the distribution of societal resources, the people who are experiencing social problems with greater frequency or intensity than others tend to be perceived as 'problem populations'. Such shifts of perceptions, from the social nature of the problem to the population experiencing the problem, distract attention from societal arrangements and effectively confirm and validate the legitimacy of these arrangements, thus validating a given social system and its structure of power. In effect, because social problems tend to be more frequently experienced in the 'lower' social classes of the population, they are perceived in class terms. However, in that perception the class structure of society is concealed because the problems are explained by the personal characteristics, real or imputed, of the affected population, and little attention is given to the problems' structural character. This is not surprising, as much research on social problems is carried out in a 'truncated perspective', being focused on the populations in which social problems are experienced with greatest frequency and intensity – a 'captive audience' of social researchers.

For these reasons, most currently prevailing theories of social problems do not adequately explain these problems' social nature and causative links. Consequently, when these theories are operationalised in intervention methods, they do not achieve the manifestly stated objectives – that is, they do not solve a problem that is intrinsically social because they do not address the source of the problem. Rather, the methods used reinforce beliefs that the problem is related to the characteristics of the affected population. Furthermore, because of the tendency for theories of social problems to perceive social problems as those of 'deviant' or 'problem' populations, the intervention methods based on such theories become a part of experience-based knowledge, or 'practice wisdom', and act more as methods of social control than as methods of problem solving. Practice wisdom becomes a kind of 'theory' acquired by people whose task is to intervene in social problems at the proverbial 'coal-face'. Here, the solution may be at best a remedy in individual cases to problems that are experienced repeatedly as the 'private problems' of the affected population. These problems are then perceived as being related to the characteristics of that population, not as social problems that are the outcomes of much wider societal arrangements.

In the study of social problems it is the society's dominant value system and the corresponding social structure of power in which a given problem occurs that have to be understood first. For example, if it is accepted that Australia is a class society – social class being the most significant dimension of social structure and its divisions, and over-riding differences of sex and gender, age, ethnicity or religion – then the presence, perception and interpretation of (as well as any methods of intervention in) phenomena perceived as social problems will be determined by that structure. Similarly, if for example it is believed that the dominant feature of Western societies is the power of patriarchy, then all social phenomena, especially those perceived to be social problems, will tend to be perceived, interpreted and acted upon from this perspective. Again, if a certain social condition such as chronic poverty or unemployment is believed to be a manifestation of 'flawed' personalities or characters of the people experiencing the condition, then intervention methods will predictably be aimed at 'correcting the flaw'.

As stated earlier, social problems are social phenomena that threaten, or are seen to threaten, the values and dominant interests of a society. Values and interests are most clearly revealed when they are threatened; or, as Martin Rein has pointed out, 'concealed sources of power and prestige come to the fore when their position is threatened' (1976:37). It is therefore in the study of social problems that sociology can achieve its great potential as a social science. By examining the kind of phenomena to which societies react or feel compelled to react, or do not react and do not feel compelled to react, the societies' manifest as well as underlying values and dominant interests are revealed.

Theoretical Assumptions of this Book

In this book we examine the existing sociological theories of social problems and then present a theory that draws on these theories while being grounded in empirical observations of social problems in con-temporary industrialised societies. We think our theory adequately reflects and explains the nature of social problems in contemporary societies. The main theoretical assumption underpinning the analysis in the book is that the so-called pathological conditions that are commonly referred to as social problems – such as poverty, unemployment, family dislocation and so on – emerge logically from societally pursued dominant values, interests and corresponding goals. These unwelcome negative conditions constitute a 'residue' of those mainstream activities directed at the pursuit of such dominant values, interests and corres-ponding goals. In other words, social problems do not arise so much from the disjunction between societal goals and institutionalised means provided for their fulfilment, as Merton (1957) has argued (however important this disjunction might be), but from the pursuit of the dominant values *per se*. The problems constitute a 'normal' by-product, a residue, of these pursuits. In this kind of dialectical relationship, 'each silver lining creates a cloud'.

The system of goal pursuit has, as it were, a built-in failure rate, and the extent or negative intensity of failure tends to be directly related to the value and difficulties attached to the attainment of the pursued goal. Paradoxically, a higher rate and intensity of failure enhances the value of the pursued goal. For example, the value of a position in an organisational hierarchy is enhanced by the number of people applying for the position, all applicants except one necessarily failing in the process. Similarly, persistence in pursuing certain goals that are promoted as universally desirable leads to directly related failures. Pursuing wealth through business activities or through gambling is a notable example of such activities. It follows, then, that the solution or attenuation of any such problems would have to entail interference in, or modification or abandonment of, the pursuit of certain goals.

In other words, the solutions of social problems are to be found in changing the structural arrangements of society. It may therefore be expected that such solutions would not be welcomed by society's dominant interests. For this reason, social problems tend to be explained either in terms of external causes (and therefore beyond the society's control), or as related to the behavioural or personality characteristics of the affected population, with solutions then sought in changing that population's attitudes and behaviour. At best, the solution is sometimes sought in marginal adjustments of the existing arrangements 'on the periphery', which might provide certain flexibility in those arrangements and perhaps a marginal attenuation in the frequency or intensity of the problem, and thus demonstrates and even reinforces the legitimacy and success of the system and its structure of power.

Being a direct outcome of the pursuit of cherished goals that are striven for through a variety of institutional means, social problems tend to acquire an intergenerational continuity. Social reproduction of values, interests and organisational structures therefore also entails a reproduction of social problems. This is particularly evident in problems emanating from the operation of social institutions concerned with the allocation of society's resources and of those concerned with education, socialisation, maintenance of social order, the labour market and industrial relations. At the same time, as the form or even the nature of activities performed by these institutions changes, this leads to new situations, outcomes, and corresponding social problems. If the means and methods of intervention designed to ameliorate or control such social problems do not take the new situations into account, they become ineffective or even irrelevant. Thus, for example, due mainly (if not exclusively) to changes in the nature and technology of economic production, the nature of unemployment in Australia and throughout the industrialised world has significantly altered in recent decades, becoming increasingly entrenched in certain sections of the population. Yet perceptions of unemployment and corresponding remedial measures have remained largely unaltered. Indeed, the prevailing recommendations for solutions are seen in the time-honoured search for greater productivity, an increase in the gross domestic product, lower wages (for workers but not for managers), freedom of employers to hire, retrench or dismiss staff, reduction of services provided by the public sector, and greater international competitiveness. None of these measures appears to be achieving the desired results, and entrenched unemployment has therefore become a 'normal', permanent state of affairs that is seemingly beyond solution.

Like all social phenomena, social problems are 'social constructs' – that is, they are social conditions, activities, attitudes and so on that at some stage may be perceived as 'problems', although they might have existed in society for some time without being seen in this way. The change in perceptions signifies a change in values, attitudes or interests, or new knowledge and awareness of a real or potential threat. Changes in attitudes towards air pollution caused by petrol fumes, towards ecology, towards the treatment of children, and towards racist views are some examples of such changes in perceptions.

On the other hand, certain phenomena that might be perceived initially as social problems but that acquire a somewhat 'permanent' character may also acquire the character of 'normalcy' and so obtain acceptance by society. Paradoxically, this change in attitude may be assisted by, and be an outcome of, the methods of intervention initially applied to control, attenuate, or solve the perceived problem. For example, single parenthood was initially perceived as a social problem, but later acquired a degree of legitimacy through public income-support measures. In Australia, such support measures were at first provided as a 'supporting mother's benefit' designed to alleviate the extremes of poverty in such situations; this has now become a 'sole parent pension', thus changing the formal quality of the support and also changing the social status of the recipients towards a degree of legitimacy. Another example of a socially significant change has occurred in the perception of organised gambling. Historically, Australian society has been perceived as a society of gamblers but, except for the past two or three decades, organised gambling (however small-scale, such as playing cards for money) was a breach of the law and was pursued as such by law-enforcement authorities. Now, organised gambling in a variety of forms – casinos in every capital city and poker machines in every hotel and club – has become one of the most actively pursued state-sponsored and state-promoted activities, being regarded as an important economic activity and a significant source of government revenue (Legge 1996, McCrann 1996). This new legitimacy, in turn, creates a new social problem defined in a personalised perspective as a 'problem gambler'.

Certain social problems function to legitimate dominant values and interests. As Christian religions, in order to maintain believers' allegiance, once needed sinners and the demonstration of the penalty such sinners would incur in a future life, so does any political and economic system need to maintain its legitimacy by demonstrating the penalty for failure to follow its values, principles and methods of operation. The legitimation function of 'failures' was well demonstrated by Emile Durkheim in his argument that crime had a positive function in increasing social cohesion and solidarity (since society felt the need to 'close ranks' in the face of a threat to its security and safety). Today, the vulnerable position of early school leavers in the labour market might be regarded as a social problem, but it also serves to emphasise the value of education; in a similar way, statistics on the increasing frequency of housebreaking are good news for the security industry.

Certain social problems appear to be intractable, despite sustained efforts to alleviate or solve them. Indeed, if we observe policies and methods of intervention in social problems we will see that such policies and methods are repeatedly used, in a rather ritualistic fashion, although the claimed or expected results are not forthcoming. Why, then, do such policies and methods of intervention continue to be used? This suggests that policies and methods of intervention might have other aims that are equally or even more important than the solution or control of a given problem – namely, the need to demonstrate that the problem is being addressed. Such demonstration shows a commitment to the maintenance of social order and serves as a public assertion, or re-assertion, of dominant values and interests, and the legitimation of such values and interests.

Theories and Methods of Intervention

The observations and propositions mentioned in the previous section are explored in depth in the following chapters. By presenting the phenomenon of social problems in a theoretical perspective that draws on a number of sociological theories and empirical observations of social problems in contemporary societies, this book aims to demonstrate and enhance the relevance and value of sociology to current societal issues and to intervention methods practised by the 'helping professions' (such as social work, psychology and related professions), and thus potentially to improve the effectiveness of their endeavours. At present, the input of sociological knowledge into the education curricula of these professions is either minimal or non-existent. If there is some sociological input, it is usually limited to the presentation of certain theories at a level of abstraction that makes it difficult for students to see the theories' relevance or usefulness in applications to professional practice. The gap between theory and practice seems to remain as large as ever, continuing the difficulties of applying theories formulated at the macro-level of social organisation to problems encountered by the helping professions at the level of individuals or small social groupings (such as families on low incomes, or groups of young people with certain common characteristics such as unemployment), or at the level of certain localities such as the 'disadvantaged' suburbs of large cities. The problem of the relationship between public issues and private problems, identified by C. Wright Mills (1959), remains largely unresolved.

In our attempt to examine the nature of social problems and intervention methods in an integrated perspective, we do not suggest any intervention methods that would provide ready solutions to social problems. However, we think that a better understanding of these processes, which we aim to achieve and convey to readers, may lead to more effective intervention methods. A sociologist interested in the study of social problems once said that a '"social problem" is, first and foremost, the problem of knowing society, both actually and potentially. What to do about improving society at any particular point depends upon assumed knowledge about the facts of social structure and social forces' (Small 1898:114).

The perception of, interpretation of, and methods of intervention in social problems are influenced by political considerations of governments and of dominant interests in society. Potentially effective solutions might not be taken because they may create other problems more threatening to the existing structural arrangements than the original problems themselves. Therefore, social problems need to be perceived in the framework of society's structure of power. Conceptually (but closely related to social reality), this structure may be presented as an interrelated three-level activity of social organisation: political, administrative and operational (Jamrozik 1992; see Figure 1.1). In this perspective, the activities that take place at one level of the structure are perceived as a form of social action that affects the actions at the other two levels. Together, actions at any of the three levels are seen to produce a sequence of interaction processes through which dominant values and interests are integrated into the existing structure of power. This perspective facilitates identification of the 'intervening variables' that fill the conceptual gap between the macro-structure of social organisation – that is, the level at which dominant values and interests are translated into policy decisions on the allocation of resources – and the micro-structure of everyday life where the consequences of these decisions are experienced. Social problems may emerge at any or all of the three levels, and the intervention methods may also be directed at the relevant level or levels. However, the perception of social problems is different at each level. Consequently, any remedial measures devised to control, alleviate or solve the problem will also be different at each level. The examples in this book, especially those in Chapters 5 and 6, identify certain social problems in Australia (e.g. unemployment) that have been converted into personal problems with attached connotations of personal pathologies. Other problems (e.g. child care) that at first emerged as personal problems have been converted into social problems, either completely or partially, and have since remained in the political sphere as issues demanding government attention.

Social problems, which from our theoretical perspective emerge as a negative residue from the pursuit of certain goals, corresponding structural power arrangements and allocation of resources, are therefore intrinsically political in nature. It follows that effective solutions for such problems can be found only in changing those structural arrangements and pursued goals. However, as will be seen in later chapters, especially Chapter 3, prevailing intervention methods practised by the helping professions focus almost solely on the micro-structure – that is, on the population experiencing a given problem. The social problem is then perceived and attended to as a private, personal problem. The problem attended to at the operative level has therefore been 'converted' from one of a social and political nature within the social sphere into a personal problem in the private sphere. It is then related to the person's individual characteristics, such as attitudes, psychological make-up, abilities of intellect, or personal relationships.

Such conversions of social problems are taken for granted, and the intervention methods pay little if any attention to the intervening variables that link the problems of a particular population group, stratum or class to the political level of social organisation where decisions affecting the well-being of the population are made, and where the source of the problem can most often be found. The processes of conversion of social problems and the social and political significance of these processes' legitimating role for the dominant structure of power in society constitute the main issues examined in this book. We think that the theoretical perspective we have developed to examine these issues is an effective heuristic tool for the study of social problems in contemporary societies and that it may lead to the formulation of a theory of social problems that has greater relevance to the understanding of social problems these societies now experience. As our perspective covers the nature of social problems as well as the methods of intervention that convert social problems into personal problems, we call it the 'theory of residualist conversion of social problems'.

This book emphasises the need for sociologists to give more attention in their theorising to conversion processes in the multi-level structural organisation of society. It aims to help sociologists achieve a more thorough understanding of the tasks performed by policy makers, administrators and especially the helping professions, so as to provide them with concepts that can be effectively operationalised in methods of intervention by including the intervening variables in assessments of individual situations.

The Scope of this Book

In the following chapters, the empirical data on social problems are drawn mainly from Australian society, but the social significance of the

Figure 1.1: Levels of Activity in Methods of Intervention

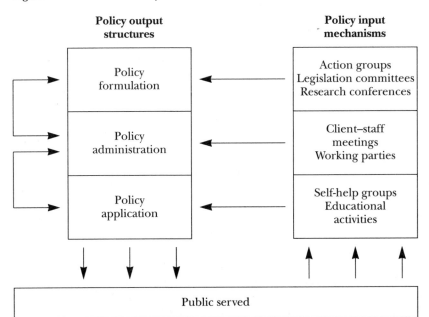

data has much wider implications. Drawing on data from one country limits the scope of generalisations, but as Australia is a country of immigrants, its population has roots in a diversity of cultures, which are maintained in differing degrees by various ethnic groupings. These diverse cultures are not always easily accommodated into the dominant Anglo-Australian culture and its values, which have remained characteristic of the monocultural core social organisations, in politics, public administration and the law (Jamrozik *et al.* 1995). The nature of Australian society and the nature of any social problems that arise or might arise in that society need therefore to be seen in the light of Australia's tenuous multicultural character. Yet, because of its cultural diversity, Australian society may be regarded as a kind of microcosm of the global society, and its social problems may to a certain degree reflect some of the current global concerns, be these concerns of an economic, cultural, social or religious nature.

Although we have attempted to include some social problems from other societies and cultures, we are aware that our frame of reference is by and large confined to Australia and to Western industrialised societies. This is a limitation we share with most current studies in sociology. As has been pointed out by Barry Smart (1992:95–6), much contemporary social analysis exhibits an 'overriding ethnocentric Western bias' that implicitly assumes the superiority of Western economic and social development and uses it as a comparative measurement in the analysis of social conditions in the Second and Third Worlds. This limitation poses serious questions about the wider application and relevance of the theories currently followed in sociology and in the social sciences generally. One might ask to what extent, if any, are some of the postmodernist theories (see Chapters 2, 5, 9 and 10) relevant to the understanding of social issues in the developing countries of Asia or Africa. Do these theories have any application or relevance to the newly industrialising countries (NICs) of South-East Asia, or to the countries of the Third World, or is their relevance confined only to the Western industrialised, or postindustrial, world?

What are the important social problems in the world today? At the level of a city or suburb an important social problem may be the incidence of petty crime; at the national level it may be unemployment; and at the global level it may be air and water pollution, increasing energy usage, waste disposal (especially the disposal of chemical waste) and, above all, the increasing gap between the affluent industrialised countries and the vast majority of countries where poverty is endemic (the North/South divide). The biggest social problem, and the source of other problems, is undoubtedly war and its outcomes, but wars are fought not only to increase a country's political or economic power, but also to preserve existing interests or to prevent a perceived direct or potential threat to the country's interests or even the very survival of a society or culture. Equally threatening on a global scale are health problems causally linked to certain human activity, such as sexually transmitted diseases (HIV and AIDS), lung cancer (the effect of tobacco smoking) and the rapidly spreading use of illicit drugs. Sexual abuse of children has emerged as another widespread problem. However, other social problems, current or potential, are created by human endeavours carried out with the intention of benefiting humanity. Research on DNA, nuclear energy, embryo transplants and cloning of animals and plants may all lead to unpredictable and not necessarily beneficial outcomes for the world and its inhabitants.

With the growing globalisation of economic and political issues, it has been suggested that studies of social problems should also aim to develop a global perspective. For example, the American Society for the Study of Social Problems has suggested that such studies should take into consideration the operation of the international political economy and should focus on three areas: the role of the state in defining and addressing social problems; development of new theoretical and empirical models for research; and cross-national or cross-regional implications of such research (Santiago 1993). James Coleman (1991) sees a number of potential social problems looming in the growth of what he calls the 'constructed social organisation' (such as the modern business or public corporation) replacing the 'primordial organisation' (e.g. the family) as the main mechanism of social control, socialisation and distribution of social product. For Aristide Zolberg (1991) the social problem of global proportions is the division between the affluent industrialised countries and the rest, and the restrictions imposed by countries on the movement of labour. Connelly and Kennedy (1994) see the unequal distribution of resources and restrictions on population movement as potentially the greatest global social problem. They paint a futuristic scenario of masses of people from Third World countries landing on European shores and spreading panic among the local population.

While a comprehensive exploration of current or potential global social problems is beyond the scope of this book, the examination of social problems in Australian society is conducted in a framework of a global perspective, especially in relation to Australia's immigration and population policy, and internal ethnic and cultural diversity. Also, the examples we use focus on problems that can be identified in most societies and that tend to affect either whole societies or significant parts of their populations, acquiring a 'perennial' character, rather than problems that emerge in some societies at certain times and then disappear. However, this emphasis does not mean we consider the latter problems to be irrelevant to our theoretical framework; we include such examples where they appear to be relevant to our analysis. Furthermore, as noted earlier, and as will be demonstrated throughout this book, certain social problems are experienced by a whole society but are particularly experienced by the lower socio-economic strata, or 'lower' social classes. If problems occur *throughout* the social structure, they tend to be differently perceived, interpreted and intervened in, according to the social class of the affected population. The class structure, or the differential 'command over resources through time' by different social classes, as defined by the late Richard Titmuss, is the main feature of Australian society, as it is of all Western capitalist or 'free market' societies. This being the case, we maintain, social class has to be considered as the main variable in the analysis of the nature and frequency of social problems, as well as in any analysis of the perceptions of, interpretations of and methods of intervention in social problems.

This book has eleven chapters, each dealing with a specific area or specific aspects of social problems. Although there is a sequential continuity of issues analysed from one chapter to the next, each chapter is sufficiently comprehensive to be read on its own.

Following this introductory chapter, Chapters 2 and 3 give a critical review of earlier and current theories of social problems, and their applications in methods of intervention. In addition to theories that may be termed 'classical', such as disorganisation theory and critical theory, more recent theories emanating from feminist contributions and various postmodern orientations also receive attention. Chapter 3 shows how theories are operationalised at the levels of policy making, administration and service delivery, and how through integration with practice wisdom, theories of social problems lose their social character and become theories of individual or group 'pathological' or 'deviant' behaviour. From such a perspective, individual behaviour is then explained with little, if any, reference to societal influences, determinants and constraints, and intervention methods focus on the correction of the perceived 'pathology' of the individual.

Chapter 4 focuses on the human agency – that is, on the social actors who play important roles in the definitions of and societal responses to social problems. These roles are played by academic researchers and teachers, members of the helping professions and political activists, and are enacted through research, authoritative writings, public debate, organised lobbying, and then in policy making and intervention methods. The chapter examines how such activities become integrated with, and often subordinated to, the values and interests of the social actors, so that public perceptions of social problems become 'mediated perceptions' that are compatible with the actors' values and interests. The role of mass media in creating mediated perceptions of social problems is especially noted in the chapter.

Chapters 5 and 6 fully elaborate the book's theoretical perspective and substantiate its applicability to explanations of currently prevailing social problems both in Australia and on the global scene. The chapter demonstrates how the global market economy, the dominant structure of economic and political power, and the corresponding distribution (or rather maldistribution) of human and material resources affect Australian internal conditions and present formidable challenges for governments and for social theorists, researchers and analysts who advise policy makers. It follows that these challenges also need to be considered by university teachers who devise educational programs, subject curricula, instruction methods and application of theories to intervention methods. Of particular importance to understanding contemporary social problems are the challenges presented by the cultural diversity on the global scene, and its reflection in the com-position of Australian society. Chapter 5 examines, in the Australian context, examples of problems experienced in Western societies, such as unemployment, degradation of the environment, reduction of the public sphere, the demise of the welfare state, and the impact of postmodernism. Chapter 6 analyses some problematic aspects of a multicultural society, and also examines the problems of child abuse and neglect, and state-sponsored gambling.

Chapters 7, 8 and 9 examine three areas of social structure that, it is argued, encompass the key areas and issues of social concern and constitute the main, although not all, sources of social problems. The first issue is *inequality*, which is examined in Chapter 7 as a universal global issue pervading all social institutions and all aspects of social and economic life, and giving rise to the most serious and seemingly insoluble social problems. Following this is an analysis of two areas of universal and fundamental importance to social life. Chapter 8 examines the first area, that of the institution of *the family*, which in Australia as well as on the global scene has been going through significant changes, resulting in increased diversity of form but also in loss of stability and economic viability. The family being the basic social institution, the effects of its changing character and its social role are differentially experienced in various social strata and sections of the population. However, the overall social significance of these effects has not received adequate attention in sociology because of the fragmen-tation of views, theoretical interpretations and underlying values and interests. The issues addressed in Chapter 8 are the relationship of the family with the state and the market, inequality in the family structure, and the effects of class perspective that are built in to methods of intervention in family problems. Chapter 9 examines the second area, that of *social order*, and the host of problems this issue entails. It is examined in a broad perspective, encompassing the institutions and processes of formal social control such as the police, courts and correctional agencies, the institutions of the labour and financial markets, and the institutions concerned with socialisation, such as the family and the education system. The analysis of these three areas illustrates what may be called a 'hierarchy' of social problems, in which problems of a universal character lead to a number of other problems affecting large or small sections of the population.

Chapters 10 and 11 provide a critical test of our theoretical perspective on social problems. It is argued, and demonstrated by empirical examples, that the theory put forward in this book offers an opportunity for sociology to be a living social science, contributing to a better understanding of society and to the well-being of the population. Chapters 10 and 11 also identify some important implications for governments and for resource allocation policies, illustrating the importance of these policies in creating social problems or in preventing social problems from occurring. Finally, particular attention is given to the role of the helping professions as important social actors in social problems. We point out that the theory presented in the book offers an opportunity for these professions to widen their range of operational variables in their perceptions and interpretations of social problems, and through such wider vision improve the effectiveness of their intervention methods.

CHAPTER 2

Contemporary Perspectives on Social Problems

There are numerous sociological perspectives on social problems. In addition to theories that entered the sociological discourse in the first half of the 20th century and that may be termed 'classical', such as social pathology, social disorganisation or social deviance theories, some newer perspectives have become influential in recent years. The conflict perspective and critical theory, which draw on the Marxian view of the capitalist society, became influential in the late 1960s and early 1970s, but have since been replaced by the constructionist perspective, which came to the fore with considerable impact in the 1970s and replaced the previously popular 'labelling theory' from which it originated. Since the early 1980s, a variety of perspectives have come into the field of sociology under the umbrella of feminism, poststructuralism and post-modernism. Now, in the later 1990s, the theoretical field of sociology is rather fluid – that is to say, there is much discussion and heated debate about the current nature of society, in which the 'old' tends to be rejected in no uncertain fashion while the 'new' might be argued for with great conviction and emotion but with much less clarity.

There is at least one distinctive difference between older and newer sociological theories, especially in the perspectives on contemporary social problems. Classical theories sought explanations for social problems either in the flaws of human personalities and characteristics (perceiving these flaws as a form of social deviance) or in social structure and social organisation (or rather disorganisation), or in both. A common feature of the new perspectives is that relatively little attention is given to structural factors such as socio-economic divisions in society and the well-established evidence of the relationship between certain problems' frequency, and socio-economic status or social class. In these perspectives, the presence and frequency of certain problems

17

are related to population groups identified on a 'life cycle' dimension such as age, or on the dimensions of sex or ethnicity. The implicit assumption is that such population groups are homogeneous in their socio-economic or social class status. As this is rarely the case, such unwitting concealment of socio-economic or class divisions in social analyses seriously flaws the perceptions and interpretations of social problems, with corresponding flaws in methods of intervention following from such perspectives. In effect, postmodernist perspectives are conservative in nature, as they present issues of equality or inequality among the multitude of social groupings and their specific interests, and overlook the reality of the overriding structure of inequality that is based on social class divisions within which the fragmentation of interests occurs.

Given the heterogeneity of ideas and perspectives in postmodernist writings, it was unavoidable that serious contradictions and incompatibilities would emerge in explanations of social problems. The relativist theoretical positions taken up by protagonists of certain causes and interests are argued from the premise of logical and moral rectitude, which eschews comparison and makes it extremely difficult to develop a debate that would facilitate a critical analysis of the issues in question. We address these issues later in this chapter, and further, in relation to specific aspects of social problems, in other chapters, especially Chapters 4, 5 and 9.

In the field of social control – that is, in the realm of policies, administration and service delivery apparatus – the classical perspectives still hold sway. Some measures of social control in fields such as juvenile justice or even unemployment tend to have distinctive features of biological determinism and social pathology underpinning their policies and practices. Such measures focus on individuals taken out of their societal context, so any successful intervention serves to validate the measures, while failures are explained by the inability or unwillingness of the 'treated' person to change. Such self-validating practices prevent critical evaluation or the introduction of practices based on another perspective.

What, then, constitutes a social problem in the contemporary industrialised society? A social problem is a social phenomenon or social condition that is perceived to potentially or directly threaten the social order. It is perceived to threaten society's interests, or to threaten or offend moral standards and values – perhaps offending aesthetic values or sensibilities, perhaps injecting a feeling of guilt. This particular feature of threat differentiates social phenomena or social conditions that are perceived as social problems from social phenomena or conditions perceived as such *tout court*. The latter might be 'interesting' and arouse intellectual curiosity in a sociological researcher, but they are not perceived as problems in normative terms. A study of phenomena that are not perceived to have a deleterious impact on society may therefore be conducted with intellectual objectivity, and the value guiding the study may simply be the value attached to the pursuit of knowledge. However, there is no presumed value-neutrality in undertaking a study of social phenomena that are considered to be social problems, nor in the interpretation of observed and recorded data generated by such a study. When we analyse a condition that is perceived to be a social problem, we might endeavour to maintain intellectual objectivity in our perception and interpretation, but we also know that someone, somewhere, will see the condition as an undesirable social problem, or as a threat.

The question is whether there can be such a clear division between these two approaches or perspectives – that is, a division between intellectual objectivity and the value-laden perception – or whether the difference is only a matter of degree. Spector and Kitsuse assert that no adequate definition of social problems has been formulated in sociology and 'there is not and never has been a sociology of social problems' (1987:1). All social phenomena present a problematic situation of a certain kind, although the element of threat might not be clearly or immediately evident. Certainly, the researcher may attempt to study any social phenomenon with a degree of detachment and emotional non-involvement, perceiving it in a perspective of normality (as suggested by Matza in 1969); on the other hand, the researcher may study a given social condition with the belief or knowledge that the subject or object studied presents some kind of real or potential threat to society – or to certain sections, strata or classes in society – in terms of values or interests.

These distinctions are important because they turn our attention to some important aspects of sociology and the social sciences generally. First, we become aware of the nature of social phenomena as social constructs, subjectively perceived without independent existence from the observer's perception. Second, the same condition may therefore be perceived, interpreted and acted upon in different ways. Third, we may study social problems for a variety of reasons and with a variety of approaches – for example, we may study a social condition and accept its 'threatening' nature; or we may study the reason (or reasons) why some people see the condition as a social problem, or why some people see it as a social problem and others do not. Fourth, we may study a social condition because, with sociological insight, we think a particular condition presents potential or direct negative outcomes for society or for some social groupings, strata or classes. The threat might not be

clearly or immediately evident because the causative links or the inter-
play of certain factors are not easily seen, or because for certain reasons
there is a reluctance in society to see them, or their existence is denied.
What the sociologist's attitude should be in such situations poses some
important ethical questions concerning the social role and social
responsibility of sociology and the social sciences generally. We examine
these issues in later chapters.

In his definition of what constitutes a social problem, Robert Merton
asserts that 'a social problem exists when there is a sizeable discrepancy
between what is and what people think ought to be' (1976:7). How large
this disparity must be before people acknowledge that a social problem
exists depends on particular conditions, people's attitudes and prevailing social norms. People's perceptions of and attitudes towards social
problems depend also on their state of knowledge about relevant issues,
and on the source of that knowledge. The source of knowledge is an
important factor, as in contemporary industrialised societies much of
people's knowledge about social problems comes from the mass media.
Their perceptions of social problems are therefore to a large extent
'mediated' perceptions. In relation to the study of social problems,
Merton points out that a social problem may be either 'manifest' or
'latent'. He sees it as sociology's task to identify conditions in the second
category, and to demonstrate their direct or potential significance for
society – that is, to make the latent social problem manifest. On the issue
of subjectivity in the perception of social problems, Merton emphasises
that sociologists are not immune from value judgements, and that
ethical issues arise not only in sociological analysis of social problems
but also 'inhere in the very formulation of problems for social research'
(1976:24).

The subjective nature of social problems or social conditions is easily
demonstrated by the example of differing perceptions of social reality
that are presented by political parties at elections. Various political
parties, media commentators and political analysts present to the
electorate a diversity of perceptions and interpretations of social reality.
Voters accept one version rather than another and act on it accordingly,
even if some voters might remain sceptical about politicians' arguments
and motivations. Voters' acceptance of a particular version of reality
increases if the version presented also includes criticism of the social
reality presented by the competing party or parties, as being a social
condition that contains a threat of some kind. Voters are also more likely
to accept the presented version of reality if the nature and extent of the
alleged threat in the opposition's version is intensified by being
portrayed as such by the mass media or by an influential political lobby.
For example, in Australia, certain conservative politicians and media

commentators frequently relate the policy on immigration to the problem of unemployment (however spurious this relationship might be), resulting in general community approval of a substantially reduced immigration intake. Acceptance of this argument is further facilitated by relating immigration to the implicit (and at times explicit) 'threat' of 'Asianisation' to the existing European or Anglo-Australian population of the country.

In summary, then, for a social condition to be accepted as a social problem, the condition has to be perceived as such. First, this means that a certain condition may not be perceived as a social problem one day, yet may be seen as one the next, or that some people will see it as a social problem and act upon it, while others do not see it as a social problem. In other words, a social problem is a social condition perceived in a normative way. Second, a social condition (such as a physical condition of certain people) may be perceived as a social problem by direct observation, or its existence may be inferred from certain physical conditions or actions, verbal or written expressions, or in the latent or potential outcome of certain conditions or actions.

This brings to light yet another feature of social problems – namely, that a social condition perceived as undesirable or threatening will not be perceived as a social problem unless it is considered to be remediable or solvable. Indeed, an undesirable or threatening condition may be perceived as a 'problem', but it will persist without any action upon it because of beliefs that the problem is 'God's will', the 'work of nature', or due to an unchangeable 'human nature' and therefore beyond the society's capacity to intervene for the purposes of attenuation or solution. There are many such conditions. For example, poverty may have observable physical dimensions, such as particular living conditions, lack of food and lack of certain amenities or services, but poverty itself is a concept, a social construct, whose existence is determined through certain arbitrarily, consensually or expediently defined criteria. Poverty might be considered 'bad', but also unavoidable. The biblical assertion that 'the poor will always be with us', or the frequent observation that 'the rich get richer and the poor get poorer' are folk wisdoms that play an important legitimising role in maintaining conditions of social inequality. By presenting poverty as somehow 'natural', these beliefs lessen the pressure to remedy the condition.

In the past, poverty was legitimised in Western Christian countries by being portrayed as pre-ordained by the divine power, and as something that would be compensated in future life. In contemporary Western industrialised and affluent societies, poverty is legitimised by a range of explanations, such as structural change in the labour market, difficult economic conditions or general scarcity of material resources. It is also legitimised by demonstrated governmental concern, which is expressed in the provision of personal services, income-support measures, and sponsorship of research designed to examine the extent and nature of poverty and to suggest remedies. The common factor in all such measures is the problem's shift from the public sphere and the conversion of its social/political nature into the personal problem of the poor themselves. Most research concerned with the study of poverty examines the poor. The processes of the allocation of resources that are the basis of both social inequality and resulting extremes of wealth and poverty are rarely, if ever, the topics of government-sponsored research. The issue of social inequality as the most significant social problem is discussed in Chapter 7.

Theoretical Perspectives

Social theories might be regarded as theorists' value-neutral intellectual observations and explanations, yet they are inevitably not only expressions of the theorists' scholarly orientations but also expressions of their personal values and interests. On a broader scale, social theories are expressions of values and interests prevalent or dominant in a society at a given time. This characteristic is especially present in social theories concerned with phenomena considered to be social problems. This is also why over the past hundred years, as societies in the industrialising world changed, new theories of social problems appeared with great frequency in sociology. Rubington and Weinberg (1995) list seven such theoretical perspectives that came into sociological studies from the late 1890s to the early 1990s. Most of these perspectives originated in the United States and, correspondingly, their theoretical frameworks and analyses were derived from empirical observations of that society. The perspectives are listed below in the chronological order in which they emerged in sociological literature, covering a period from the late 19th century to the present day. This does not mean that each emerging perspective replaced the previous one, which was then entirely discarded, or that only one perspective dominated the social analyses of a given period. Indeed, from its origins, sociology has been the source of ideas and diverse interpretations of social reality, presenting either complementary or conflicting perspectives on social issues. All seven perspectives are still very much alive, not only in sociological literature but in the minds and practices of social actors involved in social problems – politicians, journalists, psychiatrists, economists and social workers. The seven perspectives are also evident in the general public's consciousness. The perspectives are:

1   Social pathology
2   Social disorganisation
3   Value conflict
4   Deviant behaviour
5   Labelling
6   Critical theory
7   Constructionist

These seven perspectives, briefly outlined in the rest of this chapter, provide a historical overview of the changes in sociological theorisation but do not constitute an exhaustive theoretical framework of the sociology of social problems. In recent times, various new perspectives have emerged that are debated, clarified, modified and criticised. For example, the feminist input cannot be ignored, because it opened a new field of vision and has been instrumental in developing new perspectives such as the identification of the source of power in the notion of patriarchy. T. H. Marshall's theory on civil, political and social rights has significant explanatory power in the analysis of social problems. Michel Foucault's influence has been quite strong, providing a somewhat different perspective on power in society from what was presented before, especially his key concept of the knowledge/power relationship as a universal phenomenon in all human relationships. Various post-modern ideas have also served to develop new perspectives, as has the influence of some theories of culture. However, notwithstanding these developments and the differences in sociological discourse that have ensued and continue to ensue from them, no clearly identifiable theory of social problems has emerged. There might be theories that aim to explain particular problems, but there is no theory of social problems *per se* that would provide a theoretical framework for the study of social problems as specific social phenomena, uniquely distinct from other social phenomena.

1 Social Pathology

The notion of social pathology emerged in the later part of the 19th century and was very much in vogue throughout the early part of the 20th century. At the time, both Europe and the United States were going through an intense process of industrialisation. This produced unprecedented wealth for some, but for many it produced dislocation of family and kinship, poverty, and work in extremely unpleasant con-ditions in factories and mines controlled by coercive management regimes.

Early sociologists developed the social pathology perspective from examining the effects of extensive social change on the people who had been uprooted from their rural surroundings and forced to live and work in new and strange conditions. The sociologists' focus on the effects of change rather than on the causes of the change turned their attention to the 'victims of change', and they sought to explain the victims' plight as a failure to adjust to changed conditions.

The social pathology perspective developed by the early sociologists was built on organic analogy, and in that perspective explanations for such problems as poverty, crime, drunkenness and dependency were sought in the flaws of human character. Sociologists, together with 'social reformers' of the day, tried to explain, for example, why such problems occurred in a country such as the United States, which had 'noble' principles like equality of opportunity. They therefore sought explanations in the flaws of human nature, using the organic analogy borrowed from medicine of a sick or maladjusted individual. In Europe, the organic analogy was used by people interested in forensic science, such as Lombroso, in their search for the 'criminal type' whose body build, facial features and level of intelligence were believed to be distinctly different from those of the 'normal' population.

With the influence of the social pathology perspective, a corresponding notion of 'reform' was being developed at the time, meaning the reform of a 'flawed' individual. Most social welfare agencies established in that period used intervention methods that focused on the individual and that sought to change the individual's behaviour (Trattner 1979, Woodroofe 1962). Prevention measures took the form of 'child saving', implemented by removing children from poor families and placing them in residential institutions or in foster families (Randall 1896). At the same time, some early sociological analysts, still imbued with philanthropic and reformist fervour, pointed to the industrial and urban conditions under which the masses of workers lived and suffered deprivation and exploitation on a grand scale. Attempts to apply the organic analogy to what they saw as pathological forms of industrial organisation, however, had little effect on the industrial scene. As one observer wrote, 'the remedial forces for readjusting and improving social conditions beat almost ineffectively the empty air', although she noticed some parallel, hopeful signs in the enlightened movements both in America and Europe and argued for legislative measures to prevent individual and corporate oppression (De Graffenried 1896:190–201).

It is important to note that the concept of social pathology is still very much in use in various social welfare agencies, especially in the correctional services, and in those that deal with domestic violence and child abuse. Some of the current interpretations of the 'underclass' are also grounded in the pathology perspective (Murray 1984). Evidence for 'undesirable' personal characteristics is now also sought in genetics. Indeed, the concept of social pathology has proved to be a hardy perennial that survives in many forms of assessing a person's performance in education, work, social conduct, interpersonal relationships and general lifestyle. In a wider perspective, the concept of social pathology forms an important ingredient in racist theories and beliefs.

2 Social Disorganisation

The social disorganisation perspective was developed in the 1920s at the University of Chicago (Park *et al.* 1925). This perspective represented a significant shift of focus from the individual to the social and economic environment, and opened a new field of sociological research interests and a new research methodology.

Using the city of Chicago as the area for their study, Robert Park and his colleagues observed that certain social problems were concentrated in some city areas but not in others, and they related this to the city's rapid growth, the replacement of one kind of population by another, and the interaction between the population, commerce and industry. Chicago, like many American cities at the time, experienced large population growth both from European immigration and from the movement of African-Americans from the Southern states. This influx of people – who found themselves in a new and strange environment and who sought to establish a new life with few supports of family, friends or neighbours – gave rise to social disorganisation manifested in such problems as homelessness, poverty and rising crime rates.

The pioneering work of Park and his colleagues established a model for studies in urban sociology, which became increasingly important as cities increased in size and the magnitude of social problems in the urban environment presented increasing problems for social organisation.

Sociologists who studied social problems in the theoretical framework of social disorganisation identified a number of issues within this concept that led them to differentiate between social disorganisation as a *condition* and as a *process*. This distinction led to the formulation of the hypothesis of 'cultural lag', the essence of which was that 'material culture tends to change more rapidly than nonmaterial culture' (Mowrer 1941:840). Introducing the notion of culture into the concept led, in turn, to the question 'What constitutes social reality?' and to the issue of subjective perception of social reality. The concept of culture also led to the awareness of social participation and culture conflict as factors in social disorganisation (Queen 1941:307–16).

3 Value Conflict

The value conflict perspective was developed in the 1930s as an outcome of the Great Depression. Sociologists found that existing theories of social problems, which sought explanations in the concept of social disorganisation, were simply not adequate to explain what could be observed in society itself. In what was commonly referred to as a 'pluralistic society', they found that conflict arose out of competing interests, differential access to resources and, in a later phase, led to intergenerational differences and conflicts. In essence, the conflicts were conflicts of values.

A significant feature of the value conflict perspective was the observation that an objective social condition may be perceived differently by different persons, the difference being related to, influenced or determined by a person's social values. A social problem was therefore seen as an objective condition defined subjectively (Fuller and Myers 1941a,b). This observation also meant that sociologists had to be aware that their perceptions and interpretations of a social problem might be different from the laypeople's, leading to different suggestions for a solution.

4 Deviant Behaviour

The deviant behaviour perspective represented a further progression towards explaining individual behaviour from societal perspectives. It examined social institutions, finding out how they worked and how they related to people. The concept of social deviance attracted much attention in sociology and in other branches of the social sciences, as well as from the general public, as it promised to explain the causes and nature of law breaking and other anti-social activities. It came into sociological vocabulary and research relating to social problems in the 1930s, but reached its height of popularity in the 1950s and 1960s when law and order became the dominant social problem in Western countries – especially in relation to young people's social behaviour in the United States. People had great difficulty in comprehending why, in times of unprecedented affluence, the frequency of law breaking seemed to be increasing rapidly.

The search for explanations of social deviance was at first intense among social psychologists whose concepts of 'waywardness' were very similar to the concept of social pathology of a few decades earlier. In sociology, Robert Merton, who was one of the foremost exponents of the functionalist school, published his theory on social structure and anomie in 1938 and revised it later in 1957. Merton saw the cause of social deviance in the disjunction between culturally propagated and cherished goals – the American Dream – and structural arrangements whose feature was the inadequacy of, and barriers to, institutional means for many people to reach those goals. Socially deviant behaviour was seen as a form of adaptation to such structural arrangements, and adaptation might take different forms, ranging from extreme ritualistic conformism, to innovative (though law-breaking) behaviour, to overt rebellion (Merton 1957:131–94). Such forms of deviant behaviour occurred when people found the barriers to propagated social goals unsurmountable. Unable to achieve such goals through accepted social norms, they resorted to other means to reach them. Merton defined such situations of 'normlessness' as a state of 'anomie', a concept he adopted from Durkheim's classic study of suicide.

Among other theories of social deviance, Edwin Sutherland's 'differential association' theory has also been influential to this day. Sutherland's theory found acceptance particularly as the explanation for young people's law breaking, as much of their anti-social behaviour was in groups or organised gangs (Sutherland and Cressey 1978). Others (Cloward and Ohlin 1960) sought explanations in the differential structure of opportunities to engage in acts, some of which were legal but many of which were anti-social or criminal. They argued that it was the lack of legal acts and the prevalence of anti-social activities that gave rise to deviant behaviour.

Theories of deviant behaviour have retained their popularity in various forms to this day. Although these kinds of sociological theories focus on explanations of deviant behaviour in societal structural arrangements, seeking explanations in acquired or inherited personality characteristics is quite prevalent, especially in psychology and criminology. As various forms of behaviour regarded as deviant from prevalent societal norms are interpreted as mental illness or are proscribed by law, persons who manifest such behaviour become the subjects of attention for psychiatrists, psychologists and social workers employed in correctional agencies. The observed behaviour is therefore individualised, and explanations are sought in a person, not in society. These issues are explored in greater detail in Chapters 3 and 9.

5 Labelling

The labelling perspective came into the debate on social problems in the 1950s. Its main feature, which became the subject of much heated argument, was to turn attention in the first instance away from the 'deviant person' and towards the people who had the power to define the appropriateness or legitimacy of certain social conduct and apply the label of 'normalcy' or 'deviance' to those who engaged in such conduct.

Exponents of the labelling perspective pointed out that certain social conduct might be taking place, yet no one really bothered about it until someone said it was 'wrong' or 'bad' for society and that some correctional measures should be taken to eradicate, suppress, or at least attenuate it. They argued that when that view was accepted by society or its influential sections, the conduct so labelled became 'deviant'. Howard Becker, the foremost exponent of the labelling perspective asserted that:

> social groups create deviance by making the rules whose infraction constitutes deviance, and by applying those rules to particular people and labelling them as outsiders. From this point of view, deviance is not a quality of the act the person commits, but rather a consequence of the application by others of rules and sanctions to an 'offender'. The deviant is one to whom that label has successfully been applied; deviant behaviour is behaviour that people so label.
>
> *(1963:9)*

The labelling perspective led to a debate concerning the notions of 'primary' and 'secondary' deviance. Questions were raised about some people's susceptibility to deviant behaviour, exemplified by such expressions as 'wayward youth', thus bringing the social pathology perspective back into the debate. Critics argued that the labelling perspective, if followed to its logical conclusion, would mean that there was no objectively defined behaviour that could be called deviant. A related issue in the debate was the observation that the meaning ascribed to a particular social conduct (especially conduct labelled as deviant) would probably be different in the labeller's perspective and in the perspective of the person whose conduct was being labelled. This raised the issue of the 'hierarchy of credibility' between perspectives 'from above' and 'from below', which a sociologist needed to take into consideration. Related arguments arose about the degree of personal involvement of researchers in the problems they were studying, and the difference between commitment to certain values and overt partisanship in social issues (Gouldner 1975).

There has been much debate over calling the labelling perspective a theory. We do not enter into this debate here, but we need to note that the effect of labelling has acquired increasing significance in recent years with the growth of the helping professions, who indeed have power to authoritatively define social reality. Such authoritative definitions may apply to the definition of a social condition as well as to the behaviour and character of a person or group. The labelling perspective turned attention to the power structures in society and, in a sense, has unwittingly given credence to Marx's argument that whoever controls material production also controls mental production and makes others subservient to it.

6 Critical Theory

Critical theory came onto the sociological scene in the 1970s, but its origins date to the 1930s, to the critical theory developed at the Frankfurt Institute of Social Research. The scholars of that institute, Horkheimer, Adorno and Marcuse, endeavoured to apply Marxian theories to the analysis of contemporary capitalist society and attempted to reconcile or integrate some of Freud's early work with Marxism. Their focus was on the state and state power, which they saw (as Marx did) as the power of the dominant class. Their influence was particularly strong in the late 1960s and early 1970s, when increasing sections of American society, particularly university students and black youth, began to question American involvement in the Vietnam War and racial relations in the United States itself.

The essence of critical theory is the argument that the nature of social problems and their aetiology can be properly studied and understood only in the context of the social system in which such problems occur. The study of social problems in this perspective is a study of a society's political economy – that is, the study of social institutions as power structures, the roles they perform in society and their effects (Miller 1976:131–41). It follows that to effect any change in society, including finding any solution to social problems, undeniably means changing the power structure of society. The critical theory of social problems in Western industrialised societies has, in effect, been a critique of the capitalist system. Sociologists who figured prominently in studying social problems from the critical perspective were C. Wright Mills (1943, 1959), Alvin Gouldner (1971) and Richard Quinney (1977).

With a clear focus on social structure rather than on the social groupings or individuals within it, critical theorists argued that studies of social problems had to be conducted at a high level of abstraction, so that the common features and structural links of such problems could be identified. Studies of specific problems at a low level of abstraction failed to identify the structural basis of such problems and tended to lead to interpretation of problems in terms of social pathology (Mills 1943:165–80). Not much appeared to change in the study of social problems over the next 30 years. In his presidential address to the Society for the Study of Social Problems in 1976, S. M. Miller observed that 'what the study of social problems most lacks is a theoretical understanding of a specific whole society. If we think of social problems only narrowly, we are guilty of suppressing the relationship between personal problems and social ills' (1976:140).

The 'pathologising' of social problems and the assumed value-neutrality of social researchers was seen by the critical theorists as the main problem of most theories of social deviance. Frank Lindenfeld argued that:

> Psychologism and the myth of value neutrality are two major obstacles to understand [sic] social problems. Psychologism is the explanation of social phenomena in terms of the attitudes and behaviour of individuals rather than the structure of society. It is the attribution of structural characteristics to a mere sum of individual attitudes or milieux. The myth of value neutrality is simply that social scientists can be objective, when in fact they cannot.
>
> *(1973:2)*

From the critical theory perspective, a study of social problems, and any study of society, is a political act. The political nature of any such study is not seen in the subjective interpretation of a social problem, but simply in the awareness that the act of choosing a social issue as a topic for enquiry is intrinsically political because it brings the issue to public notice.

7 Constructionist

The constructionist perspective on social problems came into socio-logical analyses in the 1970s. It 'emerged from some sociologists' dis-satisfaction with the dominant, objectivist stance' in the study of social problems (Best 1989:243). The perspective constituted a fur-ther development and elaboration of the labelling perspective, and its theoretical background was the work of Peter Berger and Thomas Luckmann on the social construction of reality (1966).

The constructionist perspective is now applied to a wide range of social phenomena, not specifically to the study of social problems. The focus of the constructionist perspective is not on social phenomena *per se*, but on the processes through which social phenomena are con-structed and interpreted. The theoretical assumption of this perspective clearly distinguishes social phenomena from physical phenomena, in that social phenomena are not perceived to have an independent existence from the perception and interpretation of the observer. In the study of social problems the focus of this perspective is therefore primarily on the processes through which a social condition is per-ceived as a social problem, not on the condition itself. The focus is mainly on the social actors involved in social problems – that is, the people who make claims that a particular condition constitutes a social problem, and the effects of such claims. The identification of a social problem is therefore seen as a 'claims-making activity' (Spector and Kitsuse 1987, Best 1989). Furthermore, some theorists have emphasised the predominantly collective character of claims-making activities, arguing that 'social problems are fundamentally products of a process of collective definition instead of existing independently as a set of objective social arrangements with an intrinsic make up' (Blumer 1971:298).

As noted in Chapter 1, methods of intervention in social problems tend to focus on the population experiencing a particular problem rather than on the social causes of the problem. The constructionist perspective shifts the focus of study to those social actors who have the power to influence public opinion, or who have an acknowledged authority to make certain claims about social problems and have such claims accepted by others. This is the constructionist perspective's strength, but may also be regarded as its weakness. The weakness lies in its focus on the social actors in social problems and on the processes of their claims-making activities, but relatively little if any attention is given to the causal links of the social problem with the structural arrangements in society. The given problem itself also receives rather secondary attention, except for the notion that the problem is 'created' by the claims-makers. Notwithstanding this, the perspective's strength is in its focus on the processes through which certain conditions are brought into the public arena as social problems. Also, in identifying the social actors who engage in these processes and in focusing on their ability to make their claims 'stick', the perspective enables the identification of some aspects of the power structure in society. This feature is particularly important in the study of the helping professions' role in human services and of their power to authoritatively define social reality. These aspects are examined in Chapters 3 and 4.

Social Problems and the Sociology of Social Problems

This brief overview of the approaches taken in the study of social problems over the past hundred years indicates a range of interests, assumptions, definitions and theoretical interpretations. The approaches may be classified and compared according to their focus or according to the theoretical perspectives that guide them. The latter dimension would show the influence of three prevailing sociological theories: functionalism, symbolic interactionism, and critical theory (or Marxism). The main division in focus of these approaches is between the study of social problems as certain *social conditions*, and the study of social problems as an *activity*, usually a collective activity. The focus of earlier studies, such as those of Park and his colleagues (1925) was clearly on social conditions; the focus of later studies, such as those of Becker (1963) and Spector and Kitsuse (1987), was on activity. Certainly, these different approaches do not fall into discrete categories, as any

sociological study of a social condition undoubtedly entails a study of
related activities, and a study of activities must out of necessity refer
to the condition in which such activities take place. The problems encountered in attempts to reconcile *structure* with *action* and the assign-
ment of prominence to either one are actively debated in sociology,
especially in class analysis (Crompton 1993). In the study of social
problems the proponents of the activity focus argue, with considerable
justification, that social problems can be studied in a number of
intellectual disciplines, but that a primary focus must be on the activities
through which social problems are constructed. This means the focus is
mainly on the social actors who construct social problems, rather than
on the populations who experience or are seen to experience a problem. As explained by Spector and Kitsuse, the focus of study:

> must take the members' perspective as the starting point, focusing in par-
> ticular on definitional claims-making activities as the primary subject matter.
> Rather than investigate how institutional arrangements produce certain social
> conditions, we examine how individuals and groups become engaged in
> collective activities that recognise putative conditions as problems, and
> attempt to establish institutional arrangements.   *(1987:72)*

Spector and Kitsuse argue that the 'central problem for a theory of
social problems is to account for the emergence, nature, and maintenance of claims-making and responding activities'. In line with this
constructionist perspective, they define social problems as 'the activities
of individuals or groups making assertions of grievances and claims with
respect to some putative conditions' (1987:75–6).

In the constructionist perspective, an impression may be gained that
the sociologist studying social problems is a kind of 'uninvolved observer' of the social scene. This is never the case, and the role played by
the sociologist as an observer and interpreter of a given social condition
and related activities is an integral part of sociological theories of social
problems. The researcher is a social actor. By examining the activities of
other actors who 'construct' a problem, the researcher 'joins' the act of
construction by providing definitions and interpretations of other
actors' activities that are based on the researcher's own subjectively
perceived phenomena. Indeed, it may be argued that the study of social
problems, in whatever theoretical perspective it is conducted, is a form
of intervention in social problems – often a form of primary intervention. The role of the researcher is therefore crucial. The subjectivity
of the researcher's perception and interpretation of a social problem is
legitimately expected to be taken into account by the researcher's
specialised 'scientific' knowledge, in the light of which the problem
studied is likely to be perceived and interpreted differently from the way

it is perceived and interpreted by the public (Manis 1976:18–25). This issue in the studies of social problems has prompted much debate. For example, in a comparative analysis of American sociologists' choices of social problems for study over a period of 42 years (1934–75) and public opinions surveyed over the same period, Robert Lauer found substantial differences between the interests and concerns of each group (1976:122–30). If this is the case, it prompts the question 'Whose social reality do sociologists present?' We examine the significance of this debate in Chapters 3 and 4.

Postmodern Theories

Much of contemporary sociological discourse revolves around the transition of societies from modernity to postmodernity. Modernity meant certainty and rationality; postmodernity means relativity and uncertainty.

In the theoretical perspectives on modernity and postmodernity, most of the seven perspectives on social problems mentioned so far would fall into the category of modernity. The exceptions would be the labelling and constructionist perspectives, which have certain features of postmodern thinking such as questioning the objective reality of social phenomena and emphasising subjectivity and implicit relativism in the construction of social reality. In focusing on the processes through which certain subjective meanings are ascribed to social conditions, labelling and constructionist perspectives also aim to demonstrate that a social phenomenon may be ascribed a variety of meanings and a variety of relative values. This is a significant theoretical issue, posing some interesting questions for the sociology of social problems. In discussing the transition from modernity to postmodernity, Jeffrey Alexander argues that:

> With the Enlightenment and the growth of secular, scientific thought, the ethos of perfectionism became inseparable from the claims of reason. Reason is the self-conscious application of the mind to social and natural phenomena. Through reason, people came to believe, we can master the world. Through this mastery, we can become free and happy. The world can be made a reasonable place. It can be reconstructed ... In the twentieth century this fundamental tenet of modernity has been challenged and ultimately changed. The faith in progress has often been severely disappointed and the sense that there is a real possibility for perfection has diminished.   *(1995:66–7)*

The main feature of postmodern theories is the demonstration of the relativism of perceptions and values, which are irreducible to one agreed-upon perception or value. In such an irreducible plurality of perceptions of values, no value may be established by any objective criteria as more important than any other value, which means that no hierarchy of values may be established. 'Things which are plural in the postmodern world cannot be arranged in an evolutionary sequence, or be seen as each other's inferior or superior stages; neither can they be classified as "right" or "wrong" solutions to common problems' (Bauman 1992:102). Nor is it important what anyone says or writes, because the meaning and significance of what is said or written – the 'text' – lies with the listener or the reader. This relativism poses some important questions for the analysis of social problems and social issues in general. For example, does this mean that there are no social issues or problems that affect everyone? Does it mean that subjectivity in personal or group perceptions of social reality is beyond any critique or evaluation by 'outsiders'? Does it mean that there is no value, interest or knowledge that can be universally shared?

These questions contain important implications for postmodern thinking in the sociology of social problems. It needs to be noted that there is not one theory of postmodernity, but rather an eclectic collection of views and interpretations of social reality. As one exponent asserts, the dominant feature of postmodernity is the absence of common perceptions of social phenomena and of agreed-upon rules and common values; indeed, the concept of the 'social' itself needs to be questioned (Baudrillard 1983). 'Post-modernism is the most comprehensive of recent theories. It includes in its generous embrace all forms of change, cultural, political and economic.' Because of its eclecticism, 'post-modernism is the most difficult of contemporary theories to assess' (Kumar 1995:3,4). It is also a theory of uncertainty; the concept of modernity, which provided a promise of progress, is discarded but has not been replaced by another promise, another value. Zygmunt Bauman points out that postmodernism presents society as a picture of chaos and, in addition:

> the total absence of any precedent to go by, be reassured by, be guided by – makes the situation totally unnerving. The waters we leaped into are not just deep, but uncharted. We are not even at the crossroads: for crossroads to be crossroads, there must first be roads. Now we know that we *make* roads – the only roads there are and can be – and we do this solely by *walking* them.
>
> *(1995:17; emphasis in the original)*

This is one of many critiques of postmodernism. There are also those critics who question the validity of the concept itself, arguing that postmodernity is just another stage in the ongoing progress of modernity (e.g. Habermas 1993). Jean-François Lyotard himself, the foremost exponent of postmodernism, asserts that the postmodern 'is undoubtedly a part of the modern ... Postmodernism thus understood is not modernism at its end but in the nascent state, and that state is constant' (1993:44). Postmodern theories are also criticised for their absence of critical self-analysis. As one critic says:

> Post-modernists sometimes fail to examine their own assumptions or follow their own advice. They also fail to apply their well-honed critical capacities to their own intellectual production ... Self-deconstruction is seldom on the post-modern agenda ...   *(Rosenau 1992:176)*

Rosenau identifies a number of inconsistencies in postmodern reasoning and mentions especially the following contradictions. First, she argues, postmodernism devalues theory building, but any anti-theory argument is itself a theoretical proposition. Second, post-modernism denies the rationality of logical thinking, but the process of deconstruction, which aims to 'demystify' the value of a text, is itself a form of logical analysis. Third, in arguing that the established system of values favours certain social groups, postmodernism expresses a value preference. Fourth, while arguing for relativity of values, postmodernists elevate their own perspectives against others. In sum, Rosenau points out that any argument or judgement is based on certain criteria, even if the criteria are implicit, and this means an assertion of validity (1992:176–7).

It is beyond this book's scope to deliberate the finer points of the differences in meanings given by various writers to the terms modern, modernity, postmodern, postmodernity, and other related terms. There is clearly no agreement among the exponents of these schools of thought on the meaning, let alone the significance, of these terms. This is to be expected in situations of 'evolving concepts' or 'concepts in the making', and postmodernity is such an evolving concept. Furthermore, if relativism in meaning and values – a key concept in postmodern discourse – is taken to its logical conclusion, then no agreement on these issues can be expected because the meanings and values cannot be objectified and shared. In referring to these new perspectives, therefore, our primary concern is to examine the changes that have emerged in the study of social problems, the meanings attached to them, the methods of intervention that follow from these perspectives, and the social outcomes of these processes.

If one follows postmodern reasoning to its logical conclusion, certain problems of social organisation come into view. If there is no social reality that might be universally accepted by a society, then serious doubts may be raised about the feasibility of social order. For example, while the law of a country might be perceived to be an instrument of the dominant class, nevertheless in a democratic system there is an agreement that a system of laws is necessary to make social life feasible. In postmodern reasoning, however, the law becomes a 'text' of the dominant class and represents only one kind of social reality among many. It needs to be noted, however, that the operation of the adversarial system of law does give considerable credence to the postmodern perspective, as the judgement favours the side that presents a more convincing 'text' of the social reality under judgement. Given this feature of the adversarial system, the introduction of methods of mediation in some courts of civil jurisdiction and especially in the Australian Family Law Court may be seen as a method for reconciling different, and opposing, realities in the postmodern era.

Relevance of the Class Concept/Theory

Postmodern perspectives tend to attach little significance to, or entirely ignore or discard, the class structure of contemporary industrialised Western societies. In focusing on change and the diversity of perceptions of social reality, postmodernism makes this change and diversity visible, but fails to reveal the structural context in which these processes are embedded. The actors and activities may change, but the setting ensures the continuity of certain dominant values and interests. As Kumar comments in his observations on the processes of change: 'instruments and techniques may change, but the overriding goals and purposes of capitalist industrial societies remain the same as before' (1995:32).

Considering the undeniable evidence of distinct differences in the frequency, nature and intensity of certain social conditions that are perceived and acted upon as social problems, the rejection of class theory gives the postmodern perspectives of social reality a distinctly conservative character. The problem with the concept of social class is that, historically, it has been based mainly on the occupational position of the incumbents – that is, on their position in the relations of production. Now, as the emphasis in the 'free' post-industrial market economy is on consumption rather than production, the concept of relations of production is no longer perceived to be appropriate or adequate for the analysis of contemporary society. However, one's position in the consumption sphere still depends on one's position in the field of wealth production, whether one is a producer or financier, a worker in the workshop or a manager in the executive suite. The relations of production might be concealed from direct view, but are nevertheless there as fundamental power relations in society.

The relevance of the class concept to social issues of the 1990s has not been entirely abandoned in sociology. It continues to be examined by a number of sociologists, and a strong if not prevailing opinion leans towards a critical re-examination of class theory, but not a rejection of its relevance. For example, Lydia Morris acknowledges that profound changes in the economy – manifest especially in changes in the shifts and conditions of employment, the changing gender composition of the labour force, and high levels of male unemployment – pose a serious challenge to social class as an appropriate concept in identifying basic structural divisions in society. Nevertheless, she argues that:

> Although social class, as currently constructed and defined, does not seem able to address these questions, this does not mean that the concept itself, much less that of social structure, should be abandoned. This seems to have been one unfortunate effect of a growing awareness of fragmentation and social diversity that challenge any straightforward or unidimensional account of the nature of social divisions.   *(1995:127)*

Morris observes, for example, that unemployment does not only concentrate in certain families and households, but tends to extend spatially to kinship and friendship groups, and that these are certainly class-related (1995:128). As to the concept of the 'underclass', Morris points out differences in the meaning of the concept. In the debate on this issue, she says:

> In one branch of this literature, unemployment and social exclusion are linked with a distinctive cultural predisposition and value framework. The counter-position is that social exclusion and the denial of social citizenship are products of differential impact of social change.   *(1995:131)*

Morris further observes that 'One clear feature of social and economic change has been the polarisation of households into a two-earner/no-earner divide, notwithstanding the complexity of the intermediate positions' (1995:135).

These observations, based on empirical evidence of change in most industrialised countries, give further support to the argument that it is the family or household, rather than the individual, that is the appropriate unit of analysis in the study of social divisions and corresponding inequalities (Morris 1995:2). Morris attaches considerable significance to kinship and social networks as important elements in social division and class structure. This emphasis on the social processes rather than 'static' structures is very useful in identifying the extent of the ability of families, households and social classes to exercise 'command over resources through time'.

Rosemary Crompton also sees the rejection of the class concept in social analysis as a flaw in contemporary sociology. 'The retreat from class, it may be suggested,' she says, 'is becoming the sociological equivalent of the new individualism' (1993:8). Crompton acknowledges that although there is much confusion about the term, 'there are insufficient grounds for the wholesale rejection of class as an "outmoded nineteenth century concept"' (1993:8).

In this book, we aim to demonstrate that the concept of social class is an important heuristic tool in the study of social problems. In retaining the concept of class, we also keep in mind the importance of participation in production, considering the fact that access to employment has now become a 'scarce commodity' and is clearly class-related. Our main focus however is on consumption, consumption patterns and access to consumption. 'Access' means the ability or capacity to consume, and in a wider context means 'command over resources through time'. As Crompton notes, some people are able to satisfy their consumption needs through the market, while others have to rely on the state. This has now become a fundamental class division. However, as argued elsewhere (Jamrozik 1991, Jamrozik and Sweeney 1996), the state facilitates access to market consumption for those who hold a position in production activities, while providing minimum means for survival in conditions of subsistence for those who have lost access to the production process. We consider this division to be an important, indeed fundamental factor in the nature of social problems in contemporary capitalist societies. The division is fundamental because it entails not only a division between inclusion in and exclusion from access to society's resources, but also the loss of privacy for the excluded population strata through state control and surveillance – that is, the loss of citizenship rights that the rest of society takes for granted.

CHAPTER 3

Methods of Intervention in Social Problems

Social problems are complex phenomena composed of a range of inter-connected processes. An adequate understanding of a social problem as a social phenomenon has to include the perception of its genesis – that is, the causal links to social activities that 'create' the problem, the social actors who identify the problem, the population particularly affected by the problem, the nature of the perceived threat, and the applied methods of intervention intended to alleviate, control or solve the problem. An essential part of this understanding is the identification of the social actors in all these processes.

In this chapter we examine the methods of intervention in social problems, focusing first on the role of theories and research, and then on the activities that are implemented as the response to identified social problems. In this approach we give attention to the role of the state and examine responses to social problems from the perspective of the three-level structure of activities, illustrated schematically in Figure 1.1 (see page 11). We note that each level of social organisation does not only represent different activities, but that activities at each level are likely to be guided by different values, interests and theoretical orientations. Values, interests and theoretical orientation at one level are often incompatible with those at the other levels. At each level there are also constraints that limit the extent and nature of activities. We attempt to identify some of these constraints, especially those affecting the activities performed by human services at the operational level, where the helping professions play a leading role in service delivery. In examining activities at that level, we look particularly at social work, as this profession holds the central position in society's formal response to social problems.

Theories and Research

We suggested in the previous chapter that a study of social problems constitutes a form of intervention in social problems – often a form of primary intervention. This is so because theories of social problems underpin the various intervention methods aimed at either attenuating or solving a given problem. A study that leads to the identification and interpretation of a social condition (or certain social activities) as a social problem, manifest or latent, may invoke a societal response and even influence the choice of intervention method. A societal response is more likely to be forthcoming if such a study makes the potential 'threat' visible to the public and includes a convincing conclusion about the likely detrimental effects for society if a given condition or conduct is allowed to continue.

However, there is not always a societal response to an identified social problem, and if there is, its form does not neccessarily connect logically to the theoretical perspective projected in the study. The link between a theory and its translation and application in practice is often not evident, or might not even exist. Policy makers, administrators and practitioners in human services tend to be rather critical of theories, especially sociological theories. While they might sometimes acknowledge a theory's relevance, they are more likely to claim that their own attitudes and methods are more appropriate because these are based on their own knowledge gained from experience or 'practice wisdom'. There are also those who become so committed to a method based on a particular theory (not necessarily acknowledged but implicit in the method) that no amount of evidence of the method's inapplicability or lack of effectiveness seems to lessen their faith in its validity. The result is that intervention methods tend to be, one way or another, practice-driven. Practice develops its own theoretical legitimation and its own ontological validity, reinforced through induction of repetitive activities.

Practice wisdom often demonstrates John Maynard Keynes's observation that 'practical' people are usually the disciples of a long-departed and discredited theorist. This is often the case at all levels of intervention in social problems, from policy making to administration to service delivery. Some theoretical assumptions that have never been put to a critical test continue to underpin societal responses to social problems. They become so well integrated in practical activities and so taken for granted that their relevance or validity are not questioned and not even discussed (e.g. 'Welfare assistance breeds dependency'; 'People are *by nature* competitive'). Yet, as noted in the previous chapter, the differences in perceptions and interpretations of social issues or social problems clearly demonstrate that different theoretical assumptions are often held about an issue or problem, leading to different societal responses and intervention methods (Martin and Kettner 1996:20–30; Spicker 1995:35–6). Furthermore, intervention methods are not derived solely from theoretical perspectives, but are also influenced, if not determined, by ideological, political, financial and cultural constraints.

What, then, is the role of sociological research in social problems? Opinions on this issue certainly differ, arising as they do out of different theoretical perspectives on social problems and different views on the social role of sociology and the social sciences generally. For example, Rubington and Weinberg assert that any theoretical perspective on social problems, if it is to be adequate in its explanatory power, must be comprehensive in scope in that it must address four related aspects of such problems: *causes* – that is, ideas about the factors that produce social problems and the nature of that process; *conditions* – the background in which the causes of social problems are likely to develop; *consequences* – the likely harmful effects of the identified problems; and *solutions* – not necessarily explicitly stated, but implicit in the analysis of the problem. These four aspects imply that sociologists have a 'dual mandate – that is, to solve social problems as well as to develop sociology as a discipline' (1989:360). To fulfil this dual mandate, the four aspects imply four roles for the sociologist: theorist, researcher, applier and critic. To perform these four roles in one study is clearly extremely difficult, as the activities implied in each are not easily compatible, because of the theoretical perspective applicable to each role and the purpose of a given study. For this reason, sociologists choose broadly between approaches aimed primarily at testing and/or generating hypotheses and theories, and applied studies aimed at explaining a particular problem in a theory's framework and/or exploring possible methods of intervention in the problem studied.

Opinions certainly differ on sociology's role in the study of social problems. For example, Manis (1976) argues that sociology – being a social science discipline with legitimate claims of engaging in scientific enquiries into the human condition – confers certain obligations on the sociologist to pursue such enquiries with an awareness of the values that influence public perceptions of phenomena whose existence as objective facts may be determined by scientific enquiry. This means that in certain situations a sociologist may have a moral obligation to point out the significance of some undesirable conditions in society, which public opinion may not be able to see. Manis points out that social problems do not always emerge in a simple cause–effect linkage; the linkages may be quite complex, giving rise to primary, secondary and tertiary problems (1976:107–11). Basing his opinion on these observations and on the value premise of social obligations related to the sharing of scientific knowledge, Manis advances a definition of social problems, which he asserts serves as the basis for the knowledge-value paradigm in the study of social problems. 'Social problems [he states] are those social conditions identified by scientific inquiry and values as detrimental to human well-being' (1976:25).

A similar view is expressed by Merton, who argues that popular perceptions 'are no safe guide to the magnitude of social problems' (1976:16), as such perceptions are influenced and mediated by people's personal experiences, interests, values and the power of the mass media. The 'latency effect' of certain social problems (that is, an effect not immediately evident, but likely to become so in the future) is another important factor. The sociologist needs to take these factors into account in the study of social problems and present the findings accordingly, even if these findings differ from prevailing public opinion. At the same time, sociologists must also be aware of their own values, which undeniably influence their interest as individuals in particular issues and also their perception of those issues as social problems. These values guide the selection of research questions and methods of enquiry, as well as methods of analysing data and formulating conclusions.

Other writers (e.g. Spector and Kitsuse 1987:63–72) address this issue by pointing out that sociologists, like members of any scholarly discipline or profession, are members of their discipline but also ordinary members of the public. This means that they may hold personal views on a social problem, based on their values and moral judgements, and also views as members of their discipline. In any study of social problems they therefore need to separate these two positions, as their work will be regarded in society as a product of research endeavour conducted within the researcher's discipline and therefore based on a certain authoritative 'expert' knowledge.

There are two related and important issues involved in these arguments about the role of research in social problems – especially in research commissioned or sponsored for the explicit purpose of studying a specific problem. One is the use of research as a means of discovering a possible solution to a problem, which implies the task of translating, or converting, the social/political nature of the social problem into a technical problem. The other is the scope of enquiry such research needs to take if it is to explain a problem's nature adequately. If the scope is confined to a narrow definition of the problem and does not introduce a broad societal framework into the research design, the research will run the risk of producing findings based on a 'truncated perspective'. These two aspects have been examined elsewhere for their role in relation to policy formulation and

legitimation (Jamrozik 1991, 1992), but they acquire an added significance in the context of their specific role in methods of intervention
in social problems.

Political–Technical Conversion

Since social problems arise out of structural arrangements in society,
they are intrinsically political in nature. However, identification of social
problems, and any remedial response that might follow, depends on
many factors, not the least of these being the attitude of the government
– that is, the state. Yet for political and related ideological reasons, or for
economic or other reasons, governments tend to respond to a social
problem only if such response fits into their policies and interests. As
Alvin Gouldner observed:

> The state, therefore, does not only require a social science that can facilitate
> planned intervention to resolve certain social problems; it also requires social
> science to serve as a *rhetoric*, to persuade resistant or undecided segments of
> the society that such problems do, indeed, exist and are of dangerous
> proportions. Once committed to such intervention, the state acquires a vested
> interest of its own in 'advertising' the social problems or whose solution it
> seeks financing. In other words, the state requires social researchers that can
> *expose* those social problems with which the state is ready to deal.
>
> *(1971:349-50; emphasis in the original)*

On the other hand, governments faced with a social problem that calls
for difficult policy decisions that are likely to be met with a negative
reaction from the electorate or from an organised and influential lobby,
tend to depoliticise the issue by shifting it to either administrative or
professional 'experts' who are then expected to provide an 'objective'
technical analysis and possible solution. Commissions of inquiry, private
consultants and accredited researchers perform such 'depoliticising'
functions. This does not mean that such mechanisms and instruments
do not provide valuable inputs into policy making and in formulating
responses to social problems. Yet rarely if ever do such inputs result in
policy responses that entail the structural change in resource allocation
that might be necessary to effectively solve or attenuate the social
problem in question. On the contrary, depoliticising issues is a means of
seeking a solution to a social problem while at the same time preserving
the existing structure of power (Jamrozik 1991, 1992).

For this reason, much research into social problems that is sponsored
or specifically commissioned by governments does not examine the
political nature of such problems. Instead, it aims to present and
explain problems in the conceptual perspective, which gives the problems a 'technical' character, feasibly amenable to technical solution or

alleviation. This 'conversion' of problems effectively removes them from the political arena and enables governments to provide a response that does not disturb their overall policies and objectives. Or it enables them not to do anything about a problem, typically on the grounds of scarce resources or other, more 'important' priorities.

The social and political significance of the conversion of social problems by research is one reason why so much research sponsored or commissioned by governments is done by economists. As most social problems are related in some way to the allocation of resources, human or material, they are amenable to presentation in economic terms. The conversion of their political aspects into economic data therefore tends to present such problems in a neat, one-dimensional perspective of economic indices and equations, omitting as irrelevant any aspects that do not fit into the economic paradigm. As observed by Paul Hirsch and his colleagues, unlike sociology, which perceives society as a complex phenomenon, 'the marginalist revolution allowed economics to re-define itself on a much streamlined basis'. The style of contemporary economics 'is characterised by the development of models based on deliberately, vigorously, and rigidly simplified assumptions. The *elegance* of the models, their "parsimony" is prized and the intent is that they be predictive' (1987:318; emphasis in the original). Contemporary governments therefore prefer that research into social problems be conducted within an economic perspective, especially research carried out in the 'neo-classical' or 'economic rationalist' perspective, which focuses on the principle of 'scarcity' and examines social issues in the sole perspective of the 'free' market. Sociological research may be accepted, provided it focuses on quantifiable data and eschews any references to political issues. In effect, governments seek research that focuses on possible solutions to a problem rather than that which provides explanations.

It needs to be noted however, that governments' attitudes to social problems are influenced by the ideological orientation of the party in power. Governments of social-democratic persuasion are more likely to acknowledge structural causes of social problems and to seek technical advice or research that provides feasible suggestions for structural changes to solve or attenuate such problems. By comparison, liberal-democratic and conservative governments are less likely to acknowledge structural causes in social problems, and tend to seek advice or research that is directed at the population affected by the social problem in question, hoping that the solution can be found in modifying the attitudes and behaviour of that population. Governments that follow the ideas of the 'New Right' or the theories of economic rationalism certainly tend to look for research that provides them with the grounds to adopt such remedial measures.

Truncated Perspectives

Methods of intervention in social problems are guided and influenced by certain theories and beliefs, and also by political expediency. Historically, many theories of social problems were generated from studies that focused either exclusively or substantially on the population groupings or social classes in which a particular problem was manifestly visible. This approach to studying social problems continues to this day, and in applied research commissioned or sponsored by governments the focus tends to be entirely on such populations, for example the unemployed, the homeless, and the poor. Often, this approach appears to be motivated by researchers' concern for these populations, and it seems 'natural' for researchers to seek explanations for social problems in the populations negatively affected. However, theories of social problems that are formulated on the basis of data collected in such studies, rather than on data from studies focusing on the population as a whole, are flawed conceptually, lead to flawed perceptions of the problem and, in turn, to corresponding flawed methods of intervention. Such theoretical flaw is created by the limitations of the data – namely, the data are obtained by focusing only on the population experiencing a given problem, and comparable data on a population not affected by the problem are lacking. Furthermore, in the definition of social problems, such studies are no longer studies of social problems. They are studies of the *effects* of social problems experienced by the studied population as personal problems, the problems' nature having been converted into personal problems by such research approaches (see Mills 1959). These research approaches lead to truncated perspectives on society. Any generalisations drawn from research of this kind, when applied to another part of society or to society as a whole, are unavoidably flawed and lead to erroneous conclusions. Comments and imputations drawn from such research are frequently made about the universality of certain problems throughout the whole social structure, while the data and intervention methods focus exclusively on specific sections of the population.

Theories and Methods of Investigation

The two issues discussed previously bring into focus the significance of theoretical perspectives that guide the methods of research into social problems. Clearly, some perspectives logically lead research towards seeking explanations of social problems in social structures, while others lead to the study of populations experiencing a given problem. Correspondingly, the perspective guiding a study also suggests, implicitly or explicitly, the method of intervention. For example, the depoliticisation of social problems through the conversion of their social/political

character into that of problems explained by the putative characteristics of affected populations is facilitated by the psychologising and
pathologising features of the theories of deviance. Such theories not
only serve to remove social problems from the political sphere but also
provide the basis for intervention methods in the form of 'treatment'
for the putative pathology in the personal characteristics of the
population experiencing the problems. Through such a perspective on
social problems, the legitimacy of the dominant values of society and the
pursuit of corresponding goals is maintained. The intervention
methods' moral rightfulness is demonstrated by the manifestation of
helpful assistance rendered to the unfortunate population perceived
to be 'afflicted' by a pathological condition.

A typical example of such a conversion process is unemployment.
High levels of unemployment have been consistently recorded in most
industrialised countries since the mid-1970s, clearly indicating the sys-
temic links of this phenomenon. Unemployment has spawned volumes
of research that seeks explanations in a variety of causes, but the most
consistent attention has been given to unemployed people themselves,
examining their personal characteristics, their methods of seeking
employment and their attitude to work. In compiling an annotated
bibliography of unemployment research in Australia, Diana Encel
(1989) identified 349 items on this issue published from 1983 to 1988.
The most numerous identified categories were reports on surveys of
unemployed people, particularly young people. (See Chapter 5 for an
analysis of unemployment as a social problem.)

A different outcome could be expected if research into a social
problem were conducted in the perspective of critical theory. In that
perspective, the source of social problems is sought in the social structure, so a complete depoliticisation of the problem is not possible.
At best, the source of the problem may be shifted to administrative
arrangements, thus converting the problem as perceived into a technical problem but leaving it in the public sphere. A different outcome
again might be expected from studies in social problems conducted in
the constructionist perspective, which focuses on the processes of
claims-making about the existence and nature of social problems rather
than on the objective existence of social problems as such. Indeed, the
constructionist perspective refutes the objectivity of social problems.
This approach's concern is to study the social activities through which
certain social conditions are identified as social problems, and to show
how claims to that effect are accepted by society, or by a significant part
of society, as legitimate and valid. The focus on claims-making activities
leads to identification of the individuals and social groups who make
such claims, to their methods of operation and apparent motives and

interests, their successes and failures in having their claims accepted by society or governments, and the consequent outcomes. The constructionist approach is therefore a study of social power, which (the protagonists of the perspective would argue, with considerable justification) is the legitimate and important task of sociology. In focusing on the processes of claims-making, the constructionist approach can show how certain claims lead to the perception of social problems in the characteristics of the affected population and how intervention methods then focus on attempts to correct those characteristics believed to be the cause of the problem. The translation of a social problem into the personal problem of a certain population is then complete, maintaining the validity of the social pathology perspective.

Research into social problems is frequently of value to governments as the first form of intervention, and for this reason it is in governments' interests to sponsor it but also to control it. It is well known that sponsoring or commissioning bodies aim to retain control over the research process, including the method of enquiry and the dissemination of findings. The control of research in 'politically sensitive' social-problem areas is achieved through research conducted by organisations operating under specific contracts or through commissioning research from private consultants, in each case retaining control over the dissemination of findings. The findings of such research are likely to be made public only if they support the government's policy, or convert the political nature of the problem investigated and provide the basis for a program of technical intervention.

It can be concluded from this discussion that research into social problems poses theoretical as well as ethical issues for researchers. Sociological research that aims to explain *how* certain problems occur and *why* they occur will apply a 'naturalist' perspective to the object of research – that is, 'the philosophical view that strives to remain true to the nature of the phenomenon under study' (Matza 1969:4). However, research commissioned by a government or another sponsor would be expected to provide suggestions for the solution of the problem under study, and this would mean the research would be more likely conducted in a 'correctionalist' perspective – that is, with the assumption that the phenomenon to be studied is an 'undesirable' condition. Unavoidably, such an assumption would influence not only the method of enquiry but also interpretation of the findings.

Organisational Levels of Intervention

The depoliticisation of social problems through their conversion into personal problems of certain individuals or population groupings can be clearly demonstrated in the context of the three-level organisational structure of social action illustrated in Figure 1.1. Intervention in social problems may be initiated and take place at any level of society's organisational structure. Normally, expectations are that the response will be initiated at the political level, as the resources necessary to develop and implement the response are allocated at that level. In practice, this is not necessarily the case. A response is often made at first in some form at the operative level because it is at this level that a social problem first becomes manifest. However, whatever takes place at the operational level – that is, at the level of service delivery – is influenced and often determined by decisions at the administrative level, and at the policy making level where resource allocation takes place. For this reason, any analysis of intervention methods in social problems has to include an examination of activities that take place at all three levels. The importance of this approach may be illustrated by the following, more detailed description of activities at each level, and their interrelationship or interdependence. This interrelationship is two-directional, although in common perceptions it tends to be perceived as one-directional, from top (the political level) down to administration and service delivery.

The Political Level

The *political level* of action represents, essentially, the interaction between the public and the government. This interaction entails processes through which certain societal values and interests are translated into policies, laws and allocation of resources deemed necessary to implement the policies and enforce the laws. Interventions in social problems are also initiated at this level in the form determined by the perception of a given problem. The intervention may take the form of new legislation, an amendment to existing legislation, the restructuring of administrative machinery or the creation of a new organisation to deal with the identified problem. It may also include certain publicity, an educational program through the media, or allocation of funds to the public or private sector for specific activities designed to provide services in the given problem area. The government may also take action aimed at depoliticising the nature of the problem, or at delaying intervention by commissioning an inquiry or a research program. An example of such a response to political pressure on a government was the establishment of the Commission of Inquiry into Poverty (1975), which enabled the-then Australian federal government to demonstrate its willingness to do something about the growing poverty among certain sections of the population, but at the same time delay any concrete action on the grounds that more reliable information was first necessary.

The Administrative Level

The *administrative level* acts as a 'transmission belt' and 'conversion mechanism' that converts political decisions into intervention methods at the level of service delivery. The activities at the administrative level consist of processes that translate policies and legislative acts into administrative rules, establishing appropriate administrative machinery, developing instructions for the operative level, and thus converting the (political) social problem into a technical problem. Activities at this level also include administering resources allocated at the political level and applying them to specific programs and methods of intervention. A problem still remains in the public sphere, but is no longer political in nature, having been converted into a technical task able to be dealt with by administrative expertise, which is often assisted and reinforced by specific professional knowledge. In Australia, the establishment of numerous labour-market programs since the mid-1970s – most of which have produced rather meagre results – is an example of converting a structural/political issue into a technical problem expected to be solved or at least attenuated by technical expertise.

The Operative Level

At the *operative level*, policies, laws and administrative rules and directives are interpreted and applied to actual situations or persons. At this level, a direct face-to-face interaction takes place between the helping professions (and related occupations employed in human services) and the people who experience a particular problem. At this level of intervention a social problem is removed from the public sphere by being 'translated' or 'converted' into the personal problem of those in the affected population. At this level, a dual conversion takes place: conversion of a collective problem into an individualised, personal problem; and conversion of the now-personal problem into a form of pathology that fits into the framework of the professional's intervention method and the theory guiding that method. Employing financial counsellors, whose task is to assist people who are on subsistence incomes (such as unemployment benefits) to manage their meagre finances, is an example of such a response. Indeed, emergency financial relief services provide assistance to families who have difficulty paying their accounts for domestic expenditure (e.g. rent or power accounts), but assistance is conditional upon the recipients' willingness to accept financial counselling (Department for Family and Community Services 1995). (The three-level intervention system in social problems, identifying some of the typical responses and methods of conversion, is presented schematically in Figure 3.1. A detailed analysis of this process is given in Chapter 6 and shown in Figure 6.1.)

The Conversion Process

What kinds of activities, then, are to receive attention in the analysis of methods of intervention in social problems? While intervention might take place at all three levels of organisational action, in common perception and in much human services professional literature, attention is

Figure 3.1: Methods of Intervention in Social Problems

Spheres of activity	Methods of intervention
Political/social sphere Social problems emerge as 'negative residue' from pursuit of dominant values and interests	Structural change Legislation Allocation of resources
Administrative sphere Problem converted into technical problem for administrative attention	Administrative restructuring Applied research Use of technical expertise
Operative sphere Problem converted into personal problem of affected population	Personal intervention by helping professions (e.g. counselling, therapy, surveillance)

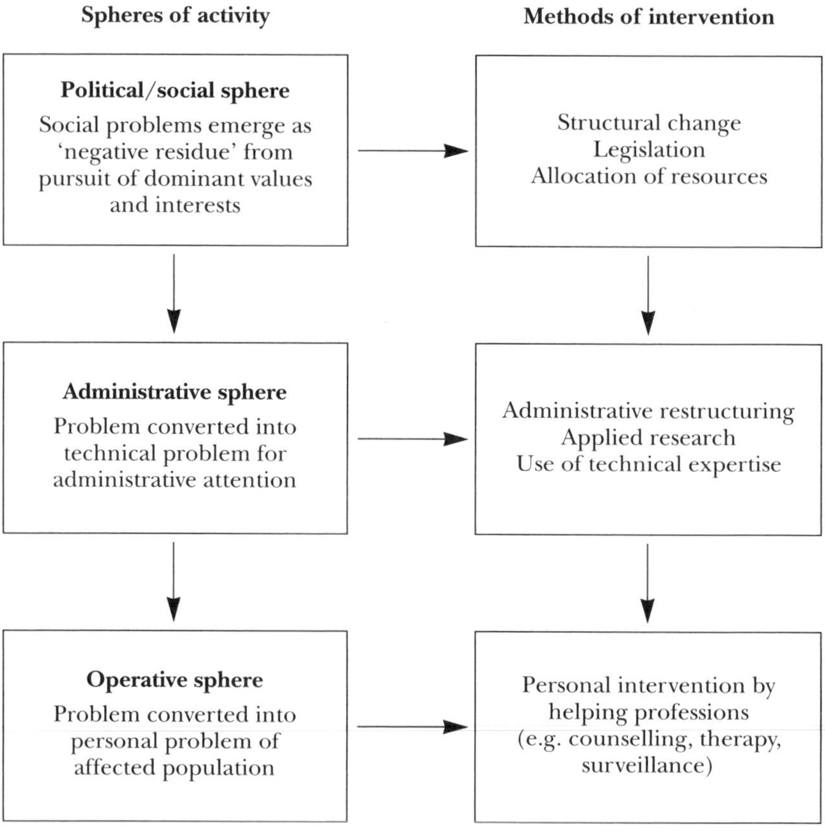

Note: For analysis of this process, see Figure 6.1

usually focused on methods of service delivery at the operative level, while the administrative and policy making contexts receive relatively little consideration. This 'disjunction' in perceptions extends also to research approaches to social problems. For example, in an overview of research on young people's health in Australia (Boland and Jamrozik 1989), the researchers found that while polemical discussions and rhetoric in the literature on young people's health presented the issue as a 'social problem' that called for policy responses at the political level, research activities (most of which were funded by government agencies) focused almost entirely on young people's health-affecting behaviour, such as tobacco smoking, alcohol consumption, illicit drug use and lifestyles. It was also evident from the data that most research was conducted by members of the helping professions who were engaged either in teaching and research at tertiary institutions or who were practising in service administration or service delivery. Their perception of the problems investigated in their research was therefore directly related to the intervention methods practised by their profession.

As shown in Figure 1.1, in methods of intervention in social problems the three distinct levels of activity involve three groups of social actors performing three distinct but related roles: policy making and resource allocation; administration; and service delivery. The fourth group of actors consists of the public who are being served. In such a composition of activities and actors it may be expected that different views and concerns and even conflicts of interest are likely to occur. People working at each level of organisational structure not only have different tasks to perform, but may also view their tasks from different theoretical and value positions or with different personal interests. People working at the same level may even hold differing views on these issues. These differences are likely to produce different perceptions of an intervention program. As Donnison and Chapman pointed out some years ago (1965:33), a study of any social program or service would find four distinct views and opinions of the program's performance, or 'four tones of voice': *manifest* (the officially approved and publicly propagated version); *assumed* (the subjective interpretation by the people working in the program); *extant* (the 'objective' reality); and *requisite* (the desirable, aimed-for-but-not-fulfilled version). These four perspectives are rarely if ever the same, offering a distinct possibility of four different conclusions that might be reached from examining a single program, with each perspective presenting its own perception of social reality.

How and why such differences occur is presented schematically in Figure 3.2, in which the four levels of activity shown earlier in Figure 1.1 are integrated with the 'four tones of voice' identified by Donnison and Chapman. In Figure 3.2, 'X' identifies the category of actors who are likely to present a particular perspective or 'tone of voice'. It may be expected that, more often than not, policy makers will present the manifest version of a program (the claim of intent or achievement), or the requisite version (the desired objective, but limited or unfulfilled by lack of resources or non-cooperation of other parties etc.). Administrators of the program are likely to present the manifest version publicly, but the assumed version privately among themselves or to people in whom they confide their personal opinions. Service providers at the operative level will have their own assumed view of the program, but will also be in the best position to see the extant reality of the program, for example its degree of effectiveness. Recipients of the intervention (the people 'with the problem') will have their own extant view of the program and also their view of what the program ideally should be.

The different perspectives on the nature of an intervention program by those actively involved in the program illustrate the intrinsic nature of social phenomena – namely, the absence of independent existence from the observer's perception. The differences in actors' perceptions and interpretations may be due to their personal values and interests, but the differences may also be due to different theories influencing the views and guiding the activities of each group. For example, policy makers' views are likely to be influenced by political ideologies and economic theories; administrators' perceptions are likely to be influenced by management theories; and professionals at the level of service delivery are likely to follow a diversity of psychosocial theories of human problems and corresponding methods of therapeutic intervention.

Figure 3.2: Comparative Framework for Evaluation of Organisational Performance

Levels of activity	'Tones of voice'			
	Manifest	Assumed	Extant	Requisite
Political	X			X
Administrative	X	X		
Operative		X	X	
Receiving			X	X

Different political and social influences also come into play at each level. These differences often result in incompatible orientations, interests and interpretations of given policies. Policy makers are influenced by public opinion, as their remaining in power depends on public support. Political expediency is the ever-present factor in policy decisions, although a decision based on expediency is always presented to the public as the 'best possible' decision or the 'only possible' decision. Policies are thus determined by what policy makers see as ideologically appropriate, economically feasible and politically expedient or necessary.

Administrators, on the other hand, follow their own theories and practice wisdom. Bureaucracies have long memories and long-established, time-proven methods of operation. Furthermore, in large organisations, the same principles and interests do not necessarily operate at each level of the organisational hierarchy. Subordinates' interests and corresponding perspectives on the task at hand are not the same as those of managers. The complexity of administration increases in line with the diversity of functions performed and the number of agencies involved. It follows that with the trend that began in the 1980s towards corporatising and privatising public sector activities, thus introducing a diversity of actors through competitive tendering for services, translation and implementation of policies are more likely to increase the differences between manifest, assumed and extant realities of the public response to a given social problem.

At the operative level (or 'coal-face') of the public response to social problems, whether government or government-sponsored, policy decisions and administrative regulations and commands are converted into direct service intervention methods and applied to individual situations or 'cases'. In this process, social problems are translated into individuals' problems – or to use C. Wright Mills's perspective (1959), public issues, which are collective in nature, are translated into individualised private problems and are treated as such by the intervention methods used by the helping professions and related occupations. The problems also have to be 'fitted' into the methods of intervention and into the theories and values that guide the interventions. Activities at the operative level are the most visible, so the translation of social problems into problems of individuals or certain social groupings means a fundamental shift in perception from social to personal and from collective to individual. This entails a corresponding shift in explanation from structural factors to the personal characteristics of the population experiencing a given social problem's effects. The helping professions might refer in their rhetoric to 'social problems', but their intervention methods are often bereft of social meaning.

The three-level analysis facilitates the identification of processes through which the rhetoric at the political level (or at any level) is not always followed in practice. Indeed, the perception of a given problem is likely to be different at each level. At the political level for example, the perception of a problem is assisted or fashioned by the mass media, which have a hunger for news and sensation. The mass media, together with public opinion polls, identify issues and present them as social problems, but they also *create* issues and influence and mould public opinion. A social problem may indeed be 'created' by a political lobby, which stimulates interest within the media to publicise the issue, and thus exerts pressure on the government to respond. On the other hand, certain issues do not attract the media's attention for long. In such cases, the problem remains while the pressure on policy makers to act on it is removed.

In the conditions of postmodernity, the question arises whether, or to what extent, the relativism of diverse values and plurality of often-conflicting interests can be accommodated in the society's response to social problems. Being subjected to pressures from business interests, professional organisations and political lobbies, and faced with social problems created by their own policies, governments seek to shift difficult-to-solve issues from the political arena, into either the administrative level or, more often, the field of technical expertise and research. In such situations the role of social research as an integral part of the response to social problems comes into focus. Governments sponsor social research by establishing specialised research institutes, by providing funds for research activities in universities, and by commissioning research into specific problems from a variety of private consultants. Most of this research converts social problems into technical problems – that is, problems amenable to management through administration or professional intervention.

Professional Interventions and Practice Wisdom

In human services the most important (and the most numerous) people are the members of the helping professions: teachers, medical practitioners, nurses, psychologists, social workers and a wide range of counsellors who specialise in certain methods of intervention in people's personal problems. From the perspective presented in this book, the intervention methods employed by these helping professions first convert social problems into the personal problems of the people they serve. The professionals then attempt to 'treat' the problems using their specialised method, usually referred to as consultation, counselling, therapy or therapeutic counselling. However, to achieve some understanding of the intervention methods used at the operative level we need to look not only at the limitations imposed by professional perspectives but also at the constraints imposed on the service delivery methods by the decisions made at political and administrative levels. Working within the three-level organisational framework, the helping professions play a dual role, represent a dual authority and perform a dual task. They act as members of their profession and also as members of an organisation; they act with their societally sanctioned professional authority, but also directly or implicitly with the authority of the state. Correspondingly, they practise their professional skill and through their intervention methods legitimise the conversion process of social problems to personal problems. The greater the success of the helping professions in carrying out the task of conversion, the less intervention is needed at the administrative and/or political level. This means that policies and administrative arrangements in the society's response to social problems are also influenced and constrained by the degree of success or the limitations of intervention methods used by the helping professions at the operative level.

The helping profession most closely identified with intervention in social problems is social work. Along with other helping professions, social workers use intervention methods that are applied mainly in encounters with individuals, or sometimes with small groups of people who are perceived to share a similar problem. More often than not, the method used is defined as counselling of some kind. 'Counselling', as an intervention method used by the helping professions, is an umbrella term that includes a wide range of approaches guided by a wide range of theories. What actually takes place in the process of counselling is difficult to know because this activity usually takes place in a face-to-face encounter in the privacy of the counsellor's consulting room or in the counselled person's home. Counselling is a method whose meaning and purpose is accepted by the helping professions as self-evident, but which is rather difficult to explain to the uninitiated. Indeed, it is interesting to ask 'What do counsellors do when they counsel?' This question is particularly apposite to social work, as this profession is actively engaged in most of the fields of concern referred to as social problems, and counselling is the method that the profession universally uses. But it is also a profession that claims considerable eclecticism in its methods of counselling intervention, the methods being derived from a range of theories borrowed from other disciplines, mainly various fields of clinical psychology. Notwithstanding social work's claim to being a profession whose intervention methods are grounded in a particular theory or theories, the intervention methods in social work are largely driven by what may be called 'practice theory' or 'practice wisdom'.

Practice wisdom is the attitude a person develops in an organisational environment under the influence of the organisation's internal culture, dominant values and history. It is a form of 'theory' that guides the organisation's activity and that is constantly reinforced by fulfilled expectations or, rather more often, by self-fulfilling prophecies. The social reality thus created is maintained by confirming instances of success or failure of repeated actions – a kind of ongoing inductive process of theory confirmation.

Practice wisdom is a feature of bureaucratic organisations and is especially prevalent in organisations in which personnel undergo rigorous in-house training designed not only to prepare recruits for the tasks ahead but also to socialise them into unquestioning acceptance of the organisation's values and the authority of superiors in the organisation's hierarchy. Typical organisations of this kind are the police, the armed forces, and all kinds of organisations defined by Erving Goffman (1961) as 'total institutions', such as prisons, ships, psychiatric hospitals, boarding schools, monasteries and convents.

Practice wisdom is particularly prevalent among occupations employed in human services whose intervention methods have a weak theoretical base and whose evaluation criteria for the effectiveness of the service provided are difficult to establish with precision. This is an ever-present issue of concern and contestation in organisations and occupations providing human services of a non-tangible nature, such as social work and a variety of related helping professions whose methods of intervention are confined to counselling, psychotherapy and various other forms of advice that aim to achieve in the recipients certain changes in behaviour, attitudes, human relationships or the ability to manage everyday affairs. Practice wisdom becomes a powerful force, especially in organisations providing services to populations experiencing certain 'entrenched' social problems such as unemployment, poverty, or the breakdown of law and order. Where such conditions remain unchanged for years and become a feature of the lifestyle, intervention methods used by the helping professions acquire the characteristics of a ritual that reaffirms the condition and, at best, impresses upon the recipient the necessity to adjust to the condition. For example, poverty-relief measures, such as issuing food vouchers, might provide temporary relief but do not change the conditions. As the service is delivered to individuals in a face-to-face mode, service providers begin to see the recipients of the service as the embodiment of the social problem – they become the 'problem population'. For the service provider, each new encounter with a member of the population experiencing the problem serves to confirm this perception and further reinforces the provider's practice wisdom.

Social work, by definition and in common perceptions, is the foremost profession engaged in the provision of services aimed to solve, attenuate or control social problems. It is also an occupation that claims professional status but that operates with a weak theoretical base, relying on theories borrowed and assimilated from other professions such as medicine, psychology, sociology and jurisprudence. To this day, the prevalent view among the helping professions and among social workers themselves is that social work does not have a theory of its own. There are also views among social workers that the social sciences and the theories these generate are of little value to the field of social work practice, which (it is argued) takes place in the 'real world'. Although there are assertions to the contrary, the relationship between social work and the social sciences has remained rather tenuous, especially the relationship between social work and sociology. As a result, social workers often refer to practice theory, which it is claimed is based on certain assumptions about society, human behaviour and problems experienced by certain categories of people. There are models of social work practice that aim to demonstrate how those assumptions can be operationalised in various forms and methods of intervention. Most social welfare agencies would have 'theories developed from experience' about 'typical young unemployed' people 'lacking self-esteem', or people with a 'bad working habit'.

Undoubtedly, there is dissonance between social work and the social sciences, and this dissonance cannot be explained solely by the reluctance of social workers to apply the theories and findings generated in social science research. For example, there is relatively little sociological research that examines the actual process of social work practice (Sheppard 1995). The problem, however, is much deeper. One reason for it is the prevalence of theories in social work that are broadly defined as 'psychosocial'. However, because the methods of service delivery in social work are highly individualistic and person-focused, the 'social' part tends to disappear in practice. Practice theory or practice wisdom then takes over. (This issue is further examined in Chapters 8 and 9.)

Practice wisdom in social work has been defined by Michael Sheppard as 'the accumulated knowledge practitioners are able to bring to the consideration of individual cases and their practice in general' (1995:279). Sheppard identifies three sources of practice wisdom: knowledge gained from 'everyday life'; knowledge gained from the ideas generated in social science research; and knowledge gained from social work practice. Knowledge gained from social work practice comes from experience with a number of cases involving the same problem and from cases involving similar problems. Sheppard considers accumulated knowledge of this kind to be valuable, as it enables practitioners to approach each new case with certain hypotheses based on previous experience. However, he acknowledges that such inductive hypotheses may also serve to confirm or verify established expectations and prejudices, and may prevent the practitioner from noticing new factors that might be present in a new case. The potential of practice wisdom to contribute to the advancement of knowledge is thus limited, especially as it tends to be an unrecorded 'personalised knowledge' or 'practice folklore', known to the individual or passed around through word of mouth, but not subjected to rigorous validity testing (1995:265–93). As a knowledge base for the methods of intervention in social problems, practice wisdom has little to offer in terms of solving or attenuating problems. Rather, it tends to serve as a means of legitimating the social problems that society or its government are unwilling or incapable of solving. In effect, practice wisdom is a conservative force, and its use by social workers makes social work a conservative profession.

Class Perspective and Social Pathology

It is to be expected that in a class society, the perception of social issues and social problems will be mediated through the class perspective. This perspective manifests itself in at least three ways: certain social problems tend to occur either solely or with greater frequency and/or intensity in some social classes rather than in others; certain social problems occur throughout the social structure but are perceived and interpreted differently according to the social class of the affected population; or certain social problems occur throughout the social structure but are concealed in some classes and revealed in others, mainly because services employed to deal with the problems, and the methods of intervention, differ between classes.

A relevant issue is the compatibility or conflict of interests between service providers and service recipients, and the outcome of these differences. Most professionals in human services operate within a middle-class perspective, but some of the services they provide are used by middle-class recipients and others are used by working-class recipients (Le Grand 1984). The services used by middle-class recipients are usually those that facilitate their social functioning, such as child care, higher education, or counselling in marital relationships. Working-class recipients are usually those who experience the effects of some social problems such as unemployment, law breaking, child abuse and neglect, or poverty. In the former service situation there is a reciprocity or compatibility of interests, as the service benefits the provider in the form of employment and is also of direct benefit to the recipient. In contrast, in the latter situation there is a conflict of interests, as the service is still of benefit to the provider, but is of doubtful value to the recipient who experiences the negative effects of a social problem and who is expected by the provider to overcome these effects by changing his or her attitudes or behaviour (Jamrozik 1991).

The most important differences between the two kinds of services are in the perception of their value, in the respective rationale behind their provision, in the entitlement of the recipient to service, and in the outcome for the recipient. Services of the first kind (child care etc.) are provided as a response to a perceived problem experienced by people who are attempting to meet and reconcile their various needs, aspirations and responsibilities. Services of the second kind are provided on the grounds of a person's perceived inability or inadequacy to meet expected needs and obligations. Services of the first kind are an acknowledgement of society's or its government's responsibility to meet these particular needs, and the needs are perceived as social problems that have to be solved by political means; those of the second kind are provided as a response to the recipient's perceived personal pathology, thus effectively removing those problems from the social sphere. Acceptance of the former services is voluntary; acceptance of the latter is frequently forced on the recipient.

The distinction between the two kinds of services and the corresponding two kinds of recipients from two different social classes is of utmost significance in the analysis of the processes of identification, interpretation and methods of intervention in social problems. In particular, the distinction leads to such questions as: which social problems tend to be converted into personal problems, and which tend to resist the conversion and remain in the political sphere? Under which conditions do such differences arise, who benefits or is penalised by these differences? What kind of social forces are at play in these processes? These issues are at the heart of our theoretical perspective on the sociology of social problems, which we briefly outlined in Chapter 1 and present in detail in Chapter 5.

Solution or Maintenance?

A statement is made now and again that by using their methods of intervention in social problems, the aim of the helping professions is, or should be, to 'work themselves out of a job'. This statement is often made in an idealistic and half-joking fashion, its potential significance rarely receiving the attention it probably deserves. If discussion of this statement continues to any length, it usually leads to two conclusions. One is that the world will always come up with new problems, and that if one problem is solved another will take its place. A second, more thoughtful conclusion might include an observation that solutions to social problems often contain the seeds of another problem. The second conclusion is more critical, expressing a degree of scepticism or even cynicism about the effectiveness of professional intervention methods. Both views are based on knowledge that has considerable theoretical validity and both can potentially be tested empirically. However, the first view is based on the observation that society is never entirely static, and any form of intervention in a particular social condition creates a new situation that again may be problematic; the second view addresses the real problem of the difficulties encountered in evaluating professional methods of a non-tangible kind such as counselling.

There is, however, another aspect of social problems and intervention methods that is also of relevance – namely, that some problems are so entrenched in societal arrangements and so much an intrinsic part of societal pursuits that the most any intervention methods at the operative level can achieve is to control the extent or the intensity of the problem. The disadvantaged position of the Australian indigenous population is an example of a problem of this kind; entrenched unemployment among some population groups is another. Some other problems have a perennial quality, and some of these acquire the characteristics of inevitability.

In examining these issues, we need to keep in mind that each method of intervention in social problems – each activity – has a dual role or function. The manifest function is to attend to the problem in question: to solve, attenuate, or maintain and control. The inherent social role or function is to assert the legitimacy of the applied method and of the policy implemented by that method. This is the role performed by all professions, especially those in human services. They do this by virtue of the dual authority they possess: the specialised knowledge, and the authority and sanction of the state. This dual authority gives these professions certain freedom of action, but also makes them the guardians of the dominant structure of power. Because of these two roles the helping professions perform, and despite the frequent claims of some, the helping professions rarely act as agents of change.

CHAPTER 4

Social Actors in Social Problems

To speak of things social is to speak of things related to humanity, to human agency. This seemingly trivial observation is of central significance when speaking of social problems. It implies that social problems are in essence caused by people, are maintained by people, and are solved, attenuated or controlled by people. It is an observation that needs to be made and fully appreciated because what appears to be simple and obvious is in practice not as simple as that, or is not acted upon as such, leading at times to interesting and/or serious outcomes.

The relationship between theories of social problems and methods of intervention is more closely examined in this chapter, with a focus on the human agency – that is, on the roles played by certain social actors in the perception and intepretation of social problems and methods of intervention. What determines the methods of intervention: theories and practice wisdom, practice interests, or both? Why do certain practices persist despite strong evidence of their ineffectiveness? Is there always a second purpose in the manifest purpose; a hidden agenda? On what evidence are new theories formed? How are new intervention methods developed? Is it usually a case of 'old wine in new bottles' – that is, does the 'real' societal purpose of social control measures (being maintenance of class and sectional interests etc.) persist in various forms and disguises? The continued use of certain ineffective measures, which are ostensibly designed to solve certain 'entrenched' social problems such as unemployment, poverty or law breaking, suggests that this might be the case.

The Importance of Human Agency

Social problems are certain objective social conditions perceived and interpreted subjectively. Examining the role of social actors in social problems is therefore of prime importance to understanding the nature of social problems, their theoretical and popular explanations, the degree of importance attached to particular problems, and the intervention methods adopted to attenuate, control or solve such problems. Identifying social actors in social problems is important for a number of reasons. First, in a society of pluralistic interests – social, economic, cultural, religious and political – opinions on social problems will differ, as will the interests of the social actors. As Merton points out, 'one group's social problem tends to be another group's solution, just as, sequentially, one group's solution becomes defined as another group's problem' (1976:10). Second, not all groups and their interests have the same degree of power to express and/or act: the power structure in society is usually hierarchical. Third, the characteristics of social problems point clearly to the political nature of social problems; their existence, magnitude and seriousness are therefore contested perceptions and concepts. Fourth, in most societies nowadays, public perceptions of social problems are (as are perceptions of all public issues) 'mediated' through the mass media, public relations experts and organised lobbies. The authoritative perceptions and intepretations of social problems by academic researchers and the helping professions are of particular significance, especially if those perceptions and interpretations are taken up and propagated by the mass media.

Two comments are apposite here. First, social problems may emerge from conditions which are not created by a human agency. For example, floods, bushfires, prolonged droughts or earthquakes are social conditions created by physical phenomena, but their outcomes will depend on the societal response – that is, human agency. The kind of social problem that will emerge from such events will depend not solely on the events themselves, although the initial cause would be those events, but on society's response to the events. For example, how rescue or emergency measures are implemented in physical disasters may cause new hardships for the affected population.

The second comment about the importance of human agency in social problems concerns what is known as a 'corporate entity', which in law is a kind of legal 'person' that can do almost all the things a human being can do, and sometimes more. Corporate entities have always existed in the form of power structures such as political institutions, religious bodies or educational institutions. However, their existence acquired much greater significance as a capitalist business institution. Indeed, corporate organisations have now replaced many informal structures, and constitute the main centres of economic, political and social power. The corporate entity is an interesting institution, an interesting creature, which can serve to absolve people from personal responsibility for their actions, sometimes to a major degree. A bad government, an incompetent bureaucracy, a firm producing shoddy goods are some examples of corporate entities that provide a screen that conceals the real human actors, their decisions and activities, and that absolves them from their personal responsibilities. Corporate entity has become a device that enables people to make and preserve their fortunes, while through the business they conduct they may lose millions of other people's money. Governments can create poverty through incompetence, bad policy or the implementation of a certain ideology. Bureaucrats can produce similar results. Professional bodies such as, for example, the Australian Medical Association, the Law Society, and the Australian Association of Social Workers, can advocate ideas, theories and methods of intervention in social problems whose effects are of less value to the people experiencing the problem than to upholding the status quo of the profession's power.

Corporate entities are power structures, many of which extend throughout a country, often transcending national boundaries, exerting their power and influence throughout the globe. Control over them and their responsibility to the public is severely circumscribed. The Bophal disaster, an accidental release of poisonous gas that resulted in thousands of deaths and thousands of chronically sick people; silicone breast implants, which were later found to leak, causing distress and necessitating surgical removal; the Dalcon shield, an IUD that was found to cause severe infections; thalidomide medication, which produced thousands of defective births; and mining and processing of asbestos, which produced lung and other cancers and consequent deaths among workers – these are some examples of the severe social problems that can be caused by such corporations and the difficulties experienced in dealing with the problems they create, especially when it comes to accepting responsibility and paying compensation. Each of these examples resulted in prolonged court cases for compensation (and in some cases for non-disclosure of information that was available to the producers), with varying results.

The corporate entity is an important concept, enshrined in law, with significant consequences for society. James Coleman observes that such an entity represents a form of social actor – a purposefully constructed 'corporate actor' whose structure consists of positions held by people who are merely temporary occupants of those positions. 'The corporate actor, as the actor that establishes the structure, holds the right to make rules or laws and to specify the structure of supervision and the sanctions associated with rule violation' (1993:9). In effect, corporate entity *reifies* a legal concept. A corporation may be endowed with a special power enacted by governments or parliaments; it can sue or be sued in a court of law; it can be fined or closed (legally 'killed'), but one cannot put a corporate entity in gaol. It may be a very useful arrangement for economic, political or administrative activity, but its effects – positive or negative – are created by human beings and are experienced by human beings. For this reason, any examination of social problems must go beyond the corporate screen that reifies social constructs and gives them a seemingly physical existence. It must aim to identify the real human actors who hold corporate power and who use it to make their personal decisions.

The awareness of the significance of corporate structures and their power brings into focus the appropriateness of the three-level organisational perspective in the analysis of social problems (see Figures 1.1, 3.1 and 3.2). While at the operational level the methods of intervention in social problems are to a large extent applied by individuals and aimed at individuals through direct contacts between them, at the policy making and administrative levels the corporation is the unit of decision-making, and the decisions may be directed at individuals, at certain social groupings, or at whole communities. Decisions might be made by individuals at certain levels of the corporation hierarchy, but the official version of such decisions becomes depersonalised, presented as 'the department has decided', 'the cabinet has decided', or 'it is the opinion of the church', and so on. Decisions then become decisions of the corporation, legally absolving individuals within that corporation of their personal responsibility, unless such individuals have made decisions not in accordance with the corporation's laws, or outside the bounds of their authority. Even at the operative level, decisions and actions taken by individuals are taken under the authority and legal protection of the corporate body, be this a welfare agency, government department, or any other public or private organisation authorised by some legal provisions to apply certain intervention methods to a given social problem. In contrast, the recipients of welfare services do not have such protection, further increasing inequality in the power relationship between recipients and service providers.

Social Actors in Perspectives on Social Problems

From the theoretical perspectives on social problems examined in Chapter 2, social actors in social problems belong to various categories and receive varying degrees of attention. In the social pathology perspective the main social actors are 'maladjusted' or 'under-socialised' people. Similarly, in the perspective of social deviance it is the 'delinquents', the 'criminals', the 'rebels' or the 'extreme ritualists' who are the object of attention. In both the social disorganisation and critical perspectives, the focus of attention is the processes and social conditions, with social actors not clearly or directly visible, since they are concealed behind social groups, social strata and power structures. The labelling and the constructionist perspectives pay particular attention to the role of social actors – that is, the role of the people who attach certain labels to other people, and people who make claims about certain social conditions.

Social actors in social problems are thus perceived in three distinct groups:

1 Those who are seen to be 'acting out' certain 'deviant' roles
2 Those whose actions and identities are subsumed into social groups, classes or power structures
3 Those who make claims about certain people being 'deviant' or claims about certain social conditions being social problems

The actors in the first group are identified by their pathological characteristics and behaviour. Those in the second group may be either the members of the power structures or the victims of those structures. It is the third group – the 'labellers' and the 'claims-makers' – whose activities are of particular interest in sociological studies of social problems, because they are seen as 'inventors' of social problems, and the effects of their activities may lead, and often do, to outcomes of considerable social significance. The aim of labelling and claims-making is to identify subjective individual or group perceptions, attitudes and values, to convert them into objective phenomena, and have such conversions accepted by society as real objective phenomena of some significance that call for corrective actions or solutions.

Social actors in social problems who engage in labelling or claims-making activities fall into a number of categories. The actors whose activities are examined in this chapter include political activists and lobbyists, moral entrepreneurs, academics and social researchers, newspaper columnists and media commentators, and members of the helping professions. These groups are not discrete categories, as a person's activities may fall into more than one category. For example, a social researcher may also be an active lobbyist, using the results of their research as evidence of the need for political action; and a political activist, by taking up a particular cause, becomes a moral entrepreneur.

Political Activists and Lobbyists

Political activism and lobbying is usually a collective activity. Political activists identify a social condition as a social problem and aim to bring it to public notice and to the attention of government. They act as individuals or aim to build up wider public support by engaging in public activities that seek to influence public opinion towards accepting their definition of the problem they see as important, and then influencing the government to act with the aim of correcting or solving the identified problem. In the vocabulary of political science, political activists are referred to as 'pressure groups' and are divided into 'altruistic' and 'self-interest' pressure groups. In the area of social problems an altruistic pressure group may take up the cause of a 'disadvantaged' or 'oppressed' population, or it may identify problems of health or public safety as issues calling for government response. A self-interest group, or lobby, would aim to identify its own position as one of disadvantage and as a real or potential problem for the whole society. In each case, the actions of political activists are likely to meet with a positive response from society and government if such actions are successful in convincing the public that the social problem of concern contains a real or potential threat of some kind to the whole society.

No less significant social actors in social problems are politicians themselves. Recognising certain social conditions as social problems of a severity or magnitude that affects significant sections of the community, and implementing any remedial actions, requires governments to respond in terms of legislation, allocation of resources and development of appropriate programs. Politicians also need to show commitment to a 'cause', which enhances the support of their electorate and assures them of gaining power or staying in power. Taking up the identification of social problems and arguing the need for government action is a frequently used path to political power.

A feature of political activists' and lobbyists' activities is their interest in issues that, from the perspective they present, in most instances call for political decisions. Any such decision endorses the perspective of the problem they identify as being in the political sphere. This is an important distinction, as any social problem presented in such a perspective lessens the likelihood of its being 'pathologised' through conversion into personal problems of those in the negatively affected population. Conservation movements and the feminist movement have been outstanding examples of successful political activism in recent decades. An example of a less successful but sustained and partly successful political activism has been the demand for decriminalisation of the possession and use of marijuana.

Moral Entrepreneurs

In a broad spectrum, all people act, in some way and at some time or another, as social actors in social problems. In our daily activity –

working, driving a car, expressing an opinion in a friendly conversation or a debate – we contribute to the creation, discovery, maintenance or solution of social problems. However, certain people, or rather categories of people, with certain characteristic attitudes and actions, play significant roles in this area. One such category of people who become significant social actors in the area of social problems is that of the 'moral entrepreneurs'.

Throughout history there have been people who saw some sort of 'evil' in society and decided to fight it. The European missionaries who brought the Christian religion to societies subjugated by colonial powers endeavoured to 'save' the souls of the 'primitive heathens' and were not always selective or gentle in their methods of religious conversion (which ranged from persuasion and bribery to open coercion and physical torture). However noble and well-intended the actions of some missionaries might have been, the effect in most cases was the destruction of cultures and social systems, and the facilitation of the people's subjugation by the invading power.

Today, moral entrepreneurs more often act as lobby groups. The methods used include lobbying of politicians, influencing the population at large, demanding legislation, organising public demonstrations, or creating issues for the mass media. Views on the environment, on abortion, euthanasia, immigration and multiculturalism – all these are formulated in moralistic terms and are propagated by some people who are committed to certain values, protecting or attacking some interests and/or seeking support for their views. Their claims-making activities (Spector and Kitsuse 1987) present a variety of issues as social problems and engage – or aim to convince others of the necessity to engage – in activities to 'fight the problem'. Such moral entrepreneurs may include journalists, academics, doctors, politicians, aspiring politicians, ministers of religion, people known as 'do-gooders', opportunists, and people with personal vested interests.

The distinct characteristics of moral entrepreneurs lie in their focus on the phenomena they perceive as endangering the morality of society, and in their location of problems in certain structures or population groups, or even in the whole society. The endangered morality as they perceive it may be interpreted in social or racial terms, or more often in religious terms related to a particular faith. The nature of the problems therefore tends to be emphasised in the projected non-tangible detrimental effects, such as a deterioration in moral values or 'moral fibre', and likely penalties in the afterlife. These characteristics of portraying social problems differentiate moral entrepreneurs from other social actors in social problems, whose perceptions of problems may be based on a range of values and interests, and who may portray the detrimental effects of presented problems in social terms such as deterioration of law and order or an increase in poverty.

Academics and Social Researchers

People engaged in tertiary education, and in writing and research in the social sciences, are of considerable significance among social actors in social problems. Through their work they identify and define the nature of social problems, develop theories and concepts, and, in doing so, also imply or even directly suggest remedies or solutions. As Alvin Gouldner observed:

> information gathering systems or research methods always premise the existence and use of some system of social control. It is not only that the information they yield may be used *by* systems of social control, but they themselves *are* systems of social control.   (1971:50; emphasis in the original)

Research in the social sciences, especially research concerned with issues considered to be social problems, is never value-free. This is not necessarily an issue, provided the value position of the researcher and the aim of the research are made public. The reason for conducting research into social issues may be the researcher's wish to explain certain phenomena, but it may also be a desire to achieve certain aims of social consequence – for example, to turn public attention to certain issues as social problems, or to provide data for remedial intervention in such problems. Sponsors of research, whether government agencies or private corporations, also have certain aims, and these may not always be explicitly or clearly stated, or be identical with the researcher's aims.

Value-committed social research may be conducted with a high degree of intellectual objectivity, but on the other hand if it is motivated by a strong or extreme commitment to a value or interest, it may acquire the characteristics of what Neil Gilbert (1995) defines as 'advocacy research'. Research of this nature aims to elicit public and government response in a desired direction by presenting a problem in an exaggerated per-spective. This, Gilbert explains, is done in a number of ways: defining a problem so broadly that extraneous elements can be included in it; projecting onto the whole society findings that may apply only to a small group; including data and evidence from other studies that are only marginally related to the problem in question; and using anecdotal 'atrocity tales' to raise emotions in society. Research conducted using such methods usually receives interest and publicity from the mass media, especially if the 'problem' makes a good human interest story (1995:108–9).

Gilbert's example illustrates an issue of importance in scientific pursuits generally, but one of particular significance in the study of social problems. As the identification, definition and interpretation of certain phenomena as social problems have a normative basis, and any such activity includes a human agency involved in or affected by any such problems in various ways, the question arises as to the degree of objectivity a sociologist may achieve in the study of social problems. Is it possible in such studies to remain (as it were) party-neutral, or does one unavoidably take one side or another when one examines a situation? To put this question in less value-laden terms, in studying a given problem does one approach the phenomenon 'from above', or 'from below'? Or should one approach it from both ends?

The question 'Whose side are we on?' was eagerly debated, with some fire, in the American Sociological Association during the 1960s. The two protagonists, each on opposite sides, were Howard Becker and Alvin Gouldner. Becker, the author of *Outsiders* (1963), argued that sociologists, because of their commitment to certain values, had to take the side of the 'underdog'. In his presidential address at the 1966 Annual General Meeting of the Society for the Study of Social Problems, he argued:

> To have values or not to have values: the question is always with us ... the dilemma, which seems so painful to so many actually does not exist, for one of its horns is imaginary ... In the case of deviance, the hierarchical relationship is a moral one. The superordinate parties in the relationship are those who represent the forces of approval and official morality; the subordinate parties are those who, it is alleged, have violated that morality.   *(1967:240)*

Becker argued that this hierarchical relationship created a 'hierarchy of credibility'. The subordinates' version of reality did not have the same credibility as the version of the superordinates. By taking the side of the underdog and studying social problems 'from below', he argued, the sociologist was able to correct this imbalance, at least to a certain extent.

Gouldner did not disagree with Becker about the imbalance in the hierarchy of credibility, but argued that this did not mean a sociologist had to take sides. To conduct a study of social issues and social problems one could, and should, present the underdog's case, he argued, but one could not identify oneself with the underdog because one was not an underdog. To claim otherwise was hypocritical. Gouldner was concerned that 'the myth of a value-free social science', which had been maintained until the 1960s, was 'about to be supplanted by still another myth', being that it was impossible for a social scientist to research and be impartial: one had to make a choice to write either from the perspective of superiors or subordinates (1975:27–8).

Gouldner's criticism was aimed particularly at researchers who became entrepreneurial in their ability to attract public funds for their research by identifying themselves as in sympathy with the values and policies of the government of the day. Such researchers became members of what Gouldner called 'the new establishment sociology'. As he expressed it, 'It is a sociology that succeeds in solving the oldest problem in personal politics: how to maintain one's integrity without sacrificing one's career, or how to remain a liberal although well-heeled' (1975:49). Through such actions, he argued, sociologists were compromising their intellectual objectivity and scholarly integrity. To maintain these values, sociologists did not have to share values with those whom they studied, or the values of those who had research funds, but follow the values they claimed as their own, however unpopular these values might be (1975:59). He argued that 'an empty-headed partisanship unable to transcend the immediacies of narrowly conceived political commitment is simply just one more form of market research ... It is to values, not to factions, that sociologists must give their most basic commitment' (1975:67–8).

The Becker–Gouldner debate brought into the public view the ever-present issue of objectivity and subjectivity in social research and in the social sciences generally, and also an added issue of partisanship. More recently, Neil Gilbert (1995) raised the issue of partisanship encountered in the form of 'advocacy research', which brings into question the integrity of social research. These debates illustrate the political implications of research into social phenomena that are perceived to be social problems, as research in such phenomena is always likely to meet with diverse reactions from those in society who may hold strong partisan views on, or particular interests in, the problem being investigated.

Partisanship in social research remains an issue, and with the greater use of research in policy making, the issue is more important than ever before. The conceptual construction of social problems, methods of research and analysis, and the publication of results affect and change the views of the public and are therefore of political importance. Social research is used by various interest groups to present their views and interests in the perspective that is to their advantage and to the disadvantage of others. This does not mean that researchers set out to deliberately create false or misleading data on the issues they investigate, but that the very fact of selecting an issue for investigation means 'creating' an issue and presenting it to the public as a 'social problem'. Partisanship may also lead to outcomes not intended by the researchers. For example, the predilection for studies of 'disadvantaged' populations is based on the belief that by learning to know them, their characteristics and living conditions, and by making this information public, such

studies may generate a positive response from society and the government, which will then alleviate the disadvantage. This often leads to an
opposite response. The focus on the disadvantaged population predictably leads to the disadvantage being related to the characteristics of
the population itself and, as a consequence, such a focus becomes
instrumental in the development of remedial intervention methods that
are aimed to relieve the 'pathology' of the population but that often
produce more effective methods of social control. This does not mean to
say that research into disadvantage should not be undertaken; on the
contrary, it is important for research to reveal disadvantage where it
exists. However, it is of prime importance not to present disadvantage
in a truncated perspective (see Chapter 3), but in a comparative
perspective, so that the true nature and extent of disadvantage is
properly revealed.

Newspaper Columnists and Media Commentators

In the age of mass communication, the media play an important and
powerful role in identifying social problems and in bringing them into
public notice. Identification also means 'creation' of problems. It is
accepted that the mass media not only report news but also create news.
Newspaper headlines are rarely created by pleasant news, but rather by
unpleasant news: catastrophes, accidents, wars, crimes, violent actions,
and problems looming on the horizon (the danger of the imminent
problem being deduced from an event or from the opinion of a visiting
'expert'). Social problems are vividly portrayed by presenting them as
'heart-rending human stories' or 'human catastrophes', described in
emotive terms and supported by appropriately selected photographs or
television images.

The presentation of issues as social problems in mass media is usually
much more effective in convincing the public than scholarly research
because the news is immediate and widely disseminated, written in a
language that readers can understand, and the intended effect is
achieved by headlines, with emphasis achieved through judicious editing. A social problem is given greater significance if it is commented
upon by an expert columnist or a well-known academic researcher.
Further significance is created by presenting public views on a problem
through the publication of the results of a telephone survey conducted
by the newspaper itself or by a contracted public opinion pollster. In
radio, significant actors in identifying social problems are the 'talkback'
personalities, some of whom command large audiences.

In Australia, commercial radio personalities such as John Laws
and Alan Jones are household names. They attract to their programs

opinions from listeners who tend to be rather conservative, even at times extreme in their views, and whose voices are interpreted as the voices of 'real Australians'. Similarly, on Radio National, a radio station of the publicly owned Australian Broadcasting Corporation, programs such as 'Life Matters' with Geraldine Doogue and Norman Swan, or 'Late Night Live' with Phillip Adams are certainly influential opinion makers among professional middle-class audiences. Press columnists such as Alan Wood (economics), Paul Kelly (international affairs) and social commentator Hugh Mackay in *The Australian*, and Michelle Grattan (politics) in *The Age* and *The Financial Review* play a similar role in the printed media and often in radio and television as well.

The media bring to public notice a mediated image of society created by reporting events that most people do not experience directly. The significance of this 'image' was vividly illustrated by Joseph Gusfield in his presidential address to the American Society for the Study of Social Problems. Gusfield observed:

> As part of this mass construction of reality, society itself is a spectacle, an object played before an audience. They may find it dull or exciting; informative or mysterious. It may be conveyed as series of separate events or as a patterned sequence of activities. In this whirligig of acts, 'social problems' constitute a constant and recurrent source of interest and, in popular culture, a basis for entertainment and even vicarious identification with evil. Crime, delinquency, drug addiction, child abuse, poverty, family violence, sexual deviance, prostitution, alcoholism make up a considerable part of news and popular drama. These provide much of the imagery with which social problems are perceived and acted upon.   *(1989:434)*

The impact of the media is particularly powerful on people whose participation in social activities tends to be limited by a restrictive employment environment and that perhaps extends to an occasional visit to a local club or hotel, shopping, communication with a small group of friends, and an occasional verbal exchange with neighbours. In such cases, watching the world mediated through television might be the activity engaged in most consistently, occupying a few hours every day. Being regularly subjected to the powerful images that are projected at them, such people's perception of social problems, like their perception of all distant world events, becomes their view of social reality. Unlike the more highly educated middle classes employed in professional occupations, who have access to wider inputs of views, people with limited social participation do not have such opportunities to compare views and form independent opinions.

The Helping Professions

Among the most important social actors in the field of social problems are the helping professions. What needs to be borne in mind is the 'problem orientation' of these professions. Their education and training curricula focus on the identification and analysis of pathological phenomena and corresponding methods of remedial intervention. Beginning with the identification and definition of a condition as a 'problem' and continuing into the devising of methods of intervention, attenuation, control or solution, these professions aim to acquire and maintain a monopoly over such activities. The more professionalised an occupational group becomes, the more it takes the pathology perspective on social issues, because such a profession works on the premise that the specialised authoritative knowledge of its members gives it the exclusive competence and right to engage in remedial or 'therapeutic' pursuits in its area. Armed with the authority of specialised knowledge and societal (often legal) sanction to apply that knowledge in certain ways, such professions have considerable influence over policy makers who determine which social condition or conditions need public intervention and the manner of that intervention.

All professions are 'predatory', in that they seek to define the world through their own perspectives and theories, and, consequently, to achieve the sanctioning of their role in the enhancement, maintenance, control, alleviation or elimination of the phenomena they identify as being within the orbit of their body of knowledge and their methods of intervention. In the helping professions, this role has traditionally focused on phenomena regarded as 'negative' or pathological, such as physical and mental pain or personal and social problems, but now the interests of some helping professions also look to extend to activities perceived as 'positive', such as promotion of health, education or life-style. It follows that if certain phenomena can be explained in more than one perspective or theory, then it is likely that competing theoretical perspectives will emerge from a number of professional disciplines. If such theories are then applied to methods of analysis and to interpretation of and intervention in social issues, social problems or personal problems, it may be expected that there will be some competition among perspectives for clients, consumers or whatever name might be applied to the potential recipients of professional services. Inter-professional competition becomes a competition for the 'ownership' of particular problems. While a number of professions and related lesser occupations might be actively involved in a particular problem, the profession that manages to 'own' the problem becomes the dominant profession in that problem area and can assert control over the methods of intervention.

Furthermore, its interpretation of the nature of the problem becomes the dominant perception of the problem in public consciousness. As stated by Gusfield:

> To 'own' a problem is to be obligated to claim recognition of a problem and to have information and ideas about it given a high degree of attention and credibility, to the exclusion of others. To 'own' a social problem is to possess the authority to name that condition a 'problem' and to suggest what might be done about it. It is the power to influence the marshalling of public facilities – laws, enforcement abilities, opinion, goods and services – to help resolve the problem.   *(1989:433)*

The essence of professional power lies in specialised authoritative knowledge and its application, through which the professions *authoritatively define social reality*. In human services, professional people authoritatively define whether one is healthy or ill, sane or insane, educated or marginally literate, and responsible or not responsible for having committed an illegal act. This is a universally accepted professional authority based on publicly recognised specialised knowledge. Similar to professions based on the social and behavioural sciences, acceptance of specialised knowledge occurs in professions based on physical sciences. Engineers define whether a bridge or building has to be repaired or pulled down, biologists define the extent of harmful pollution, and physicists measure and determine the level of harmful radiation. The quality or validity of specialised expert knowledge can rarely be effectively questioned, except by other experts from the same or related professions.

The helping professions define social problems as problems of individuals, as pathological conditions that require the intervention of the professions' specialised knowledge translated into a particular method of assistance, usually referred to as 'therapy'. The 'ordinary' though no-less-important functional aspects of social living and corresponding personal issues and problems encountered in everyday experience are relegated to the attention of semi-professionals or laypeople – volunteers and amateurs. The effect of this division of labour is that while perhaps the most valuable remedial as well as preventive work is done by those 'lower ranks', it is the 'important' professions that maintain the climate of certain beliefs in individual or group pathologies. As a result, the social conditions that come to be seen as social problems tend to reflect the perspectives and interests of the various helping professions and associated political lobbies, which have managed to dominate public discourse by attracting the attention of the mass media, thus keeping the issue or problem in the public consciousness and maintaining politicians' attention.

The power of the helping professionals lies in their authoritative knowledge of identification, definition, interpretation and attempted solution of social problems. The issue, which is a problem in itself, is the lack of awareness or acknowledgement (and in some cases the denial) of this power. The success of a profession in obtaining and maintaining public endorsement of its perspective and activities depends on that profession's ability to convince the public – first of the objective nature of a problem, and second of its members' capacity, through their specialised knowledge and expertise, to solve, attenuate or control the problem. The success is greater if the profession obtains exclusive rights by legal sanction to intervene in the given problem, and if the practice of its expertise is underwritten by public funds.

This issue, however, goes deeper. Over the past two or three decades, the helping professions have grown in numbers and diversity through the development of specialisations of interests and intervention methods. Does the growth of professions, especially of the helping professions, suggest that some social problems are 'created' by professionals' desire to develop their field of competence, extend their influence, and thus secure status and privilege as well as income? Is such a suggestion too simple? It may be considered, following Merton's view of sociology's role in identifying the latency of problems in certain social conditions, that laypeople would not see the 'creation' or 'invention' of some problems as falling into such a category, provided the identified 'problem' posed a potential threat to society. On the other hand, the 'invention' of certain problems may be not much more than a profession's public action aimed to ensure society's notice, with the response enhancing demand for the profession's services. Situations where the identification of a 'problem' is linked with advice to seek professional help suggest that this may be the case. However, it must be emphasised that the dividing line between the 'real' and the 'invented' problem is likely to be blurred, or that the 'problem' may be seen as such by some population strata or classes, while others do not give it a thought.

It is apposite to note, at this point, an earlier observation by Martin Rein (1970) that professions identify and define social problems within the parameters of their own competence and methods of intervention. While professions, especially the helping professions, claim with considerable justification that their authoritative knowledge is theoretically based, it is not difficult to see that their practice and the theory behind it are largely method-driven. The theoretical perception of a given problem is built into the method of intervention. Indeed, as expressed by Gusfield, 'To give a name to a problem is to recognise or suggest a structure developed to deal with it' (1989:432). At times, it seems, it might not be so much a case of a problem that calls for a method of intervention but, rather, a developed method of intervention in search of a problem.

Professional Power and Class Power

In the capitalist system, the frequency and nature of social problems are class-related and the perceptions of social problems are also mediated through the perspective of the class structure. Most social actors discussed in this chapter, especially academic researchers and members of the helping professions, belong to the (new) middle class, by education, training, and by and large their social origins. It may be expected, therefore, that the social problems examined in research and the intervention methods practised in the field will be influenced, if not determined, by these social actors' class perspective. The issue of class perspective is certainly significant in the selection of problems and human subjects for examination, but is particularly important in the work performed by the helping professions. The encounters between the helping professions (armed with the authority of their specialised knowledge and state sanction) and the recipients of their services, particularly those in the lower socio-economic strata who depend on that service for help of some kind or have to depend on it by legal coercion, are encounters of differential power relationships. These differential power relationships, so extensively examined by Michel Foucault, seem to receive relatively little attention from the helping professions in the context of their intervention methods, although Foucault's emphasis on the significance of the knowledge/power relationship in everyday activities is quite frequently discussed in professional curricula. This gap in perception serves to conceal the everyday exercise of power by these professions, since they work mainly with relatively powerless individuals and social groups such as the unemployed, the poor, poor single parents, the aged, children, people in the correctional system, and people from ethnic minorities.

For a social condition to be seen as a social problem in a class society, it has to be acknowledged as such by the dominant class. It is to be expected that from another perspective the condition may not be seen as a social problem, or that the nature of the condition may be differently interpreted. For example, people who experience a given condition as a problem may see it as such, although the condition would not necessarily be seen as a problem by professions engaged in that area of activity, or by administrators or policy makers. For the sociologist, this presents the issue of the hierarchy of credibility that Howard Becker saw as important in any study of social problems.

The role of the helping professions is of considerable political significance. Whatever the value base of a profession might be, professional perspectives on social problems and their corresponding intervention methods are essentially technical in nature. In providing technical solutions or remedies to social problems – that is, problems that are causatively linked to structural arrangements and/or political decisions – professional intervention methods effectively remove such problems from the political arena, an action that unwittingly serves to retain existing arrangements and maintain their political legitimacy. This does not mean professional intervention methods have no value; however, such methods are directed at the effects rather than the causes of social problems, and thus serve to maintain the legitimacy of the existing structural arrangements. This 'dilemma of helping' is examined in the chapters to follow. Here, it is apposite to note that professions perceive social problems from different perspectives when such problems represent a threat to their own interests. For example, the threat of constraints on professional activity would be perceived by professions as a threat of reduced quality of their service to society.

Social Actors in Postmodern Perspectives

As noted in Chapter 2, the relativism of postmodern perspectives on society presents particular issues for the study of social problems. These issues attain greater complexity and intensity when considering the role of social actors in social problems, especially social actors engaged in providing intervention methods. In the perspective of the three-level activity discussed earlier (see Figures 1.1, 3.1 and 3.2), it may be expected that postmodern relativism would be likely to create greater differences among the three levels, especially in the assumed roles of actors at each level. For example, political decisions in response to a perceived social problem might be influenced by a powerful lobby whose values and interests are not widely shared in the community. Administrative decisions are likely to be guided by managerial rationality. And perspectives at the operative level are likely to show considerable diversity, displayed by different theoretical and value orientations of the professions operating at that level. The differences among professions as well as within particular professions unavoidably create a climate of uncertainly and confusion in the minds of the people at the receiving end of professional intervention methods, increasing their powerlessness and social anomie.

CHAPTER 5

Challenges of Contemporary Social Problems

Social problems, like all social phenomena, occur in the context of a particular time and place, and have to be perceived in that perspective. This is the approach used in the overview of perspectives on social problems in Chapter 2. The perspectives examined in that chapter vary in their degree of theoretical abstraction and generalisation, but have one feature in common – namely, that they were formulated from empirical observations in one particular society, the United States. They were also formulated over the period of a century, and each perspective reflects the issues as well as the sociological interests of a particular period. This does not mean these perspectives are not applicable to the study of social problems in other societies or even to the study of contemporary issues, but the context of time and place in their origins needs to be kept in mind. Indeed, there has been acknowledgement in recent years among American sociologists themselves of an existing parochialism in the American social sciences. Although comparative international research has been encouraged, research questions and data analysis still rely heavily on American theoretical frameworks and there is a serious lack of cross-cultural components in sociology curricula (Santiago 1993:207).

As we approach the end of one millennium and the beginning of another, more and more problems that may be called 'social' are of global proportions, or at least of global significance. Not many social problems occur universally or with the same intensity across the globe, but they can attain global significance because the effects of certain actions in one part of the world may be experienced positively or negatively in another part. In the economic sphere, for example, the gap between affluent industrialised countries and undeveloped Third World countries – the 'North/South divide' – has been widening for some years, and there are no indications that this trend might be arrested or reversed in the near future. At the same time, in a somewhat parallel fashion, social divisions within industrialised countries have also been widening. This is evident in differential income distribution, access to education and employment, lifestyles, and also in family disruptions, the state of health, and law breaking and law enforcement.

How significant are these developments in the occurrence, extent and intensity of social problems in various countries, especially in industrialised societies like Australia? As stated in Chapter 1, the perspective we have developed to address these issues defines social problems as social conditions arising out of structural and cultural arrangements in society, which cause social and economic malfunctioning of those arrangements and which are perceived to be in some way a threat to the established order and power structure. These 'negative conditions' are by-products of values and goals that a society, especially its dominant power structure, seeks to maintain or pursue: they constitute a logical 'negative residue' of the activities directed at the pursuit of such dominant values, interests and corresponding goals.

In this definition we accept that a social problem is a social condition that may be objectively defined within a broad understanding and agreed meaning, but that will always be subjectively perceived by the observer, the nature of that subjectivity being determined by the observer's position in the social structure, their cultural background, personal values and interests. The key point in the definition is the assertion that social problems are 'residual effects' of the pursuits and maintenance of dominant values and interests in a given society. This means that social problems are a 'normal' occurrence and their emergence in some form can feasibly be deduced from identifying the dominant values and interests in a given society. Furthermore, it may also be expected that the prevalent and legally sanctioned intervention methods for such problems in that society will aim to alleviate or solve the problems in a way that does not disturb the society's existing structural arrangements and will thus legitimate the dominant values and interests of that society. We have already demonstrated these processes of intervention and legitimation by using the three-level analysis of social organisation, discussed in Chapters 3 and 4 and illustrated schematically in Figures 1.1, 3.1 and 3.2.

We contend that a study of social problems needs to include the identification of four related aspects:

1 The dominant values and interests in society, and the structural and cultural arrangements through which these values and interests are pursued

2 The social condition that emerges from these pursuits and is perceived as a social problem
3 The intervention methods aimed at solving, attenuating, controlling
or legitimating the condition
4 The social actors who play their various roles in the identification and
interpretation of the condition, and in applying the intervention
methods.

The 'structural and cultural arrangements' mentioned in this definition may be considered in the context of a particular society as well
as at a global level. The global level is of great significance in the 1990s
because of the global dominance of the capitalist ideology on an unprecedented scale and magnitude. In the economic sphere, the two
most powerful institutions – the World Bank and the International
Monetary Fund – exert their power and influence throughout the
world, especially in undeveloped and developing countries where,
together with the transnational business corporations, they control all
major economic activities. In the political sphere, the ideology of
what may be called 'democratic capitalism' or 'free-market democratic
capitalism' now faces no serious challenge except perhaps from the
incipient and growing religious fundamentalism in some undeveloped
and developing countries. Indeed, capitalism – or, as it is more commonly referred to, the 'free' market system – is equated with democracy
and is actively propagated throughout the world. The powerful leaders
of this faith are not averse to the use of economic or even political
sanctions against countries that show some signs of resistance to
embracing the system. For these reasons, the examination of social
problems in a particular country needs to be considered in the global
context so as to identify causal links between internal and external
activities, and the outcomes of any such connections.

Global Challenges

A belief prevalent in the world today, and also in the social sciences,
perceives the world as experiencing profound processes of change in
all aspects of social organisation: economic, cultural and political.
Barry Smart observes (1992:1) that some analysts consider the change
to be so profound that it warrants speaking of the 'end of history'
(Fukuyama) or the 'end of the social' (Baudrillard). At the same time,
Smart points to the continuity of processes of the capitalist industrial era
and to these processes' effects, which are manifest in the rising living
standards in industrialised countries and the impoverishment of human
masses in countries that provide the 'developed world' with much of its

raw materials, food and cheap labour. These 'undeveloped' countries are also used as distant sites for the production of potentially dangerous commodities and for the dumping of industrial waste. Furthermore, within the industrialised countries themselves, Smart observes: 'Capitalism continues to generate unacceptable forms of inequality and exploitation, to stimulate individual and private interest to the detriment of public or community provision, and to contribute to the disorganisation of communities and damage of the environment' (1992:3).

A phenomenon related to these developments is the disaffection with and cynicism towards the liberal political system, manifest in a low level of participation in the political process, and in increasing problems experienced by public institutions that provide important social services such as education, health and welfare. In addition to these 'local' problems, Smart notes significant problems encountered on the global scale: population growth, depletion of natural resources, nuclear and chemical weapons, environmental pollution, and the danger of serious climatic change that may threaten human survival (1992:3–4).

The world has indeed entered the 'Global Age' (Albrow 1996). While the nation-state is still the universally recognised political and economic unit, circumscribed by geographical boundaries, autonomous political order and a system of economic management, the autonomy of this unit is now effectively reduced by the dominant world-economic order. The world-wide information network – the information 'super-highway' – creates advantages for the economically powerful and disadvantages for the economically weak. As the globally thinking financial institutions are able to see the best investment opportunities on a world-wide scale and act accordingly, the economically weak also become known world-wide, and drop further back in the queue for access to capital. The information super-highway does not lead to less inequality on the global scale: on the contrary, it leads to more.

In raising the issue of global challenges that societies face in today's world, this book provides some examples of social problems that exist in most countries or that have world-wide implications. We need to acknowledge however that it is beyond this book's scope to engage in a detailed analysis of global social problems. It is nevertheless appropriate to note that the outstanding social problem on the global scale is the great and increasing inequality in access to and utilisation of material and human resources, and the corresponding discrepancy in living standards and quality of life. Integral parts of this problem are the degradation of the natural environment in certain parts of the globe and the exploitation of natural resources. If continued at the present rate, these must unavoidably lead to a crisis that may threaten the very survival of populations in affected regions, and in due course lead to negative effects in affluent industrialised countries as well. One does not have to be a prophet of doom to say what has been said many times before – namely, that exploited energy sources such as oil will eventually run out, and that the destruction of rain forests will have a detrimental effect on the earth's climate.

A global perspective on social problems helps to identify the diversity of social problems, and their interrelationships, in various parts of the world, but it also suggests caution when generalising theories that are based in one society to other societies. For example, the disappearance of manual labour occupations in industrialised countries, which is portrayed as a characteristic of a post industrial society, acquires a different significance if the issue is examined in a global perspective. The countries of the industrialised West, exercising economic advantage due to their technological and economic power, produce goods and services with an increasing capital intensity and a decreasing input of labour. They also develop industries that promote the consumption of diverse forms of leisure activities, giving these countries characteristics that increasingly resemble those of Ancient Rome during the Empire. More and more, industrial activities in 'developed' countries revolve around manipulating finance and providing 'circus games' of a growing frequency and intensity. These activities generate income for some (the state included) and stimulate consumption, but do not produce wealth.

Postindustrial societies are those that rely on the production of mass-produced goods manufactured elsewhere. They exercise the power of a new form of economic imperialism. 'Elsewhere' not only means other (developing) countries: the North/South divide seems to be replicated on a smaller scale within the industrialised world itself, in that within the industrialised countries, the producers of goods and services who work at the lower ranks of the occupational scale are under constant pressure to increase productivity and accept lower wages, on the grounds that it is necessary to lower the costs of production so as to maintain competitiveness on the global market.

With the demise of socialist political systems, capitalism has acquired the force of a religious faith, unchallenged by any other political ideology except perhaps some forms of religious fundamentalism. Capitalism is now accepted as the only viable form of social and economic organisation; it is also equated with democracy. In such a climate of belief, social problems are increasingly perceived as the problems of individuals and are explained as such. Intervention methods are correspondingly individually targeted. Individuals and social groupings who experience problems are usually those whose attitudes, abilities and behaviour indicate some form of failure to practise the virtue of capitalist philosophy. By demonstrating the locus of a problem to be in the characteristics of the people experiencing it, the capitalist system is both exonerated and legitimated.

The social problems experienced on a global scale but particularly in Third World countries, such as chronic poverty, malnutrition and disease, are undoubtedly due to a number of interrelated factors, but the relentless pursuit of higher and higher living standards in industrialised countries, which is measured by increasing rates of material consumption, is one of the main determinants. It is well established that the rate of consumption in affluent countries cannot be matched in undeveloped and developing countries simply because of insufficient earth resources, especially where the consumption of energy is concerned. A simple equation would suggest, therefore, that any significant improvement in the quality of life in poor countries would depend greatly on the redistribution of resources on a global scale. This would necessarily mean lowering consumption in affluent countries. Such redistribution would certainly not be a sufficient measure on its own, but would have to be one of the primary measures necessary to bring about improvement in the quality of life in poor countries. However, redistribution of this kind is most unlikely, as in the present dominant world-economic and political system, such global measures would be regarded as an impossible solution, or as empty rhetoric and a Utopian notion. Yet the current distribution of natural resources is an acknowledged world-wide social problem that poses a potential threat to the world's social, political and economic system as we know it.

This illustrates the central point in our perspective on social problems – namely, the causative links between the pursuit of certain values and interests and the negative 'residue' of such pursuits. Causative links similar to those found on the global scale are also found within certain geographical regions and within countries, both undeveloped and poor, and industrialised and affluent. It is the sociology of social problems in the latter countries that we mainly examine in this and in following chapters, focusing on Australia and referring to other countries for purposes of comparison. The examples used in this chapter are unemployment, degradation of the natural environment, and the reduction of the public sphere. We also offer brief comment on a related issue of great significance – namely, a trend in social policies that we interpret as the demise of the welfare state. In the following chapters, we present other examples and examine in greater detail some methods of intervention and their effects.

Unemployment

Unemployment, or forced idleness, is a world-wide phenomenon, but its causes and extent as well as its meaning are not the same in all societies.

In most Third World countries, the organisation of the labour market is such that concepts of employment and unemployment differ from one place to another. By the standards of industrialised countries, unemployment in Third World countries is very high, especially in rural settings and in the large cities to which people from rural regions have moved and live in adjacent shanty towns. In industrialised countries, there is more uniformity in the meaning of the terms employment and unemployment, but each is now classified into various categories and the meaning of these categories is imprecise. There is 'full-time' employment, 'part-time' employment, and 'casual' or 'sessional' employment, and corresponding forms of unemployment such as 'transitional', 'seasonal', 'long-term', 'structural', and so on. There is however a universally present phenomenon of unemployment encompassing all these categories, which in 1997 varied from about five per cent of the labour force in some countries to over twelve per cent in others (Gregory 1993).

Despite constantly expressed concern about high levels of unemployment, and fears that such levels present a potential threat of social disruption, vulnerability to demagoguery or even the threat of totalitarian regimes, industrialised societies appear to be helpless in reducing what is acknowledged to be a social problem. Why is this so?

In a simple explanation, unemployment results from the imbalance between a growing capacity to produce goods and services and the capacity to consume these goods and services. This equation was postulated by Theobald in the early 1960s. He argued then that observed trends, if they continued, would mean a widening gap between production and consumption and would lead to increasing unemployment, which would become entrenched in certain sections of the labour force and would not be solved by any increase in the rate of economic growth (1965:46–70). However, the relationship between production and consumption is not a simple equation, as the capacity to consume is not related simply to the volume of production, but depends on access to goods and services. There are millions of people in the world – outside as well as within advanced industrialised countries – whose capacity to consume is limited by lack of financial means. The explanation for unemployment, therefore, must be sought in the allocation of resources to the production of goods and services, and in the distribution of the capacity to consume goods and services – that is, either financial means at an individual level, or collective provisions on certain conditions that do not entail monetary exchange, such as free public transport, education and health services.

How does this situation fit into our hypothesis on the nature of social problems? In regard to unemployment, we need to note that in addition to the particular allocation of resources and the system of valuing certain activities and rewarding them accordingly, other factors also are at work. First, notwithstanding frequent assertions and expressions of concern, governments in industrialised countries have found high levels of unemployment to be manageable, both economically and politically. Unemployment constitutes a form of 'trade-off' for efficiency, as well as a trade-off between the contentment of the majority and the disaffection of a minority. In the perspective of the dominant theory and ideology of the 'free' market, productive efficiency is of paramount value and the main objective of economic activity. It is seen to ensure the maintenance of living standards and competitiveness on the world market, and it acts as a stimulus for the maintenance of effort, inventiveness, initiative and so on. Above all, efficiency means return of income on capital invested – that is, profit. The 'human surplus' that might be created through increased efficiency is of no concern to private enterprises: it is shifted across to the public sphere as a problem of the state.

In economic terms, an 'unemployed person' means a 'surplus productive capacity', but in social terms it means a person deprived of a social role, a 'human residue'. A high level of unemployment thus presents a challenge to the value of productive activity and has also been traditionally perceived as a potential threat to social order. However, the potential for social disruption by high unemployment levels is now lessened because the contemporary state has much greater power and capacity to control the consequent discontent by using financial compensation through unemployment-benefit schemes and associated services. Human services also play an important role in the management of discontent: expert advisers such as psychologists, social workers and other counsellors are used to provide various forms of material and psychological assistance, which 'keeps the lid on' discontent. Frequent, manifest assertions by parties in power about government efforts to find solutions, and promises of solutions in the 'near future', further assist in maintaining social order. Finally, and most importantly, the potential 'threat' from high unemployment levels is not seen to be so great as to outweigh the benefits of the existing situation enjoyed by the majority of the population. In other words, unemployment of the relative few (a minority) is regarded as a necessary if rather unfortunate price to pay for the benefits of the majority. By keeping the majority reasonably satisfied, the system is legitimated.

Furthermore, from the point of view of the dominant ideology of the 'free' market, high unemployment levels create certain advantages for employers and investors. High unemployment reduces the power of trade unions and reduces demands for higher wages. It also facilitates the establishment of working conditions that are sanctioned by laws giving employers greater power in 'hiring and firing' workers; the power to organise the mode of production so as to enforce greater effort from workers; and the power to reduce various benefits previously enjoyed by the workforce, such as paid sick leave, penalty rates for night or weekend work, or unhealthy work conditions. In 1996, Australian Commonwealth legislation, *The Workplace Relations Act 1996*, reduced the power of the unions as well as the power of the Industrial Relations Commission, eliminated previous rules on unfair dismissal, introduced individual enterprise agreements and individual contracts between employer and employee, and put in place a host of regulations that increased the power of employers. In times of full employment, it would not be possible for any government to enact such legislation. Politically, therefore, the issue for the government is to ensure that unemployment is 'manageable' and does not raise societal discontent to a level that would erode the loyalty of the electorate to the party in power. There are considerable advantages for a conservative government in maintaining the system as it is, as this ensures the loyalty of those who support that system, maintains the efficient operation of the economy, and also gives government ministers opportunities to admonish those who are 'unwilling to work', and maintain unemployment benefits at a low level. For the society as a whole, the fundamental effect of such conditions is a massive transfer of income and wealth from labour to capital.

In sum, a high level of unemployment is a 'residual condition' of a deliberate and rational pursuit of certain goals by society. While it might be acknowledged as a social problem, it is maintained because to remedy it would mean to devalue the existing ideology and corresponding goals and pursuits, as well as diminish the advantages that the conditions ensure for the dominant classes in society. This might not be an entirely satisfactory outcome, but in the perspective of neo-classical economics and in the current liberal-democratic ideology it is a rational solution, a rational management and control of a social condition that might be portrayed as 'unfortunate' but that has been 'normal' since at least the mid-1970s.

Unemployment is therefore a social condition that is defined, with a high degree of consensus, as an objective condition. Such consensus is possible because the issues of work, employment and unemployment have been discussed, analysed, compared, exchanged and written about for a long time at an international level, and this has been instrumental in establishing common definitions and meanings. Unemployment has been extensively researched, mainly by economists, with the implicit and explicit notion that it is an 'undesirable condition' that calls for some remedies. At the same time, there is a partly tacit, partly implicit (by inference) and sometimes even explicit acknowledgement that in the 'free' market system a certain level of unemployment is unavoidable but that this does not necessarily constitute a big problem, provided unemployment is confined to an 'acceptable' level. It is on the 'level of acceptability' that opinions differ.

Despite the manageability of high unemployment levels, evidence indicating that unemployment is a logical outcome of the 'free' market system presents a threat to the legitimacy of that system. In order to maintain and reinforce the system's legitimacy, the causes of unemployment are explained by structural changes in the labour market, by international conditions, by political constraints, and by a host of other causes. Among the 'true' economic rationalists, unemployment is also explained by the lack of full implementation of 'free' market principles – that is, the lack of complete freedom for investors and employers to conduct business without 'government interference', to organise labour in the most efficient manner and to have complete control over working conditions and rates of pay. Above all, whatever acknowledgement might be given to certain causes, one of the main causes of unemployment that has survived the test of time is the belief that there is a character deficiency in some individuals, which is defined as 'unwillingness to work'. Duncan Gallie, in his research on unemployment in England, noted that:

> In the conservative view, unemployment is attributed to the personal characteristics and work attitudes of the unemployed themselves. The distinctive characteristic of the unemployed is that they are people who have failed, either because of innate personality deficiencies or because of a breakdown in the system of primary socialisation, to assimilate the work ethic. They are characterised by a degree of behavioural instability that makes it difficult for them to hold any job for long, or they are people with low commitment to employment, the 'work shy'.   *(1994:737–8)*

It is this particular 'pathological affliction' that receives most attention from the authorities. This attention ranges from professional advice and counselling, training and re-training programs, to frequent reporting, work tests, form-filling and other surveillance methods.

There is also recognition, somewhat implicit in some remedial programs (e.g. *Working Nation*, see Keating 1994), that the threat of sustained high unemployment lies in the alienation of the unemployed from economic and social life, thus presenting a potential threat to social order – the threat of the 'underclass'. The best outcome that may be expected from such programs is only a limited success in re-inserting the unemployed into the labour market, as the programs seek to remedy the negative effects of the 'free' market system but do not change the basic premises on which the 'free' market economy is built.

Nevertheless, it is argued, partial re-insertion into the labour market is better than complete separation from it.

In Australia, unemployment has been at the forefront of public concern, policy debates and much research. Unemployment rates began to rise in the mid-1970s and accelerated early in the 1980s when the rate doubled in the space of two years, due mainly to loss of employment in manufacturing industries. There was some reduction in unemployment during the mid-1980s, but this was followed by another sharp increase in the early 1990s. Since then, there has been some reduction, but the rate remains high at close to nine per cent of the labour force (see Table 5.1). As shown in Table 5.1, the number of unemployed people in 1996 was nearly ten times greater than in 1966, and the unemployment rate was five-and-half times that of 1966. Another dimension of significance is the mean duration of unemployment per person, which in 1996 was more than 16 times that in 1966. This mean duration indicates that unemployment is concentrated in one section of the labour force, becoming for some an almost permanent condition.

Table 5.1: Labour Force and Employment, Australia 1966–96

(N = '000)

Labour force		1966	1996	Change 1966–96 N	Ratio
Population 15 years +	*N*	*8180.3*	*14384.3*	*6204.0*	*1.76*
Labour force	N	4902.5	9090.8	4188.3	1.85
Labour force	%	59.9	63.2	3.3	1.06
Employed	N	4823.9	8319.7	3495.8	1.72
– Full-time	N	4348.8	6236.2	1887.4	1.43
– Part-time	N	475.1	2083.5	1608.4	4.39
– Part-time	%	9.8	25.0	15.2	2.55
Unemployed	N	78.6	771.1	692.5	9.81
Unemployed	%	1.6	8.5	6.9	5.31
Mean duration of unemployment – weeks		3.0	50.0	47.0	16.67

Sources: ABS (1986) *The Labour Force Australia, Historical Summary, 1966–1984*, Catalogue No. 6204.0
ABS (1996) *Labour Force Australia, August 1996*, Catalogue No. 6203.0

Table 5.2: Employment in Industry Sectors, Australia 1966–96

(N = '000)

Industry sector	1966		1996		Change 1966–96	
	N	%	N	%	N	%
All employed persons	*4823.9*	*100.0*	*8319.7*	*100.0*	*3495.8*	*72.5*
Material production[a]	2222.6	46.1	2304.4	27.7	81.8	3.7
Distribution services[b]	1368.9	28.4	2290.0	27.5	921.1	67.3
Management services[c]	945.4	19.6	2852.7	34.3	1907.3	201.7
Other service industries[d]	287.0	5.9	872.6	10.5	585.6	204.0

Notes: a Agriculture; mining; manufacturing; energy and water; construction
b Wholesale and retail trade; transport and storage; communications
c Finance; insurance and property; government administration; health, education and community services
d Accommodation; cafes and restaurants; cultural and recreation services; personal and other services

Sources: ABS (1986) *The Labour Force Australia, Historical Summary, 1966–1984*, Catalogue No. 6204.0
ABS (1996) *Labour Force Australia, August 1996*, Catalogue No. 6203.0

The causes of high unemployment levels are numerous, and a detailed analysis is well beyond the scope of this book. Technological change in industrial production, and competition from global industries (especially from low-cost, developing countries) are two causes frequently mentioned, but two other related causes have also been significant. One is the shift of employment from industries producing material goods to those industries managing finance, property, public administration and providing community services such as health, education and related social services. These industries have provided unprecedented opportunities of employment for professionals of both sexes (see Graycar and Jamrozik 1993). Those who have found employment in these growing industries are therefore not the same people who lost jobs in the industries of material production (see Table 5.2). The other related factor has been the increase in the participation rates in the labour force. As shown in Table 5.1, the participation rate in 1996 was 3.3 percentage points higher than in 1966. In terms of the 1996 population 15 years of age and over (14 384 300), the 3.3 percentage points means 474 700 people. This means that if the number of employed people in 1996 was as shown, and participation rates were the same as in 1966, unemployment would have been reduced by 474 700 people.

The 771 000 unemployed people shown in the table constitute the human residue of a number of factors affecting the labour market. The industries that manage material and human resources have become the main employers of tertiary-educated professionals and para-professionals of both sexes. These new employment opportunities have given rise to the growing incidence and affluence of two-income families among professional people, and declining employment opportunities in industries of material production have produced entrenched unemployment among manual occupations. The magnitude of this 'human residue' of the market economy is illustrated by the number of people who rely on unemployment benefits as their income. In 1990–91, the mean weekly number of people who received benefits in Tasmania (19 357) was greater than the mean weekly number of recipients in 1965–66 for the whole of Australia (14 927), and Tasmania accounts for less than three per cent of the Australian population (Department of Social Security 1975, 1991). The legitimation of these conditions is achieved through claims of the necessity to improve the efficiency and competitiveness of industries. However, the pursuit of higher profitability for investors is an important pursuit, manifest in the interesting phenomenon of rising share prices whenever an industry reduces its labour force.

Degradation of the Environment

The importance of the natural environment is an issue that seems to sink rather slowly into public consciousness. On the one hand, frequent comments appear in the press about air and water pollution, gas emissions, ozone layers, waste disposal, nuclear energy, over-population, deforestation (especially the large-scale deforestation of the Amazon region), or the exhaustion of oil reserves. All these phenomena are presented as real or potential dangers to the quality of life, and as carrying the threat of eventual destruction of life on this planet. On the other hand, despite national and international conferences at which these issues are discussed, and from which reports of the debates are publicised, very few measures seem to be taken on a scale that would effectively slow down these dangerous trends and prevent the ultimate catastrophe. This dissonance between rhetoric and action appears to indicate a kind of fatalistic belief that 'things will sort themselves out somehow', if only for the reason that they have always sorted themselves out before.

As we have only a layperson's knowledge of issues relating to the natural environment, our brief excursus into this terrain is mainly to serve as an example of a social issue – an important social problem of universal significance, which has not received much attention either in sociology or in the teaching curricula and practice of the helping professions. Yet, although environmental issues are perceived mainly as concerns of biology or health, the attention given to such matters within these disciplines, and in the corresponding research, is facilitated or constrained by the dominant forces of the market and the social and economic policies of governments. Indeed, studies of environmental problems and methods of intervention show considerable similarity to the processes we have observed in social problems in other areas. There are also some distinct features in environmental issues that impede the acknowledgement that neglect of the environment is a social problem that calls for intervention at all three levels of the structure of social organisation.

The degradation of the natural environment is clearly a *social* problem. First, it is socially created, by individual actions of everyday living, and because it is an increasing by-product – a predictable residue – of deliberate rational actions by business, industry and governments, carried out for commercial or political purposes. Second, it has an immediate or potential negative effect on human beings and other forms of life, both animal and plant. These effects are universal and global; as the Chernobyl disaster showed, an accident in one place may sow widespread and long-lasting damage throughout an entire continent. Third, although the detrimental effects of this problem are global, they are manipulated by powerful states and corporations so that the effects are not universally experienced. Industrialised Western countries become 'post industrial' by shifting environmentally dirty industries to Third World countries, and also by sending them the chemical waste residues of their own industries. Within the affluent industrialised countries themselves, the location of industries and the urban land management and control measures create beautiful 'leafy' suburbs and rather barren working-class suburbs. In effect, on the international scene, degradation of the environment is a political and economic power issue; within the countries, it is a class issue.

The conservation of the natural environment is clearly incompatible with the market economy, which is driven by high consumption levels and which allocates so many resources, human and material, to the 'seduction industry' whose task is to promote the consumption of all kinds of goods and services as the desirable way of life (Bauman 1987). The negative social aspects of the pressure to consume and of its corollary, the pressure to produce the desirable objects of consumption, receive little attention in social and economic discourse when compared with the attention given to arguments advocating continuous growth in the gross domestic product (GDP) as the main solution to unemployment and all social ills. A significant departure from this direction is the work of Ulrich Beck, who argues within the framework of his 'risk theory' that the social production of wealth in the contemporary world 'goes hand in hand with the social production of risks' (1989:86). The risks include those with 'potential threats to ourselves', such as harmful and poisonous substances in foodstuffs, air and water pollution, atomic weapons and energy, and genetic engineering. These risks show a global tendency, crossing national boundaries. They 'pose a potential threat which is supra-national and not class-specific'. These risks also create 'new international inequalities, not only between third world and industrialised states but also among the industrialised states themselves', the dying forests being an example. 'The politics of an increasingly uninhabitable earth is generated in steps and bounds, in more and more critical catastrophes, through the unrestrained production of modernisation risks' (1992:88–93).

Criticisms are now being expressed of the traditional methods of calculating the GDP, pointing out that the method does not allow for the calculation of the cost of destruction of the environment. The critics advocate instead a genuine progress indicator (GPI) as a means to calculate the value of real progress. Using this method, for example, the United States economy shows a decline in per-capita income growth since the mid-1970s, while on the GDP indicator, the growth has been continuous to this day. The most significant factor in the discrepancy between the GDP and GPI measures is the use of energy. This is still growing in industrialised countries, and such growth is aspired to in developing countries. The protagonists of the GPI argue that unless environmental destruction costs are taken into account, the notion of 'sustainable development' calculated by the GDP method is entirely wrong because the notion does not adequately consider the value of irretrievable losses incurred by development.

Australia does not have a very good record in the conservation of its natural environment. This is typical of attitudes and policies in most colonial settlements, where the exploitation of natural resources has been conducted with a disregard for destructive effects similar to the disregard shown for the well-being of indigenous inhabitants, their social systems and cultures. In Australia, the colonisers' attitudes and practices were more destructive than in other colonies because the perception of the country as a *terra nullius* included not only its human inhabitants but also animals and plants. Even now, despite an active conservationist movement, the old attitudes and policies persist. For example, the current policy for forest preservation is to preserve the level of forest coverage at 15 per cent of that at the time of European colonisation. This would leave about five per cent of the country covered by forest, compared to about 25–30 per cent forest coverage in densely populated Europe. Government policy displays similar attitudes towards air pollution and the danger of global warming, with Australia refusing to agree to the international treaty (under which countries agree to reduce gas emissions to below the 1990 level) on the grounds that this country is a high energy producer and such restriction would be economically damaging. Certainly, Australian governments, both state and federal, have manifest policies that aim to ensure the protection of the natural environment. However, the intervention methods typically take the form of research or committees of inquiry, designed to demonstrate that a particular economic development venture does not produce any damage, or only produces 'manageable' damage to the environment. A system of 'environmental impact statements' (EISs) has been introduced, but the findings of this measure can be highly speculative. The argument that a venture is essential to the economy usually wins the day. So far, no significant mining development project, factory with high gas emissions, or chemical pollution of waterways appears to have been prevented on environmental grounds, except the hydroelectric dam on the Franklin River in 1983 and a paper mill in the early 1990s, both in Tasmania.

Some environmental commentators have linked the problem of damage to the environment, especially the deterioration of the urban environment, to population increase through immigration. While growth in the size of cities undoubtedly brings some problems, especially if that growth is not planned and is driven by profit without regard for environmental consequences, the concern seems to be misplaced. However motivated, this argument has been used mainly as one against further immigration, especially immigration from neighbouring South-East Asian countries. This attitude was noted by the House of Representatives Standing Committee for Long Term Strategies, which wrote in its Report that the Committee was 'troubled by the prevailing fatalism in many submissions which suggest that changing migration intake is the only variable in determining Australia's future population resource use, waste disposal and urban form ... without any attempt to suggest more appropriate land management, developing new techniques in waste disposal and treating pristine water as a premium product' (Parliament of the Commonwealth of Australia 1994:18–19). Undoubtedly, while population size cannot be ignored as a factor in the preservation or destruction of the natural environment, the damage inflicted on the Australian ecology was much greater when the population was considerably smaller (Hassan and Jamrozik 1996:11).

In the human services, especially among the helping professions engaged in services for 'people with problems', concern with the natural environment has been virtually absent. Somehow, the perception of the degradation of the natural environment as a social problem does not seem to have entered into the consciousness of these professions. (An exception is the section of the medical profession involved in public health, and important research has been done in this field (e.g. McMichael 1993).) What reasons might there be for this lacuna in professional perspectives? In social work, there is a notion of an 'ecology approach', but ecology is taken to mean 'human ecology', and the perception of the environment is confined to the 'social environment' (e.g. Fook 1993). The natural environment's relevance receives some attention from Stuart Rees (1991) in his argument on the common interests between social workers who seek to develop community-based developmental methods of intervention rather than solely individualistic therapeutic methods dealing with 'pathologies'. The most theoretically developed environmental perspective and its application to social work methods of practice was developed by Jim Ife (1991, 1995, 1997), who argues that such an approach needs to be based on a new paradigm in thinking about the economy and the natural environment.

The relative absence of concern with the natural environment by the helping professions might be due to the concept's novelty as a 'social issue' and a corresponding failure to see the degradation of that environment as a social problem. Furthermore, the 'residue' of the problem lies in the whole community, not in individuals; its negative effects are first noticed in other forms of life, so the identification of a direct or potential threat to the entire population is not presented. The helping professions – educated, trained and socialised into perceiving and interpreting social problems as pathologies related to certain population characteristics – do not have the methods in their catalogue of interventions to deal with the consequences environmental degradation has for the population. It has to be noted that all three writers mentioned above, who see the natural environment as an issue, see possible solutions in perceiving this issue as one of power within the political and economic structure, and in intervention methods aimed at changing that structure – not in therapeutic methods offered to or targeted at those individuals and families in the population negatively affected by environmental degradation.

Reduction of the Public Sphere

A prominent feature of the 'free' market ideology is the devaluation of the public sphere. In the first instance, this ideology is propounded with the aim of reducing the activities carried out by the state through the public sector. Reduction takes place through various arrangements under the concepts of 'corporatisation', 'privatisation', 'contracting out' and 'purchasing services'. The main rationale for these actions is the argument that the public sector tends to be inherently (that is, by its very nature) inefficient and is therefore too costly for society. For this reason, it is argued, the smaller the public sector, the better for society. In line with this argument, the reduction of the public sector in Australia has proceeded on a large scale since the early 1980s, first under the umbrella of the then Labor government's policies, and now (in the late 1990s) under the Coalition government's policies. Under the privatisation policy, some significant services in the economic infrastructure have been removed from the public sector: the Commonwealth Bank, the national airline Qantas, energy generating industries, and water supply. Privatisation has also entered the area of formal social control through the introduction of privately operated prisons. Private organisations have increased their activities in two other important service areas in which they were already involved: health services and education. Legislation was also passed in late 1996 to sell a portion (one-third) of the telecommunications corporation Telstra, and further sales of airport facilities and armament industries are envisaged in the near future.

The reduction of the public sector is an excellent example of an objective condition that by a subjective perception may be seen as a social problem. Does the reduction of the public sector and shift of services into the private, profit-driven sector constitute a social problem? If the performance of services in the public sector is evaluated solely by the criteria of the 'free' market (that is, the criteria of efficiency), then the result may or may not show comparative inefficiency in the public sector facility, but this would not demonstrate that such inefficiency is intrinsic or inherent in the public sector. The question is whether the criteria of the 'free' market are sufficient or even appropriate for the evaluation of public sector services. There are some fundamental assumptions upon which public services are established and are expected to operate. In the traditional democratic perspective, the public services constitute the core infrastructure of community services, access to which is expected to be available to every citizen. They are also owned collectively by the public, and the sale of such services is seen by many people as the expropriation or alienation of public property.

The division between private and public sectors is not clear-cut. There are some aspects of the public sector that play an important role in the provision of essential services and that are not immediately visible because they have been taken for granted for a long time. As illustrated

by the examples in Figure 5.1, the public sector provides a range of
human and material resources that enable private pursuits to take place
for private gain, but at considerable public cost. For example, the very
structure of laws and the structure of public health provide the setting
for private professional practitioners. Similarly, academic lecturers and

Figure 5.1: Examples of Human and Material Resources – Public/Private
Sector Configuration

Use of human resources

		Public sector	**Private/ subsidised**	**Private sector**
Use of material resources	**Public sector**	Teachers in public schools Salaried medical practitioners in public hospitals Librarians in public libraries Academics in universities	Medical practitioners in public hospitals Barristers/ solicitors paid by Legal Aid funds	Barristers/ solicitors in court work Consultants in public organisations Contracted workers in the public sector Assistance to industry
	Private/ subsidised	Public personnel seconded to private agencies Provision of office space to non-profit organisations	Non-government welfare organisations Medical practitioners in private hospitals Work-based child care Private schools	Private workers in subsidised organisations Community organisations with taxation concessions Religious organisations (churches, religious orders)
	Private sector	Public organisations in leased private premises	Medical practitioners in private practice	Private (not subsidised) universities Private community organisations

Source: A. Jamrozik and C. Boland (1993), *Human Resources in Community Services: Conceptual Issues and Empirical Evidence,* Kensington NSW

teachers in private schools practise their profession in buildings either owned or partially funded by the public purse. Most private welfare organisations rely almost entirely on public funds for their operation. The list is practically endless. Most of these arrangements mean that collective public resources are used for the benefit of individuals and private corporations. These arrangements also mean that any social problem that arises out of private corporations' operations is translated into a 'human residue', which becomes the responsibility of the state and is then 'cared for' by policies and services that are either funded and/or provided by the public sector.

The problem, however, goes much deeper. With the shift of activities from the public to the private sector comes also the growth of the cult of individualism. The cult of individualism devalues the public sphere, and with it the notion of 'the common good' and the common interest. The erosion of the public sphere took root when private-sector notions of efficiency and profitability began to be applied to the public sector. Certainly, the public sector needs to work as efficiently as possible, but in certain areas it cannot be evaluated solely on market criteria, as in a similar way the value of the domestic economy cannot be evaluated solely by market criteria (Jamrozik 1989). While public sector efficiency is important, it is the *effectiveness* of a given service and its social purpose that are most important, and one important aspect of such effectiveness is equality of access irrespective of the user's ability to pay – something the 'free' market cannot deliver. Access to health, education, a clean environment and a range of social and cultural provisions is a public matter, based on well-grounded rights of citizenship in a democratic society. For this reason, infiltration of the public sector by the values and attitudes of the market corrupts the value base of the public service. This negative result is not easily measured quantitatively, but is evident in people's attitudes to public issues, and in the declining interest in community activities and political participation.

The Demise of the Welfare State

Social problems arise from a variety of events and social conditions. Not the least of these are the social and economic policies of governments. David Gil, in his analysis of the sources of social problems, observes that:

> It should also be noted that 'social problems' perceived by various groups in a society concerning the quality and the circumstances of life, or intra-societal human relations, must be understood as intended or unintended consequences of the existing configuration of social policies. Such policies are therefore viewed not only as potential solutions to specified social problems,

but all past and extant social policies of a society are considered to be causally related to the various social problems perceived by its members at any point in time. This conceptualisation of the relationship between social policies and social problems does not negate the significance of specific policies as potential solutions to perceived problems. Rather, it provides an expanded theoretical basis for the proposition that valid solutions of social problems require appropriate modifications of the key processes of social policies.

(1976:17)

Some of the major social problems in the world today, especially in affluent countries of the industrialised Western world, may be directly linked to profound changes in the policies of these countries, the effect of which may be defined as 'the demise of the welfare state'. The welfare state, which came to be accepted in the 1960s as the model of the contemporary industrialised state, enjoyed its social and economic acceptance for only a brief period. The optimistic prediction of Wilensky and Lebeaux (1958) that the welfare state would in the foreseeable future lead to a 'welfare society' never came to fruition. Doubts about the viability of the welfare state in a capitalist system were expressed in the early 1970s by O'Connor (1973), who wrote about the 'fiscal crisis' of the state. Critique was further extended by concerned critics such as Marshall (1981), Offe (1984) and others, as well as collectively by the Organisation for Economic Cooperation and Development (OECD 1981).

The welfare state also has a growing number of critics who are openly antagonistic. They perceive the welfare state as a social institution responsible for the loss of self-reliance and for the growth of dependency (e.g. Murray 1984). These criticisms come not only from conservative liberal-democratic governments but, in Australia, came also from the ostensibly social-democratic Labor government of the 1980s and early 1990s, which gradually adopted the philosophies of economic rationalism and corresponding social and economic policies (Jamrozik 1991).

Under these growing pressures, the concept of the welfare state as envisaged by the optimistic predictions of the 1960s was to all intents and purposes dead or at least mortally wounded by 1975, although the term continued to be used and is still used in the 1990s. In liberal democracies, social policies have focused increasingly on 'targeting' benefits towards those in 'greatest need', with stringent eligibility criteria, ongoing surveillance and reviews to detect fraud, and public exhortations about the need to prevent abuse and curtail social welfare expenditure.

The welfare state also created new inequalities. More and more benefits and policy priorities focused on providing incentives to work; changes in the labour market provided new opportunities for professional and related work for both sexes; and employment in manual occupations began to disappear. The welfare state became the source of new benefits to the affluent 'new middle class' and of new exclusions to the lower working class (Jamrozik 1991). Esping-Andersen argues that:

> Social stratification is part and parcel of welfare states. Social policy is supposed to address problems of stratification, but it also produces it. Equality has always been what welfare states were supposed to produce, yet the image of equality has always remained rather vague. In some analyses it is simply taken for granted that social benefits diminish inequalities. In others, the focus is on the eradication of poverty. The really neglected issue is the welfare state as a stratification system in its own right. *(1990:3–4)*

Esping-Andersen further argues that the acceptance and consolidation of the welfare state 'came to depend fundamentally on the political alliances of the new middle class', and that the new middle classes have been very successful in having their demands met by the state as well as by the market, thus ensuring their historically relatively privileged position (1990:31). What emerged over the two decades from the 1960s to the 1980s was a 'two-tier' welfare state, bestowing valuable benefits onto the middle classes, which enabled them to function to their advantage in the 'free' market economy, and 'survival' benefits to the working and increasingly 'non-working' classes, in the latter case accompanied by complex bureaucratic control and surveillance to uncover and prevent 'fraudulent' claims on the state.

The welfare state, which was expected to attenuate the excesses of the capitalist system, became in effect an organisation whose priority was facilitating the working of that system. Neil Gilbert, writing about the changing philosophy of social protection in the United States, argues that 'what is emerging in that country is not just a variant of the conventional welfare state but an alternative form. It is a change in kind; the system of social protection is being transformed from that of a welfare state to that of an "enabling state"' (1995:151). He observes that a similar trend has emerged in England. 'References to the enabling state are often couched in the language of "empowerment", "privatisation", and "responsibility", the principle of this approach being "public support for private responsibility"' (1995:153). Gilbert draws a comparison between the welfare state and the enabling state as follows:

Welfare State	**Enabling State**
Expanding social rights	Linking rights to obligations
Relying on direct expenditures	Increasing indirect expenditures
Transfers in the form of service	Transfers in cash or vouchers
Delivery by public agencies	Delivery by private agencies
Policy focused on individuals	Policy focused on the family
Welfare benefits for consumption	Welfare benefits for investment
Reducing economic inequality	Restoring social equity

(1995:154)

What, then, is meant by social equity? Gilbert explains that 'An implicit assumption of social equity is that welfare transfers ought to result in a fair distribution of public resources among those with competing needs and problems' (1995:160). However, we need to note that 'equity' is a concept with diverse meanings and applications. It is often interpreted as a principle of allocating 'just desserts' – a principle that does not advance the clarity of the concept of equity because the expression 'just desserts' is based on certain values that are not made explicit. Indeed, the changes in resource allocation by the state have clearly been directed at benefiting those who benefit most from the market. In the logic and values of the 'free' market philosophy, this is certainly regarded as 'just desserts', as it enhances the functioning of the market.

The residue of these arrangements is the growing number of people who are excluded from the market and who become dependent on public support for their survival. In Australia, the latest available data obtained from the Australian Bureau of Statistics (ABS), based on a survey conducted in 1994–95, show that 28.8 per cent of the population 15 years and over relies on government pensions or benefits as their primary source of income (ABS 1996, No. 6227.0). This issue is further discussed in Chapter 7.

Postmodernism, Change and Progress

The big issue for industrialised societies today is to find ways of reconciling the 'old' with the 'new' – that is, to accept the social reality of postmodernity without destroying the positive achievements of modernity.

The rationality of modern thought that emerged in the 18th century from the Enlightenment has been instrumental in the advancement of science and technology, creating conditions for the development of art, culture and living conditions, which by any objective criteria would be regarded as progress. However, modernity has now exhausted itself and become sterile. With the demise of socialist political and economic systems, the capitalist system has become more narrowly one-dimensional than ever before, and its dominant ideology is to pursue 'more of the same', driven by a kind of fatalistic faith that nature and human inventiveness will always come up with something new to prevent the ultimate disaster.

On the other hand, postmodern ideas, while questioning the rationality of modern thought, its values and social organisation, do not offer anything new in terms of alternative directions, except a 'discourse' or 'deconstruction'. Furthermore, with its relativist philosophy, postmodernism fails to offer a critique of one of the fundamental shortcomings of modernity and the capitalist system – namely, the vision (or illusion), for some, of a never-ending 'progress' that is measured by an increasing quantity and diversity of consumable goods and services, at the price of exploitation and misery for others.

The central notion guiding modernity was the idea of progress, perceived as an ongoing advancement of science and technology, with corresponding improvement in living standards and quality of life. Carlo Mongardini argues that 'the idea of progress is closely linked with the idea of culture and tradition. It is impossible even to conceive of progress if there is no consolidated and robust cultural system' (1990:53). He sees danger in postmodern ideas, which question all existing values and the basis of knowledge and human culture itself, thus making it difficult for people to establish any stable social relationships. Mongardini explains that:

> Progress is synonymous with evolution, development, and not fragmentation, segmentation, dissolution. Progress means generating a new culture in which values are transformed, reshaped, but not cancelled or rendered meaningless ... progress is a process of society's structuring its new social forms; change that produces culture and not change that destroys it ... In assuming change as the only value, and the aesthetic experience as the only common bond, postmodern culture destroys itself as a culture.   *(1990:54)*

Mongardini argues that postmodernism 'offers us a culture without history (and therefore a negation of culture) and a history without culture (post-history)'. He sees both culture and history being anchored in the present, located in the experience lived out here and now, which he says 'is not the experience at all, as the term implies past accumulation to be compared with the present. Life cannot be reduced to the present: it needs a past and a future. Reduction to the present is simply an attempt to petrify the status quo' (1990:61).

In searching for a solution to this 'impasse', Mongardini looks to various social groups and institutions such as young people, churches and others who look beyond the pursuit of material goods. He finally focuses on intellectuals, by which he does not mean the 'stage-intellectuals' who act as contemporary ideologues of modernism or postmodernism, but 'those for whom the goal is still the truth attained by reflection and research'. He thinks that, if intellectuals 'can relearn to perform a critical function, and present a valid defence against the temptations of totalitarianism', they will be 'able to play a decisive part in the solution to the problems of culture that face us as we come close to the twenty-first century' (1990:63).

In Australia, as in many other countries, three important elements play an increasingly significant role in the management of resources and politics generally. These elements – globalisation of the economy, cultural influences from outside, and internal ethnic/cultural diversity – are seen by some people as sources of social problems. The first element has forced a comprehensive restructuring of economic activities, especially in manufacturing, as well as the disappearance of certain industries unable to withstand the competition from abroad. The second element has led to more 'open' lifestyles, but also to growing anxieties and fears of 'cultural contamination' from neighbouring countries. It has also led to a resurgence in attitudes of chauvinism and xenophobia, which are propagated by new forms of populist politics adopted by some 'independent' politicians. Related to anxieties and fears about cultural influences from outside is a growing antagonism to ethnic diversity *within* Australia, and also to the politics of multi-culturalism. This antagonistic attitude also extends towards the Australian indigenous population, whose progress towards regaining their cultural identity is again under threat.

These are some of the challenges facing Australian society in the late 1990s. These challenges hold particular significance for current social theorising, for research into social problems, and for the curricula and instruction methods in higher education, especially the curricula and teaching methods used in the applied social sciences and professional education, such as social work, medicine, nursing and community services generally. In particular, the trend in the educational curricula of these professions, especially in social work but to a varied extent in all helping professions, is to focus on the development of more efficient and more effective methods of intervention in social problems at the operative level, where the problems are perceived and treated as personal pathologies. The outcome of this trend is that the more successful these professions become in their intervention methods at that level, the more their success serves to legitimise the system of values and resource allocation that produces these pathologies. An awareness of this 'dilemma of helping' is the essential prerequisite such professions need to develop if their work is to achieve the results they often claim to be the aim of their endeavours.

CHAPTER 6

Social Problems in the Residualist Conversion Perspective

Social problems reflect society and its dominant values and interests. Expressing concern about certain conditions in a society is perceived as a threat to those values and interests – that is, to the power structure in society. To maintain the legitimacy of those values and interests, the power holders seek to remove social problems from the social sphere either by shifting them through explanation or deliberate action to places and forces beyond the control of the state, or by relating such problems through residualist conversion to the characteristics of the population strata experiencing them. Sometimes, a problem may remain in both the public and private spheres, its position being contested by parties with conflicting interests, according to their respective perceptions and interpretations. For example, unemployment has been explained by government policy, by unfair competition from other countries, or by the influence of some imported films or fashions being reflected in young people's 'disruptive' social behaviour and unwillingness to accept the discipline of formal and sustained employment obligations. Once a social problem is effectively located in a particular population group, it may further serve to maintain the legitimacy of those dominant values and interests by being used as an illustration of the penalty suffered by those who 'fail' to actively pursue the dominant values and corresponding goals.

In reflecting society (or perhaps showing a 'flipside' of its power structure), social problems indicate either the stability or the changing nature of society's dominant values, interests, and corresponding pursuit of certain goals. Some social problems come and go, others display continuity and persistence, and still others tend to recur at certain times in the same or a modified form, thus demonstrating that continuity and change are two societal processes that occur in a parallel fashion in most

103

societies. As society reproduces itself biologically, socially, politically, economically and culturally, but never entirely in the same form, it also reproduces its social problems – the 'negative residue' of the pursuit of its values and interests. It may be expected, then, that methods of intervention in social problems will also display a similar reproduction of continuity and change, perhaps different in external form but essentially the same in aims.

If social problems emerge as a residue of the pursuit of the dominant values and interests in society, then it follows that the intervention methods sanctioned by the state will aim to solve, attenuate or control the problems in such a way as to maintain the legitimacy of those values and interests. The perceived nature of the problems will determine the nature of the remedial response. Intervention methods may therefore take various forms, not necessarily mutually exclusive, ranging from coercive methods imposed by legislation and its enforcement through the police and the courts, to methods of assistance or 'therapy' rendered by the helping professions. However, if the political nature of a social problem is accepted by government either as a matter of policy or through public pressures the government cannot ignore, the problem will remain in the political sphere and attempts are likely to be made to solve it at that level.

As we argued in Chapter 5, in the perspective we present, the intrinsic nature of social problems is political. To maintain and re-assert the legitimacy of the structure of power and its values and interests, intervention methods must shift the focus of attention to the population negatively affected by a given social condition by identifying the problem in the characteristics of that population. Efforts can then be employed to solve, attenuate or control the problem through methods that focus on these characteristics. Through this process of conversion, the problem's political nature is first translated into a technical problem and is then further converted into a private problem of individuals, families, or certain population groupings or classes. This final stage in the conversion process is largely determined by the intervention methods used by the helping professions and by the theories that guide these intervention methods.

However, certain social problems remain in or are returned to the political sphere, whereupon governments accept responsibility for intervention at either the political or administrative level, or both. The responsibility is accepted either through a deliberate policy or through political pressure exerted by the organised activity of an interest group, which becomes an effective political lobby. There are also some public issues that continue to be contested and that are the subject of much debate and conflict between social groupings, strata or classes who want a given issue to remain in or be accepted into the public sphere as a political matter. Others may want the issue to be regarded as a private problem or, at most, be acknowledged as peripheral to the policy area. In this chapter, we examine these processes in our perspective on social problems, using as examples the issues of multiculturalism, child abuse and child care, and the state-sponsored gambling industry. As the focus of our perspective is on the conversion processes of social problems from one level of social organisation to another (changing through these processes the perceived nature of the problem and corresponding methods of intervention), we refer to this perspective as a 'theory of residualist conversion of social problems'.

Residualist Conversion of Social Problems

As mentioned earlier, if social problems emerge as a logical 'negative residue' of the pursuit of dominant values and interests in a society, it follows that the intervention methods sanctioned by that society and its government will be expected to attenuate, control or solve the problems in such a way that the legitimacy of the power structure and its pursued values are maintained and enhanced. Depending on the perception of a problem's nature at the political and administrative levels, these methods may take diverse forms, not necessarily mutually exclusive. Often, such methods are employed in a complementary manner. The response may include new legislation, which is then enforced by the police and the courts; an increase in some regulatory powers and corresponding activities; the creation of a special task force or even a new department in the public service; or a public campaign through the media. At the operative level, the most likely response will be the engagement of the helping professions, who then use intervention methods such as counselling, therapy, expert advice, or surveillance and documentation.

One frequently used method of intervention in social problems that are seen to present a serious threat to dominant values and interests (that is, to the structure of power) is state-sponsored research, either through establishing special research institutes and/or providing funds for research projects that are submitted to the funding bodies for examination and approval. The organisation of the sponsorship for such research aims to ensure that the funded or commissioned research provides useful findings but does not question the legitimacy of the dominant values and interests. This is ensured by a number of related actions, and the first and most important of these is the control of the research agenda. Such control is achieved by a range of measures, such as allocating research funds for predetermined areas of policy, commissioning specific research projects from selected consultants, appointing 'politically reliable' people to advisory committees and boards of management in government-sponsored research institutes, and prescribing certain methods of enquiry as a condition of sponsorship. Another area is the control over the ownership of intellectual property and the dissemination of research results. In research institutes funded by governments, decisions on publishing research findings are controlled by directors of such institutes or by boards of management, and research reports are published only after approval by such bodies and sometimes even by government ministers. Some research reports are never released for publication, and some are released only to certain people or institutions.

As a result of such controls, commissioned research into social problems serves to validate political and administrative measures and can produce rather trivial results, usually presented in an array of impressive statistics. Such research tends to focus on the symptoms or effects of the underlying causes rather than on the causes themselves. The symptoms thus acquire an ontological existence and, having been conceptualised as such, are objectified by quantified data selected and collected on the basis of value assumptions that are not always made explicit. The data produced by such research illustrate in technical terms concerns that have already been expressed by the government and present interesting but rather 'harmless' interpretations, conclusions or suggestions for action. Any such suggested or recommended action tends to focus on remedial measures at the operative level, and while it might include some suggestions for modifications of administrative measures, it will certainly not engage in any critique of policy. The task of such research is therefore to convert, or translate, the political nature of the problem into a technical problem, capable of being solved, attenuated or controlled by technical means such as legislative or administrative measures, with perhaps some infusion of material resources and specialised human skills. It is in such situations that the helping professions perform their social role as the next stage in the legitimation process.

Social research converts a political issue into a technical problem, but the problem still remains in the social sphere, although it may be identified in relation to a particular population group with certain defined characteristics such as educational level, occupational group, age, gender or ethnicity. The task of the helping professions is then to complete the legitimation process by a further conversion, which removes the problem from the social sphere and translates it into the personal and individualised problem of the affected population. Any successful assistance rendered to recipients of professional services also serves to legitimate the given policy and its underlying values and interests by demonstrating the effectiveness of the intervention methods employed. If an intervention method fails, this is seen as evidence that the recipient has a difficult-to-correct personality or character 'flaw' or 'unwillingness to respond'. In either outcome, the system that is the source of the given social problem is exonerated.

It needs to be noted that the helping professions continue to develop more and more sophisticated intervention methods, which are based mainly on a variety of psychological assumptions and theories not amenable to rigorous scientific tests. This does not mean that such intervention methods are not effective; yet the objective of these methods is not commonly stated with sufficient clarity, meaning their effectiveness can only be evaluated on similar 'soft' criteria. It is important to note, however, that any success or failure of professional intervention will be explained in relation to the individual recipient, or group of recipients. The legitimation of dominant values and interests, and of the structure of power, comes from the 'symbolic role' the professional performs in representing that structure of power. This issue illustrates the 'dilemma of helping', in that the professional's intervention, while attempting to alleviate the negative effects or 'negative residue' of a particular policy, also serves to legitimate that policy.

Our theory of residualist conversion of social problems is presented schematically in Figure 6.1. The processes that convert a social problem into a 'negative residue' that is located in the population experiencing the problem's effects are shown as a series of activities on the left side of the diagram. The activities shown on the right side of the diagram illustrate the processes through which a problem is forced by a political action to remain in the political sphere as a *social* problem and a government responsibility. It is important to note the distinct and significant difference between the two processes: the conversion of a social problem into a negative residue (left side) entails *individualisation* of the problem through intervention methods employed by the helping professions, while the retention of a problem in the political sphere (right side) depends on the perception of the problem as one affecting a *collectivity*. The individualisation method facilitates the conversion of a social problem into the problem of a person with certain characteristics that are perceived as the 'cause' of the problem. Maintaining a collectivity perspective also maintains the view of a problem as an issue for political and/or administrative action.

The Problem of a Multicultural Society

Cultural diversity is an issue that acquires the characteristics of a social problem in many contemporary societies. The problem may be manifest

Figure 6.1: Theory of Residualist Conversion of Social Problems

SOCIAL (POLITICAL) PROBLEM
results from

| Pursuit of dominant values and interests **(power structure)** | GENERATES → | 'Social problem' social condition **(negative residue)** |

PERCEIVED THREAT TO SOCIAL STABILITY

| Problem is addressed within the political and administrative spheres **Perceived threat continues** | Research into the 'new condition' and its effects — Research directed at the 'problem population' | Problem is addressed within the political and administrative spheres **Perceived threat is reduced** |

| The phenomenon is translated into a technical problem (e.g. through research activities) | | Political recognition of the needs of a particular group due to public pressure |

| Technical problem is translated into a personal problem of a particular segment of the community | Group in question has power — Group in question has no power | Group successfully resists acceptance of the problem as a personal problem |

| Problem is individualised and explained in normative terms as a 'pathology' | | Problem remains as collective issue/need, explained in terms of rights – call for a collective response |

| Problem is located in the person/group, confirmed through the endorsement of the helping professions | Decreased pressure on problem person/group — Increased pressure on problem person/group | Social problem is translated into 'new' social condition/reality within the political sphere |

| Continuation of social problem is perceived to be located in the failure of particular individuals and groups to respond to help provided at the political, administrative and technical levels | | Political response to initial conflict of interests results in redefinition of problem, demonstrating that existing social structure has responded responsibly to 'new' social condition |

Through confirmation of pathology → Existing social structure is legitimised ← Through political change simply in the differences in certain attitudes, habits and pursuits, such as attitudes towards the family, relationships between men and women or parents and children, or language and religion. Differences of this nature lead to communication difficulties and tensions in some public institutions such as schools, health services and legal institutions. However, the problem may also explode into violence and open warfare. This happens when one ethnic or cultural group either remains or seeks to become dominant in political and social institutions through its command over material resources in business, industry, employment access, and/or the society's culture. Such pursuit of dominance by one ethnic or cultural group – that is, with the aim of retaining or gaining advantage over other groups – leads to defensive efforts by disadvantaged groups trying to maintain or gain access to society's resources. A social problem thus becomes manifest in the conflict between the dominant and the dominated, with each side perceiving a threat from the other in regard to its own relative position in society.

Social conflicts of this nature are multidimensional, in that they may include political, economic, religious or language issues, and in a broader perspective may be perceived as cultural. Andrew Milner defines culture as 'that range of institutions, artefacts and practices which make up our symbolic universe. The term thus embraces art and religion, science and sport, education and leisure and so on' (1991:3). Milner sees differences between the aspects of society that are 'cultural' and those that are 'political' or 'economic'. However, he acknowledges that the dominant force in the world today, which influences all aspects of social life, is capitalism. For this reason, he argues, it is not only the case that 'capitalism represents the dominant form of economic organisation in the modern world' but that capitalism is also 'the dominant form of organisation of modern cultural production' (1991:4).

There are many societies today in which ethnic and cultural diversity is a characteristic of their populations. According to studies conducted in 1993 and 1994, 'the world's 184 independent states contain over 600 living language groups, and 5000 ethnic groups. In very few countries can all citizens be said to share the same language, or belong to the same ethnonational group'. This diversity is not a new phenomenon, as 'most organised political communities throughout recorded history have been multiethnic' (Kymlicka 1995:1–2). However, in the 20th century the intensity of ethnic and cultural diversity probably increased in many countries through mass migration movements early in the century and again after World War II. Population movements across national borders still occur in various parts of the globe, especially when ethnic differences within a country explode into open warfare, as was the case in Yugoslavia and Rwanda.

Australia is one country with a population of high ethnic diversity, which consists of over 100 ethnic groups with corresponding languages and cultures, as well as an indigenous population of Aborigines and Torres Strait Islanders that itself is multicultural. The data from the 1991 census show that one-quarter of the Australian population was born in another country (see Table 6.1), but the data also show that 43 per cent of people were either born in another country or had one or both parents born in another country. As to people's ancestry, the Anglo-Celtic background was the largest group, with the 'pure' Anglo-Celtic population being estimated at 48 per cent of the total population (National Multicultural Advisory Council 1995:1). There are significant differences in the ethnic compositions of large Australian cities and those of country regions, the latter being far less multi-ethnic. There are also differences in ethnic make-up among the cities. For example, Table 6.1 shows that, in 1991, Sydney had a smaller proportion of its population born in Australia than had Adelaide, and both cities had a larger proportion of overseas-born people than the country as a whole. In 1991, 43 per cent of Australia's total population had either been born in another country or had at least one parent born in another country, 54 per cent of Sydney's population was in this category, and in Adelaide this figure was 49 per cent. The different ethnic composition in these two cities reflects differences in the ethnic composition of successive immigration intakes and in the settlement pattern of migrants over the past decades.

Is the multicultural nature of Australia a social problem? If so, how does the problem manifest itself and what are its effects? One manifestation is Australia's 'symbolic universe', as defined by Milner (1991). This consists of a core of social institutions and corresponding beliefs, values and interests inherited from colonial times, which have remained largely monocultural both in structure and in personnel. The National Multicultural Advisory Council comments that 'the overseas-born, particularly those from non-English speaking background countries, are not well represented in our corridors of government'. This is equally so in parliamentary representation, in statutory bodies, and in the public service generally – especially its higher echelons such as the Senior Executive Service. These institutions 'remain unrepresentative of Australia's diverse population' (1995:13–18). As a result, the structure of political and cultural power is largely monocultural, being surrounded by a periphery of multicultural population whose ethnic and cultural diversity is extensive (Jamrozik et al. 1995).

Another related feature of this problem is the class nature of Australian society, which means that cultural differences are class-mediated – that is, from the perspective of the dominant symbolic universe of

Table 6.1: Australian Population by Country/Region of Birth 1991, Australia, Sydney, Adelaide

(N = '000)

Country/region of birth	Australia N	%	Sydney N	%	Adelaide N	%
Total population	*16851.0*	*100.0*	*3539.3*	*100.0*	*1023.7*	*100.0*
Australia	12725.2	75.5	2366.9	66.9	739.5	72.2
Oceania	351.2	2.1	95.9	2.7	9.9	1.0
Europe and ex-USSR	2300.8	13.7	517.7	14.6	212.8	20.8
Middle East and North Africa	172.4	1.0	99.8	2.8	4.5	0.4
South East/ North East Asia	687.9	4.1	275.2	7.8	30.5	3.0
Northern America	75.2	0.4	20.0	0.5	3.7	0.4
South and Central America	72.0	0.4	35.4	1.0	2.3	0.2
Africa, except North Africa	94.4	0.6	27.4	0.8	3.3	0.3
Others and not stated	372.1	2.2	101.1	2.9	17.2	1.7
Born overseas	4125.8	24.5	1172.4	33.1	284.2	27.8
Born in Australia	12725.2	75.5	2366.9	66.9	739.5	72.2
– Both parents Australian born	9424.0	55.9	1593.5	45.0	509.7	49.8
– Both parents born overseas	1362.0	8.1	376.0	10.6	102.8	10.0
– One parent born overseas	1777.3	10.5	366.7	10.4	117.6	11.5
– No adequate data	161.9	1.0	30.8	0.9	9.4	0.9

Sources: ABS (1991) *Census of Population and Housing: Basic Community Profile,* Catalogue No. 2722.0 (1,4)

monocultural institutions, cultural differences are perceived and acted upon in class terms, being seen to be inferior in relation to the dominant culture. In such a perspective, 'ethnicity signifies subculture. Ethnicity is a term that contains within it the presumption of structured class inequality' (Aronowitz 1992:53). In such a perspective, too, a social problem experienced by a particular ethnic group – a problem created by government policy – is perceived to be related to the cultural characteristics of that group.

The situation is further exacerbated by the explicit or implicit perception of cultural differences in terms of race, with racial differences being presented as a threat. The nature of this threat is related to cultural differences, but the nature of those differences is not always made explicit, enabling the person airing such views to claim that he or she is 'not a racist'. For example, this threat is conveyed in the view that 'today's immigrants look as well as sound different from most Australians … The issue is the sort of Australia we want our children to inherit. Will it be a relatively cohesive society … or will it be a pastiche of cultures with only a geographic home in common? … race matters – but only because it usually signifies different values, attitudes and beliefs. The real problem is not race, but culture' (Abbott 1990).

The dominant culture in Australia is the British (or more specifically English) culture, which was imported into the country through the colonial invasion in 1788. The colonisation of Australia meant importing the population from another part of the globe, taking possession of the land by force, establishing new laws, supplanting the population which was already there and destroying it physically, economically and culturally to the point of extinction (see Australian Broadcasting Corporation 1997). The imported English culture and its political, social, economic, religious and cultural institutions became dominant, and Australian society was formally portrayed as homogeneous in all these aspects, although the social reality was always somewhat different. Since the late 1940s, however, two social movements have occurred, which came to be perceived as a threat to the advantage enjoyed by the adherents of the dominant culture. One movement of great significance has been the mass immigration of a diversity of ethnic and cultural groups whose members have endeavoured to retain their cultural identity, and who have begun increasingly to question the advantages and disadvantages created by the continuous dominance of the English culture in the core social institutions. The other movement has been the awakening of the cultural identity of the suppressed indigenous population and their demands for some restitution of the property that was expropriated from them by force.

Both these movements are seen by the dominant power structure as a considerable threat entailing dangers to the established laws and government, to the nation's economy, to its cultural institutions and to its social cohesion. Actions taken to maintain the dominant structure include arguing for the necessity of maintaining a common language, reducing or discontinuing the immigration program, changing laws relating to land tenure so as to preclude further claims by the indigenous population, and curtailing the power of the Australian High Court and changing the manner of appointing its judges. Efforts have also been made to maintain the perspective on history that presents the English colonisation of Australia in an exclusively favourable light and that rejects some less attractive interpretations as a 'black-armband' view of history. In effect, attempts are made to ignore or erase the country's history prior to colonisation, to reject the more recent history of mass immigration, and to ignore the evolution and growth of demands from the indigenous population. In other words, these efforts aim to present contemporary Australian society in the image of the late 1940s, as if the pre-colonisation period and the period since the early 1950s did not exist – a form of 'historical cleansing'.

Ethnic and cultural diversity has a demonstrated potential for creating a socially cohesive society under the umbrella of multiculturalism. The perceived threat in such diversity is in effect the threat of social change, through which the established dominance and corresponding advantages of one ethnic group might be reduced in relation to those of other ethnic and cultural groups. The advocated methods of intervention in the perceived social problem of multiculturalism include the conversion of its intrinsically political nature into technical problems. These methods include careful selection of immigrants based on the criteria of Australia's economic needs and immigrants' command of English. They also include questions and assertions on the effects of immigration on unemployment, on the balance of payments, on population growth and its pressure on urban resources in large cities, and on the cost of social services. The demands of indigenous people are portrayed as a form of 'new racism' and as unwarranted demands for advantages not available to the rest of the population. The most interesting arguments are those against the restoration of (some) land to indigenous peoples, any such restoration being portrayed as a 'loss to the country and its economy', thus creating a symbolic image of the land being towed away to some unknown place. The common factor underpinning actions aimed at legitimation of the resistance to change is the projection of fear of its unknown effects.

The concept of multiculturalism remains a contested area. In 1989, the Australian government accepted the concept of multiculturalism as an official policy in the framework of its National Agenda for a Multicultural Australia. The Agenda was built on three principles: the right to cultural identity of all Australians; social justice (i.e. the right to equality of treatment); and economic efficiency, utilising effectively the talents and skills of all Australians. These principles were to be implemented by all government departments (and by implication, by institutions in the private sector) through an Access and Equity program (Office of Multicultural Affairs 1989). However, the implementation of the Access and Equity policy has not proceeded as expected. The 1996 report on the program's progress stated that:

The annual reports on access and equity have shown that many agencies, in the main, have still been thinking of access and equity as an 'add on', not as an integral part of their policy, planning, budgeting, evaluation and reporting. Much of the input to the annual reports has also been focused on activities undertaken in accordance with the access and equity implementation requirements rather than on strategies for achieving effective outcomes for clients from diverse cultural and linguistic backgrounds.

(Department of Immigration and Multicultural Affairs 1996:5)

Contention surrounding the concept of multiculturalism revolves around the meaning of the concept and around the extent to which the core social institutions – government, the legal system, the education system, the professions – are to become multicultural. In the rhetoric of the National Agenda, the concept of multiculturalism conveyed mainly the principle of 'equality of opportunity' and freedom of cultural expression; it did not include any structural change to the political or legal system. The 1996 evaluations of the Access and Equity program indicate that the principles of the program have been interpreted and implemented rather narrowly, being perceived mainly as a 'policy of assisting migrants with their problems'. A similar perspective is evident in most writings by members of the helping professions, in which the operative term appears to be 'sensitisation to migrants' needs'. The 'problem' is therefore perceived as a 'migrants' problem' to which 'real Australians' should extend sympathy and understanding. Certainly, there are degrees of acceptance of multiculturalism among the professions, but the acceptance usually means acceptance that a dominant monoculture exists, not building a multicultural structure of social institutions. In the language of politicians, of many political and social commentators, and of professions, multiculturalism means a divide between the somewhat mythical 'real Australians' and the 'ethnics'. The concept of multiculturalism has not entered the consciousness of the dominant core of the Australian power structure; it has remained peripheral to it.

Child Abuse and Neglect

Child abuse emerged as a social problem in the 1960s, with the identification and recorded frequency of 'non-accidental' injury to children. It was referred to in terms of pathology as the 'battered child syndrome' (Kempe *et al.* 1961). Since then, it has grown in professional and public perceptions to become one of the outstanding social problems in industrialised societies. The perception of the nature of the problem has also changed; it is now no longer the 'battered child syndrome', but 'child abuse and neglect', and the problem now includes physical, emotional and, increasingly, sexual abuse as well as neglect.

In Australia, the concern with child abuse began to be expressed in the 1970s among professionals engaged in the field of child welfare. As was the case in the United States, the 'discovery' of child abuse in Australia began with concern over reports of 'non-accidental' physical injury to children, and corresponding pressures were exerted on state governments to enact legislation that would authorise intervention where such injury was reported. At first, the recorded incidence of the maltreatment of children was presented with caution, aiming to impress on the public that the increase in recorded cases did not necessarily mean an increase in the frequency of maltreatment, but rather an increase in attention given by the helping professions to the well-being of children. For example, in South Australia, an Advisory Committee Inquiring into Non-accidental Physical Injury to Children was established in the early 1970s, but statistics of reported cases of injury first appeared in the Annual Report of the Department for Community Welfare (DCW) for the year 1977–78. In that report, 149 cases of reported injury to children were recorded for the year and referred for assessment by specially formed multidisciplinary panels in various regions of the state. The duties of these panels included assessing reported cases of injury, but panels were also expected to conduct seminars and meetings with the aim of educating the public about the problem of children's maltreatment and the development of preventive intervention methods. The report stated that the recorded number of cases of injury to children 'does not necessarily imply an increase in the underlying rate of child abuse; it may simply reflect the fact that increasingly the resources and expertise of the panels become known' (DCW 1978:23).

Over the following years, investigation of reported or suspected cases of child abuse became the top priority of the South Australian Department's activities. The reported frequency of child abuse has grown at an almost exponential rate since then, and now, in the mid-1990s, the increase in reporting still continues. In the 1995–96 annual report for the Department (now renamed the Department for Family and Community Services), 7206 cases of child abuse were reported, investigations were finalised in 6229 cases, and, of these, 2454 cases (39.4%) of abuse were confirmed. Of the confirmed cases of abuse, 36 per cent were classified as physical abuse, 30 per cent as neglect, 21 per cent as sexual abuse, eight per cent as emotional abuse, and three per cent as 'threatened or likely' abuse (DFACS 1996:33). For the whole of Australia, it is not possible to ascertain the extent of reported frequency of child abuse in the 1970s, as the first national data were for the year 1990–91. In that year, 46 769 cases of child abuse were reported, and of these, 20 868 (44.6%) cases of abuse were confirmed (Angus and Wilkinson 1993). By 1993–94, 74 436 cases of abuse were reported nation-wide, with 64 787 of these finalised, and of these, 28 711 cases (44.3%) confirmed (Angus and Woodward 1995).

How can one explain the startling phenomenon of such a rapid increase in the reported maltreatment of children? A simple answer that is usually proffered is the growing awareness in the community of the abusive treatment that children receive in some families and of the need to provide adequate protection for children under the power of state law. To this end, child protection legislation has been enacted in all states of Australia, providing legal and administrative frameworks for investigating and assessing reported suspected cases of abuse, and for criminal proceedings where such proceedings are considered to be appropriate. Legislation also provides for mandatory reporting of suspected child abuse for a wide range of occupations in human services: medical practitioners, nurses, teachers, social and welfare workers, child care workers and many others, even university lecturers. The public at large has also been invited to report suspected cases of child abuse, with assurances of confidentiality and legal protection for those reporting it. Child protection has become the major activity in state child welfare agencies as well as in many non-government welfare agencies. Police departments have established special branches to investigate and prosecute reported cases of child abuse, especially sexual abuse. Furthermore, the criteria of child abuse have been widened, first by the inclusion of sexual abuse and emotional abuse, and then by the addition of various categories of children 'at risk', the latter enabling continuing surveillance of families in which child abuse has not occurred but where circumstances have been identified that suggest abuse may occur (DFACS 1994:27). Indeed, concern with child protection has evoked the most comprehensive, reactive – as well as the most pro-active – response in recent decades from government services and associated agencies to a perceived social problem.

A number of observations on the available data suggest possible explanations for this remarkable growth in reported cases of child abuse. First, published Australian data indicate clearly that the system of mandatory reporting, direct involvement of various agencies, and invitations to the public to report suspected child abuse have been effective measures in producing reports from a wide range of sources. In 1993–94 (the latest report available at the time of writing), close to a quarter (24.2%) of all reported cases came from relatives, friends and neighbours, but in 58.4 per cent of these reports no abuse or neglect was found, compared to the mean of 47.6 per cent of negative findings in reports from *all* sources (see Table 6.2). Second, the major perceived source of child abuse is the child's family and, in the cases where the maltreater had been identified, the parent or adoptive parent was the person most often identified (74.9%) as the person believed to be responsible for maltreating the child (see Table 6.3). This in itself might not be seen as an explanation for the increase in reported cases of child abuse. However, available research data (see the following discussion of Hood 1997) indicate that the majority of parents whose children are reported to have been abused or neglected are in receipt of income support from the government, either as single parents or as unemployed. These parents are therefore already under surveillance by social security and state welfare authorities, and their child caring practices are under constant scrutiny.

The suggested explanation of the factors that might account for the increase in the reported incidence of child abuse may be regarded as somewhat speculative. Unfortunately, a significant deficiency in the published data on child abuse is the absence of socio-economic or ethnic identification of the child's family – a rather typical deficiency in social welfare reports. The exception is that data are shown separately for children of the Aboriginal and Torres Strait Islands population, and the reason for this exception is not provided in the reports. Aside from this exception, the child and his or her family are presented in a social

Table 6.2: Sources of Reports of Child Abuse and Neglect, Australia, 1993–94

Source of report	(1) Reported cases		(2) Substantiated cases		(3) No abuse or neglect found		(4)* Child at risk or no action possible	
	N	%	N	% of (1)	N	% of (1)	N	% of (1)
All reported calls	*64787*	*100.0*	*28711*	*44.3*	*30871*	*47.6*	*5205*	*8.0*
Child, parents, siblings	10791	16.7	4927	45.7	5010	46.4	854	7.9
Relatives, friends, neighbours	15704	24.2	4980	31.7	9169	58.4	1555	9.9
Health personnel	6140	9.5	3225	52.5	2434	39.6	481	7.8
Social work, schools, day care	12828	19.8	6858	53.5	5231	40.8	739	5.8
Police	7956	12.3	4529	56.9	2932	36.9	495	6.2
Other government and non-government services	3962	6.1	1864	47.0	1698	42.9	400	10.1
Anonymous others and not stated	7406	11.4	2328	31.4	4397	59.4	681	9.2

Note: Child at risk: 2605; no action possible: 2600
Source: G. Angus and S. Woodward (1995), *Child Abuse and Neglect, Australia 1993–94*, Canberra

Table 6.3: Relationship of the Person Believed to be Responsible for the Maltreatment, Substantiated Cases, Australia, 1990–91 and 1993–94

Relationship to the child	1990–91		1993–94		Change 1990–91/ 1993–94	
	N	%	N	%	N	%
All reported cases	*46769*	*100.0*	*64787*	*100.0*	*18018*	*38.5*
Substantiated cases	20868	44.6	28711	44.3	7843	37.6
– Maltreater identified	13487	64.6	15627	54.4	2140	15.9
– Maltreater not identified	7381	35.4	13084	45.6	5703	77.3
Maltreater identified	*13487*	*100.0*	*15627*	*100.0*	*2140*	*15.9*
Natural/adoptive parent	9407	69.7	11711	74.9	2304	24.5
Step parent	960	7.1	964	6.2	4	0.4
De facto parent	610	4.5	820	5.2	210	34.4
Foster parent/guardian	110	0.8	118	0.8	8	7.3
Sibling	293	2.3	305	1.9	12	4.1
Other relatives	788	5.8	776	5.0	–12	–1.5
Friend/neighbour	1319	9.8	933	6.0	–386	–29.3

Sources: G. Angus and S. Wilkinson (1993), *Child Abuse and Neglect, Australia 1990–91*, Canberra, and G. Angus and S. Woodward (1995), *Child Abuse and Neglect, Australia 1993–94*, Canberra

and cultural vacuum. However, whenever any socio-economic data on child abuse are published, it is clear that the reports come mainly from low socio-economic geographical areas. For example, in the analysis of data on child abuse in Sydney, Young *et al.* (1989) found the frequency of reported abuse to be from six to eleven times greater in the lowest socio-economic areas than in the highest socio-economic areas. Similarly, Mary Hood's recent study of child abuse in Adelaide found that in the sample of 334 substantiated cases of child abuse, 82 per cent of children came from suburban areas of Adelaide that were in the lowest socio-economic clusters. A further indication of families' socio-economic status was the high percentage of single-parent families (40%), of whom 53 per cent lived on a government pension, with the source of income of a further 41 per cent unknown (Hood 1997:167–72).

The growth in the frequency of reported child abuse and the prevailing methods of intervention pose some important and interesting questions concerning the social construction of social problems, the causative links of social problems to the dominant values and interests in society, and the processes through which social problems become converted into 'private problems' of individuals, families, or certain identified social groupings or classes whose characteristics are perceived in a social pathology perspective. The concern with child abuse is widespread throughout industrialised countries, and interpretations of child abuse and intervention methods display some common features. (There is certainly also widespread concern about the conditions for children in Third World countries, but the perception of the problems in those countries is different. This issue is briefly discussed in later chapters.)

The outstanding feature in the concerns with child abuse and methods of intervention is the focus on child abuse in the family context, with little attention given to external factors such as social or economic conditions. This has certainly governed the conceptualisation of the problem in Australia (see Table 6.3) and appears to be a common perspective in a number of countries. As observed by Katherine Beckett in her study of the American scene:

> In the early period immediately following the 'discovery' of child abuse, discussions of the issue emphasised the deviant nature of extremely violent individuals who beat their children and ignored the social conditions that might be related to this social problem ... The passage of the federal Child Abuse Prevention and Treatment Act in 1974 depended upon this 'classless' construction of the child abuse problem.   *(1996:58–9)*

Focus on the family as the locus of child abuse appears to be prevalent in Western countries. In England, 'the conceptualisation of child abuse as a problem that required treatment of the abusive parent had become conventional wisdom' (Whitmore 1984:247). Similarly, in Sweden, concern over child abuse, especially the sexual abuse of children, focuses on the family (Hallberg and Rigne 1994). In his observation on the problem of child abuse in industrialised countries, especially English-speaking countries, David Archard comments that:

> the agencies presently involved in the prevention of abuse have a stake in its continuing to be represented as something affecting individual families and which must be dealt with at that level. Indeed what can be called the 'disease' or 'medical' model of child abuse predominates. Child abuse is seen as pathological individual behaviour with a specific aetiology ... and remediable through appropriate forms of treatment. Such a model obscures both the abuse which is social and the social causes of even individual abuse.
> *(1993:157)*

Of major significance in the concern with child abuse is the removal of the problem from the social sphere as a public (political) issue and the placing of it firmly in the family context, the child's parents and home environment being perceived as the setting that requires public surveillance and control. The family that is kept under surveillance is in most cases a malfunctioning family in the low socio-economic stratum, in the lower social class. In this perspective, society can claim its concern for children by demonstrating its efforts to control the deviant behaviour of parents, and by this demonstration of concern distracts attention from the structural factors that provide the societal context of child abuse. As Archard points out, 'more children suffer significantly reduced life opportunities as a result of their socio-economic circumstances than are injured as a result of parental behaviour ... there is a significant correlation between poverty and what is standardly understood as child abuse and neglect' (1993:156).

The methods of intervention in child abuse and neglect now focus mainly on reporting and investigation. In his analysis of the problem in England, David Howe notes that in earlier intervention methods the emphasis was on 'rehabilitation of poorly functioning families', but since then the emphasis has shifted to 'protecting children from dangerous parents'. This shift has led to intensification of surveillance activities and more elaborate methods of collecting data. Social workers have become investigators and 'gatherers of evidence' – a bureaucratic solution to child abuse (1992:491–508).

In Australia, from the time child abuse was 'discovered' in the late 1970s and the response by state authorities was intensified in the 1980s, concern with the social aspects of child and family welfare has effectively disappeared from social work practice. The 'discovery' represented a radical regressive shift from concerns with inequality in the allocation of and access to society's resources, to earlier-discarded and theoretically discredited concerns with individual and family pathology (which were always found among the working classes and the poor). Investigation of child abuse has become the top priority of state welfare agencies. A wide range of occupations has been drawn into mandatory reporting, and the public at large has been encouraged, through publicity, to report suspected cases. Special courses have been offered to train people in how to identify and report suspected child abuse. Investigation of child abuse has also become a significant part of police work, and social workers now work in tandem with the police: reported cases are automatically recorded on police computers. Police are especially interested in sexual abuse, and in cases where police see the possibility of instituting criminal proceedings against the suspected or identified maltreater, this aspect takes precedence over any counselling of the child, for fear of 'contaminating' possible court evidence.

The focus on the family as the place where child protection is seen to be most needed presents something of a paradox. Undoubtedly, some

children suffer neglect and abuse in the family setting. This may be per-
petrated by their parents or by other people. As Mary Hood observes,
due to the loss of stability in the family, children now also come into
contact with a wider range of people than before, and at an earlier age
(1997:179–86). However, recent public inquiries have uncovered widespread cases of child abuse in schools and welfare institutions (including
religious institutions), as well as organised paedophile activities on the
international scene. Yet in the data on child abuse and neglect collected
by state welfare agencies, none of these forms of child abuse appears to
be reported. This rather selective attention, focusing on families who
are mainly working-class and poor families and ignoring other institutions where child abuse also occurs, suggests that concern with child
protection is closely related to the surveillance and social control of
'pathological' families. (The problem of 'pathological' families is discussed in Chapter 8.)

Child Care

Child care services constitute one of the two parts of the child and
family welfare system. The other part is normally referred to as 'child
welfare' and includes a range of services, the main one now being child
protection, which is concerned with child abuse and neglect. The two
parts are commonly perceived as two discrete services, each performing
a distinctly different function in society. In Australia, the distinction is
formalised in the organisation of services: 'child welfare' is regarded as
the responsibility of state governments, and 'child care' is primarily the
responsibility of the federal government, although state governments
also play a part in the provision of the latter service, mainly in the
supervision of standards and advisory services. The distinction between
the two parts is maintained even within states' services, each part being
the responsibility of a different government department.

Yet both parts of the system perform essentially the same function,
and are provided to meet the same need: they are provided as an
acknowledgement that 'in contemporary society the family unit is not
able to fulfil all the functions expected from it without support from the
community or society' (Jamrozik and Sweeney 1996:115). Despite the
essential functional unity, each service (as well as the need for each
service) is perceived differently. 'Child welfare' carries an imputation of
pathology in the characteristics or behaviour of the service recipient;
'child care' is regarded as being the state's obligation to assist the family
in fulfilling the child caring function. Consequently, the former is
provided using overt or covert coercion and carrying inherent stigma
for the recipient, and receipt of the latter is voluntary and is even

claimed as a right. This distinction is also reflected in the social class of the recipients: those under the attention of child welfare are mostly working-class and poor families, while the users of child care services are mainly the relatively affluent middle classes.

An in-depth exploration of the reasons and antecedents of the differences between the two parts of a service that perform essentially the same function is beyond the scope of this book. This area has a long and complex history, which has been extensively examined elsewhere (e.g. Jamrozik and Sweeney 1996, Sweeney and Jamrozik 1982, 1984, Sweeney 1989, Brennan 1994). In the context of the issues examined in this book, a brief venture into the history of child care is nevertheless necessary to consider the important question, which is: why is the perception of child care so different from the perception of child welfare, especially child protection services, and what are the differences in the outcomes of these differing perceptions?

The antecedents of child care services in Australia are found in the provision of creches and nurseries for working mothers early this century. These were established to take care of the 'street urchins' who played in the streets while their mothers worked, usually as domestic servants for well-to-do families. Later, the creches began to apply the philosophy of Froebel's Kindergartens and gave rise to the growth of the Kindergarten movement in Sydney and then in other cities. However, as the value of kindergartens for child development became recognised, kindergartens began to attract the interest of middle-class families, and children of working-class mothers were gradually excluded from them, finding alternatives in a variety of informal, often 'backyard' child-minding arrangements (Sweeney and Jamrozik 1982). Formal kindergartens focused on the emotional, intellectual and social development of the child and were not regarded as child-minding institutions. Also, children would spend only a limited time each day in the kindergarten (usually a maximum of three hours), which did not make this a very useful service for a working parent.

The federal government first entered the field of child care during World War II, by giving financial assistance to organisations that provided child care services for mothers employed in war-related industries. Later, the government also provided child care in migrant hostels, so that parents could take up employment. The acceptance of the federal government's responsibility (always expressed as 'assistance') on a more or less permanent basis came in the 1960s, under increasing pressure from industry, which sought female labour, and also from women's organisations, especially lobbying, middle-class women who began to enter employment in increasing numbers. The formal acknowledgement of responsibility for assistance came through the *Child Care Act* of

1972. Since then – through much public debate, intensive lobbying, arguments between competing perspectives over pre-school education versus child care, and frequent changes in policies – child care has become an established and widely used service, with a current budget outlay of over $1 billion ($1140.1 million in the 1996–97 financial year: Commonwealth Government 1996–97 *Budget Statements, Paper No. 1*:3–115).

Child care is an example of a social problem that remained in the political sphere as a problem for political solution, its conversion into a personal problem having been successfully resisted by well-organised political actions that were sustained for a long period and that showed renewed vigour whenever the party in power showed signs of wanting to lessen the government's responsibility or shift it onto the family. However, the political action has been only partially successful, as entitlement to child care has been established on certain criteria that by and large have made the service available to the more affluent middle classes almost as a right, while the availability of the service for poor families is usually conditional upon a claim of special need. The provision of and access to child care services have in effect become a class issue. As shown in Table 6.4, the frequency of child care use, especially formal child care, correlates positively with the level of family income: the higher the income, the greater the frequency of service use.

Table 6.4:   Children Under 12 Years: Use of Child Care and Family Income, Australia, June 1993

(N = '000)

Weekly family income $	(1) Children in families		(2) Formal care		(3) Formal and informal care	
	N	%	N	% of (1)	N	% of (1)
All families	*3085.9*	*100.0*	*596.2*	*19.3*	*1504.9*	*48.8*
Less than 160	68.9	2.2	7.6	11.0	25.9	37.6
160– 479	1010.3	32.7	171.2	16.9	427.0	42.3
480– 799	943.2	30.6	171.8	18.2	442.9	47.0
800–1039	419.1	13.6	89.2	21.3	238.8	57.0
1040–1279	242.1	7.8	61.3	25.3	142.0	58.7
1280 and over	263.3	8.5	75.1	28.5	178.9	67.9
Not stated	139.0	4.5	20.1	14.5	49.6	35.7

Source: ABS (1994) *Child Care Australia, June 1993*, Catalogue No. 4402.0

The history of child care, and the assumptions on which child care services are provided, demonstrates the significance of the subjective nature of problem construction within a perspective through which the problem remains in the political sphere and is not converted into a personal problem of a 'pathological' nature. The basic criterion for the acceptance of responsibility for the provision of child care by the government is 'the inability of the family to discharge its child caring function without assistance from society'. Stripped of its moralistic connotations, the provision of child protection services is based on the same criteria. In the case of child care, 'inability' in the majority of cases is the inability to reconcile the parent's task of child caring with the parent's pursuit of employment or other public functions; in the case of child protection, 'inability' is perceived to be some form of pathology in the parent's functioning. Corresponding with these very different perceptions of the same problem, access to the service in the former case adds advantage to an already advantageous position for the recipients; while investigation and surveillance in the latter case contributes additional stress to the recipient's already stressful situation. Access to the former service is voluntary and is exercised as a right; receipt of the latter service is enforced by law.

In the schematic presentation of the theory of residualist conversion of social problems (see Figure 6.1), the process of retaining the problem of child care in the political sphere has clearly followed the path illustrated on the right-hand side of the diagram. The political actions of powerful middle-class interests have successfully prevented the problem from being converted into the personal problem of families. In these actions, the problem is maintained as a problem of a collectivity, not as a problem of individual families. However, for a number of related reasons – such as changes in the occupational structure of the labour market, which have provided new employment opportunities for tertiary-educated middle-class professionals with priority of access given to parents in employment, and also the voting power of such professionals, which neither of the two major parties could ignore – the successful political solution has benefited mainly the middle classes.

Organised, State-sponsored Gambling

Gambling has been a social activity and a social problem since ancient times, and has been perceived as either a universal human attraction and active pursuit, or as a weakness or addiction. It is known and practised in some form in most contemporary societies. In some countries, it has become a legal business activity authorised by governments, or a government-sponsored activity promoted as entertainment while at the same time raising state revenue. Gambling has also been regarded as a social problem, or in some religious beliefs as a sinful vice. Whichever way it is perceived, engaged in or acted upon, gambling has been and continues to be a succinctly human social activity.

In Australia, gambling has traditionally been regarded as one of the defining characteristics of the population, and as part of Australian folklore. At the same time, it has been a strictly regulated activity, allowable only under rigidly defined conditions and confined to certain events and places such as horse racing venues. Unauthorised gambling has been prosecuted as a serious misdemeanor and the participants in such activity have usually been fined. It seems that in the past, laws regulating and controlling gambling acted like a religious commandment, reminding people of the sinful nature of their affliction and predilection.

Now, all this has changed dramatically. Governments in all Australian states have authorised organised gambling in widely diverse forms: casinos, and poker machines in clubs and hotels, in addition to state-sponsored lotteries introduced earlier. States compete with one another through a variety of means, aiming to attract local people and internal and external tourists to spend time in casinos. Every hotel and club now has rows of poker machines; there are also Keno, state lotteries, and the long-established gambling attached to horse racing, with its individual bookmakers and state-controlled but increasingly privatised TAB (Totalizator Agency Board) agencies. At last count, there were 13 casinos in Australia, with a total of 1136 gambling tables of all kinds (cards, roulette, etc.) and 9125 gambling machines. The number of visitors per year was estimated at 36 million, and the mean loss per visitor ranged from $29 to $70. The total state tax revenue from casinos in the year 1995–96 has been estimated at $367 million (Forbes 1997). The new Crown casino complex, which opened in Melbourne in May 1997, is reported to have cost around $2 billion and is claimed to be the largest casino in the Southern hemisphere. In addition, most hotels and clubs in Australia now have poker machines, with the number of machines in the country probably exceeding 100 000.

Organised gambling has become an important source of state revenue, accounting for 12–14 per cent of tax revenue collected by the states. State-sponsored gambling was introduced in the face of strong protests from churches and welfare organisations. As a compromise, the states agreed to allocate a small proportion of their gambling taxes to church and other welfare agencies in order that these organisations could provide services for people experiencing difficulties through gambling. Funded by the small share of state revenue from gambling, these agencies have developed new specialties in professional counselling, which they offer to people faced with difficulties directly related to gambling. Names such as Gamblers Anonymous and Break Even have entered the local vocabulary, as have anecdotes of broken marriages, ruined businesses, and homes repossessed due to defaults on mortgage repayments. There is also 'gambling addiction', regarded as a form of mental illness and treated as such by clinical psychologists and social workers using special forms of therapy.

It is clear that the problems experienced by people through gambling are their personal problems, causatively linked to the state's pursuit of a particular goal and within a particular value system, rationally organised and promoted as an activity that contributes to the economic well-being of society. These people's personal problems are therefore residualist conversions of a state-created and state-induced social problem. Political decisions to pursue that goal were taken with the knowledge that the activity would produce a negative residue of personal problems. The removal of the problem from the political sphere has been carried out by the conversion of the state-created social problem into an individual-ised personal problem of people who become addicted to a state-sponsored and state-promoted activity. The conversion has thus created new forms of personal pathologies, which are treated by professionals who are employed by agencies and remunerated by a proportion of the revenue extracted from the activities that lead to those personal pathologies. The circle of activities is thus completely closed, or perhaps squared.

The relationship between this government-sponsored and govern-ment-promoted activity (for the purpose of collecting tax revenue), and the agencies that are financed by a part of the resulting revenue to provide therapeutic assistance to the activity's victims raises some interesting questions about the management of the 'residue' of this activity. The organisations that previously campaigned against this government activity have now effectively become integral participants in it. What are such remedial agencies expected to do? Are they expected to discourage people from gambling? Are they expected to engage in public campaigns against gambling? What would happen if they did so? Would they still receive government money? None of these actions is likely. Instead, the intervention methods used by the agencies to assist 'problem gamblers' seek to relate gamblers' problems to and explain them by other causes, such as loneliness, marital difficulties, depression or other pathological personality characteristics.

The management of the social problem created by state-promoted gambling is an excellent example of the conversion process through which a social problem created by a deliberate political action is so thoroughly reconstructed that the problems of the people directly affected are explained and ostensibly 'treated' as personal pathologies derived from events completely removed from the public sphere. It is a conversion process that takes place in all social problems created by the pursuit of certain values and interests that are dominant in the social structure, although the process is not always as visible as it is in this problem area. The effectiveness of this conversion process is clearly illustrated in two of the four examples of social problems presented in this chapter: child abuse and state-sponsored gambling. On the other hand, the child care example demonstrates a social problem in which the conversion into personal pathologies is successfully prevented by the maintenance of a perspective on the problem as the problem of a collectivity. And the example of multiculturalism is an illustration of a public issue that is perceived as a threat by the dominant monocultural power structure of Australian society. The nature and meaning of the threat are contested by a diversity of opinions and interpretations, and the outcome of the contestation remains uncertain.

CHAPTER 7

Inequality – The Underlying Universal Issue in Social Problems

An underlying factor in most social problems is social inequality. Inequality has many dimensions and is present in most societal arrangements and relationships (interpersonal, inter-institutional or personal-institutional). In the perspective advanced in this book, we consider inequality to be the fundamental and universal issue pervading most societal arrangements and pursuits, as well as the corresponding factor in the emergence and continuity of social problems. This chapter illustrates this assertion by analysing societal arrangements and processes through which the pursuit of dominant, desirable goals takes place. Examples used are from the areas of income distribution, education, the labour market, and allocation of resources on a spatial scale in the cities. (As a further illustration of these arrangements and processes, social problems in two institutionalised areas – the family and the social order – are examined in greater depth in Chapters 8 and 9.)

Our concern with inequality as an underlying factor in social problems is based on recognition of the ubiquitous presence of some forms of inequality in all known societies. It is therefore an important subject for sociological studies. Indeed, social inequality has been one of sociology's main concerns, and the issue of inequality is present in some form in any sociological enquiry. Indeed, as Bryan Turner asserts, seeking to understand the nature of social inequality has been sociologists' concern 'since the origins of sociology itself', and this concern is so important that it can be defined as 'the core of sociology' (1986:30). Sol Encel supports this view by saying that 'The task of the social sciences, and especially of sociology, begins with the exploration of the social division, cleavage and conflict arising from the tension between natural equality and established social inequality' (1970:6). Our concern in this book is more specific, but nevertheless the issue of the relationship between inequality and social problems is an indication that social problems in any society can be adequately understood only in the context of the dominant values underpinning that society's structure.

Inequality in History

Inequality is deeply embedded in Western civilisation and views on it have differed widely. On the one hand, there have been thinkers who believed that although inequality was prevalent in society, it was not 'natural' but socially contrived, and society should strive for equality. The Idealists, such as Jean Jacques Rousseau and Karl Marx, saw equality as highly desirable. They asserted that inequality was socially created and that the main reason for this was the concept of private property. Rousseau argued in his *Du contrat social* that the first person who drew a circle on the ground and claimed 'this is mine' should have been called a liar, and it would have been better for humanity if he had been killed there and then because 'people belong to the earth and earth belongs to nobody'. Marx believed that a good society – a society of equals – would arrive only when private property had been abolished.

On the other hand, the Realists, such as Thomas Hobbes and Herbert Spencer, believed that inequality was natural in humanity because people were by nature selfish, self-seeking, and prepared to trample over others for selfish gains. Hobbes argued in *The Leviathan* that people knew this and so voluntarily controlled their selfish impulses and surrendered their individual liberty by appointing an absolute ruler who then provided them with safety, security and protection from one another. Without such power, he argued, social life would be impossible, and life itself would be 'nasty, brutish and short'. In a somewhat different perspective, Spencer believed that inequality in society was natural, as it was everywhere in nature. He believed human beings differed in their natural endowments, and consequently the quality of their contribution to the common good also differed: while the strong members maintained society's strength, the weak members became a burden. Spencer believed that supporting the weak members of society weakened the society's whole physical, intellectual and moral fibre, and that the quality of social life therefore depended on the 'survival of the fittest'.

Inequality may be seen to be natural in all living things, but this does not necessarily mean that a different endowment of certain attributes bestows any particular advantage or disadvantage. On the contrary, in nature, inequality in size, strength or any other attribute may be complementary. Nevertheless, in many instances inequality does entail advantage or disadvantage, and some people argue convincingly along these lines and apply the argument to human society. Aristotle expressed such a belief, which centuries later was incorporated into Christian theology and philosophy by Thomas Aquinas. Later again, it was incorporated into the core of Calvinist reformation as a Divine Order. However, while Aristotle argued that inequality was a functional part of nature itself, with elements of inequality being complementary, Aquinas aimed to reconcile what he saw as natural law with divine law, and Calvin argued that inequality was pre-ordained by the supreme power.

In the Athenian city-state of the fourth century BC, equality was a desirable goal sought in the democratic system. The feature of this system was participation of all citizens in government and in law, which secured equal justice for all, irrespective of their station in society. However, this notion of equality did not extend to women and slaves, and Aristotle sought to establish the legitimacy of this by recourse to nature. In his *Politics*, he argued that:

> It is thus clear that there are by nature free men and slaves, and that servitude is agreeable and just for the latter ... Equally, the relation of the male to the female is by nature such that one is superior and the other inferior, one dominates and the other is dominated ... Indeed some things are so divided right from birth, some to rule, some to be ruled ... Again, as between male and female the former is by nature superior and ruler, the latter inferior and subject. And this must hold good of mankind in general ... It is clear then that by nature some are free, others slaves, and that for these it is both right and expedient that they should serve as slaves.   *(1962:32–3)*

The 13th century theologian and philosopher Thomas Aquinas incorporated Aristotle's argument on natural inequality into the Christian doctrine. Using Aristotle's argument, Aquinas aimed to reconcile the egalitarian philosophy of Christ with the inequality accepted and practised at that time by the Church. Aquinas identified four types of law in descending order of importance, each deriving its authority from the preceding one: divine law, natural law, canon law and civil law. This order became part of the Western value system, with its structure of power legitimating inequality of power and wealth, the divine right of kings, and inequality between men and women. Based on this legitimacy, and supported by empirical evidence, social inequality became accepted as 'natural'. Inequality became God-ordained and was inculcated in people's minds; to argue against it was heresy. For example, the doctrine of the divine right of kings was upheld until 1776; it was only abolished by the American Declaration of Independence, which asserted the 'self-evident' truth that 'all men are created equal'.

However, Aristotle's argument about natural inequality has survived the test of time. It has been used in a variety of situations by a variety of people, with some incredible outcomes, for example the legitimation of the slave trade by Western colonial powers, the suppression of indigenous populations in the colonies, and even mass genocides. Viewing this issue in a historical perspective, it is interesting to note that to this day, there are people who believe that social inequality is natural; also, whole systems of belief have been built, within which this 'naturalness' is continuously demonstrated. For the powerful, the legitimacy of the belief in the naturalness of inequality has to be sustained and constantly reinforced lest the powerless see through the lie and threaten the powerful. The notion of social equality is thus a threat and potentially a social problem.

The problematic nature of the equality versus inequality issue began in Ancient Greece (Athens particularly), where equality was at times presented as a desirable societal goal, but where this ideal always constituted a threat to those in power, be their power political, religious or economic. People in power would therefore attempt to develop arguments through which they could uphold equality as an ideal, but at the same time maintain the inequality that gave them advantage, privilege, power and control over others.

Inequality in Contemporary Industrialised Societies

Contemporary Western industrialised societies are by definition class societies, their class structure being the fundamental feature of capitalist 'free' market economies. The distribution of societal resources in these societies, driven by the power of market forces, is characterised by inequality (which is the structural basis of class societies). Class inequality is reflected in a variety of societal arrangements and in access to resources, which broadly follow class divisions but that also include certain differences and inequalities within classes themselves, such as inequalities related to gender, age, social status, ethnicity or religion. Inequality between classes and inequality within classes are not discrete phenomena, and both may be observed in a society at the same time. However, inequality between classes may be regarded as a 'higher order' inequality, since a person who occupies a lower position *within* a class may still experience the advantages or disadvantages of that class's position in the class structure. For example, the wife of a judge may experience an inferior position within the household, but in society she still enjoys (via her husband) the prestige and other advantages of her class position. Similarly, a 'junior accountant' is still a member of his profession, although his position in the firm and his salary might be relatively low. And a medical practitioner in the first year of practice is, and is seen as, a 'doctor'.

If the characteristic feature of the contemporary industrialised 'postmodern' society is its high degree of diversity, then it may be expected that an accompanying feature will be diverse forms of inequality. Some of these will be perceived to be cutting across social class lines, but this may often be a misleading impression. The class structure, being the dominant feature of contemporary capitalist societies, overrides other structures of inequality, acting like a cauldron in which the various contents fight for their place but do not spill out of the cauldron itself.

Social division along class lines is so fixed and accepted in the perspectives on social problems that the response to certain common needs is differentiated by the use of different social constructs, which result in different services and consequently different outcomes for recipients. A typical example is the well-known division between 'child care' and 'child welfare' discussed in Chapter 6.

Social division along class lines does not mean that inequality in the class structure is one-dimensional. On the contrary, social inequality within classes and between classes is a multidimensional phenomenon. It may be inequality in the distribution of income; inequality in access to societal resources such as employment, education and health services; or inequality of participation in political or cultural activities. Inequality in any of these aspects may arise unintentionally, but it may also be institutionalised in a society's power structure. It may arise out of traditional prejudices or fears, or it may be based on certain social theories. Extreme forms of inequality may take the form of exclusion from society, or various forms of oppression – political, religious, economic, cultural or physical. Examples of such forms of inequality are easily found in various parts of the world today. The multidimensional nature of social inequality poses a number of questions, such as: which dimensions are significant and in what way? Do certain dimensions tend to occur in the same social group, social stratum or class? What is the effect of any such trends? Is the effect simply additive, cumulative, or compound? Indeed, the multidimensional nature of social inequality suggests a multidimensional or cumulative effect of inequality, or even a compound effect. Moreover, inequality in one sphere of social life leads to inequality in other spheres, because social institutions and institutional arrangements such as industry, financial enterprise, the education system and the legal system are interdependent – that is, an unemployed person cannot obtain credit from a bank, and a person with a low level of education finds it difficult to obtain a good job.

Measurements of Inequality

The multidimensional nature of inequality calls for a range of measurements of inequality. Typically, the most frequent measurements are those generated in studies of income distribution. This is an important indicator of inequality, as income is the most important factor in access to other resources, and is therefore a determinant factor in the standard of living. However, measurement of inequality by the distribution of income alone is not a sufficient measure, as it does not provide adequate information about the dominant societal forces that produce inequality of income. Furthermore, the quality of life concept, notwithstanding its susceptibility to subjective and imprecise interpretations, is a much broader concept and a more appropriate measure of social inequality than the concept of standard of living, which is measured almost exclusively by the economic variables of income and consumption of goods and services. Focusing on income tends to distract attention from the societal context in which the distribution of income is generated. It also distracts attention from other resources, access to which is essential to social functioning. As Gough Whitlam stated, when commenting on contemporary society:

> increasingly, a citizen's real standard of living ... [is] determined not so much by his income but the availability and accessibility of the services which the community alone can provide and ensure. The quality of life depends less and less on the things which individuals obtain for themselves and can purchase for themselves from their personal incomes and depends more and more on the things which the community provides for all its members from the combined resources of the community.   *(1985:3)*

The value of individual income may be increased or decreased by the relative availability of and conditions of access to goods and services in the community, such as health services, education, public transport, and recreation and culture. If, for example, these goods are provided free or at publicly subsidised low cost, then the value of individual incomes effectively rises, but if a 'user pays' principle is applied to them, the value of individual incomes falls.

Income, Employment and Education

Notwithstanding the limitations of measuring inequality by income distribution, income is an important indicator of inequality and therefore cannot be ignored, especially as since the mid-1970s the distribution of income has become increasingly unequal. This has certainly been the trend in Australia. For example, as shown in Table 7.1, from

1973–74 to 1994–95, the share of the total incomes of couples with dependent children decreased in the lowest 20 per cent of the population and increased in the top 20 per cent, the ratio between the two extremes increasing over this time from 3.7 to 6.4.

Income inequality is present in all kinds of income units (see Table 7.2). The data in Table 7.2 come from the most recent national income distribution survey, held in 1994–95. It needs to be noted in these data that differences in the degree of inequality are due not only to differences in people's earned income from employment or private sources, but also to the extent of people's reliance on public sources for income support. As shown in Table 7.2, income from wages or salaries as the main source of income varied from 32.8 per cent in one-parent families to 76.0 per cent for couples with dependent children. The reliance on income from government pensions and allowances as the main source of income was exactly opposite, at 61.3 per cent and 11.6 per cent respectively. It also needs to be kept in mind that aggregate data in Table 7.2 are based on the means in each quintile and do not show the extremes. For example, the Australian Bureau of Statistics 1994–95 survey identified 168 000 income units with income exceeding $2000 per week, and a survey conducted by the *Independent Monthly* in June 1996 identified 45 people in Australia with annual incomes over $1 million, the highest being $3.765 million ($19 231–$72 404 per week) (O'Neill 1996).

Table 7.1: Distribution of Income: Couples with Dependent Children, Australia, 1973–74 to 1994–95

Population quintiles	1973–74	1981–82	1985–86	1989–90	1994–95
			% total income		
Lowest	9.7	8.1	7.3	7.4	6.3
Second	14.4	14.2	13.3	13.1	12.8
Third	17.7	18.2	17.9	17.9	17.5
Fourth	22.3	23.1	23.2	23.5	23.1
Highest	35.9	36.5	38.4	38.1	40.3
Total	*100.0*	*100.0*	*100.0*	*100.0*	*100.0*
Ratio highest/lowest quintile	3.70	4.51	5.26	5.15	6.40
Gini coefficient	0.26	0.28	0.31	0.31	0.33

Source: Income distribution surveys from selected years, ABS Catalogue No. 6523.0

Table 7.2: Income Distribution Australia 1994–95: Couples, One-parent Families and Individuals

Population quintiles	All income units	Couples With dependent children	Couples Without dependent children	One-parent families	One-person units
		% gross weekly income			
Lowest	3.3	6.3	5.1	8.5	3.7
Second	8.9	12.8	9.6	13.5	9.6
Third	15.2	17.5	16.0	17.8	15.1
Fourth	24.0	23.1	25.4	23.2	25.2
Highest	48.6	40.3	44.0	37.0	46.4
Gini coefficient	0.45	0.33	0.39	0.28	0.43
Gini coefficient in 1989–90	0.42	0.31	0.34	0.30	0.38
		Mean gross weekly income ($)			
All income units	*579*	*950*	*729*	*388*	*356*
Lowest	96	299	186	168	67
Second	261	611	349	259	169
Third	439	829	581	338	269
Fourth	695	1091	927	436	447
Highest	1407	1921	1604	722	827
Ratio highest/lowest quintile	14.66	6.42	8.62	4.30	12.34
Ration in 1989–90	9.72	5.20	7.05	4.24	6.89
Main source of income (%)					
Wages or salary	56.2	76.0	51.6	32.8	52.0
Business/other private	12.5	11.7	19.9	5.0	10.6
Government pensions /allowances	28.8	11.6	29.3	61.3	33.2
Units with nil or negative income	2.5	0.7	1.2	0.9	4.2

Source: ABS (1996) *Income Distribution Australia 1994–95*, Catalogue No. 6523.0

Despite a high proportion of the population relying on public pro-vision for their main source of income (28.8%, compared to 10.8% in 1966 – Department of Social Security 1975), the majority of people's main source of income derives from employment in the labour market. Employment is a source of income but also of income inequality. The inequality of income derived from employment is determined by a number of factors: occupation, type of industry, hours worked, pay rates and a variety of fringe benefits. Fringe benefits are most frequently enjoyed by people in the higher echelons of the occupational structure and organisational hierarchy, being included in what is known as an 'income package' (Raskall 1994). Looking at the labour market as a whole, the outstanding feature of the differences in access to employment and conditions of work is post-secondary school education. Compared with people who have no post-secondary qualifications, those with post-secondary qualifications have higher participation rates, higher frequency of full-time employment and also record a substantially lower rate of unemployment (see Table 7.3).

Education, especially post-secondary education at degree level, is now the most important prerequisite for access to employment, particularly employment that is qualitatively better and more secure. Access to higher education is also one of the most unequally distributed resources in Australian society, the main factor of inequality in this area being the division between private and public education systems (see Jamrozik 1991). One indicator of inequality is the difference in the outcomes of secondary schooling and continuation of education at a higher level. As shown in Table 7.4, of all people 15–24 years of age who left school in 1995, 57.1 per cent continued their education in 1996. However, while only one-half of the school leavers from public schools continued their

Table 7.3:   Labour Force Status and Educational Attainment, May 1996, Australia: People 15–64 Years

(N = '000)

Labour force status	All labour force		Educational attainment			
			With post-secondary qualifications		Without post-secondary qualifications	
	N	%	N	%	N	%
All people 15–64 years*	*11406.9*	*100.0*	*5090.8*	*100.0*	*6316.2*	*100.0*
In labour force	8725.5	76.5	4326.5	85.0	4399.0	69.6
Employed	8017.5	91.9	4095.9	94.7	3921.6	89.1
– Full-time	6164.7	76.9	3344.3	81.6	2820.4	71.9
– Part-time	1852.8	23.1	751.6	18.4	1101.2	28.1
Unemployed	708.0	8.1	230.6	5.3	477.4	10.9

Note: * Excludes 635,200 people still at school

Source: ABS (1996) *Transition from Education to Work*, May 1996, Australia, Catalogue No. 6227.0

Table 7.4: Transition from School to Higher Education or Work 1995–96, Australia: People 15–24 Years

(N = '000)

Location	(1) All schools		(2) Public schools			(3) Private schools		
	N	%	N	%	% of (1)	N	%	% of (1)
Attended school in 1995	*269.1*	*100.0*	*188.2*	*100.0*	*69.9*	*81.0*	*100.0*	*30.1*
Attending in May 1996	153.6	57.1	93.2	49.5	60.7	60.4	74.2	39.3
– Bachelor degree or higher	69.8	25.9	33.2	17.6	47.6	36.5	45.1	52.3
– Diplomas	27.2	10.1	18.3	9.7	67.3	8.9	11.0	32.7
– Vocational and others	56.6	21.0	41.6	22.1	73.5	15.0	18.5	26.5
Not attending	115.6	43.0	95.0	50.5	82.2	20.6	25.4	17.8
Those not attending:								
In labour force	107.4	92.9	89.0	93.7	82.9	18.4	89.3	17.1
– Employed	74.4	69.6	60.0	67.4	80.3	14.7	79.9	19.7
– Unemployed	32.7	30.4	29.0	32.6	88.7	3.7	20.1	11.3

Source: ABS (1996) *Transition from Education to Work,* May 1996, Australia, Catalogue No. 6227.0

formal education, three-quarters of private-school leavers did so. The differences were even greater in enrolments for degrees: 17.6 per cent for the former group, and 45.1 per cent for the latter. Among those who did not continue their education, a higher percentage of public-school leavers went into the labour force (93.7% as against 89.3%), but their unemployment rate was almost three times higher than the rate of those from private schools (32.6% as against 11.3%).

Multidimensional Measurements of Inequality

It is now generally accepted among sociologists that no single dimension can be a sufficient measure of the multidimensional nature of inequality. Researchers also recognise that inequality cannot be adequately measured by static variables alone, as such approaches do not explain the dynamic aspects of inequality, in that they do not identify the societal mechanisms through which inequality is produced and maintained. Therefore, methods had to be developed to include dynamic as well as static indicators of inequality. The concern with finding an adequate method for measuring inequality arose especially in the 1960s, at the time of the 'rediscovery' of poverty in Western affluent societies. Studies such as J. K. Galbraith's *The Affluent Society* (1958) brought to public attention aspects of inequality that were manifest in the disparity between the 'private affluence' of the wealthy and well-to-do middle classes, and the 'public squalor' experienced by the poor in the deteriorating inner suburbs of large cities. Concern with poverty then spawned numerous and varied research approaches. Researchers with an interest in economics concentrated their efforts on income and in due course devised a 'poverty line' that was meant to indicate the level of living standard below which people would be regarded as living in poverty. However, researchers with socio-logical orientations attempted to develop wider conceptual frameworks, arguing that poverty was a complex phenomenon with both objective and subjective aspects, and furthermore was a dynamic phenomenon, meaning it was important to measure not only what income people had but also what lifestyle they were able to lead. One such study, which attracted much attention and argument, was Peter Townsend's study of poverty in Britain (1979). It included value judgements on what con-stituted quality of life as an important aspect of daily living and was therefore seen to be strongly value-laden. In Australia, R. F. Henderson and colleagues' study of poverty in Melbourne (1970) became a model for subsequent volumes of research. The study was conducted mainly by economists and was rather narrow in scope because of its primary focus on income, but it provided grounds for the establishment of the Commission of Inquiry into Poverty (1975), and did consider other aspects of poverty such as access to services and housing. However, income was the only dimension measured with precision. The study introduced the concept of a minimum income that would be required to obtain the basic necessities for people's survival, and referred to this minimum as the 'poverty line'. This concept has since been used to estimate the extent of poverty in Australia.

Multidimensional approaches in studies of inequality that have attracted much attention among social policy researchers have come from Sweden. The Swedish approaches arose from the recognition that one-dimensional studies were inadequate to measure living standard. As Robert Erikson comments: 'By the 1950s it had already become clear that, in spite of its widespread use, per capita GNP is an insufficient measure of the well-being of citizens' (1993). Researchers at the Swedish Institute of Social Research came to the conclusion that inequality should be measured using a number of different components that together made up the 'level' of living. Nationwide surveys based on these assumptions were conducted in

Figure 7.1: Components and Typical Indicators in the Swedish Level of Living Surveys

Components	Indicators
1 Health and access to health care	Ability to walk 100 metres, various symptoms of illness, contact with doctors and nurses
2 Employment and working	Unemployment experiences, physical demands of conditions of work, possibilities of leaving place of work during working hours
3 Economic resources	Income and wealth, property, ability to cover unforeseen expenses of up to $1000 within a week
4 Education and skills	Years of education, level of education reached
5 Family and social integration	Marital status, contacts with friends and relatives
6 Housing	Number of people per room, amenities
7 Security of life and property	Exposure to violence and thefts
8 Recreation and culture	Leisure-time pursuits, vacation trips
9 Political resources	Voting in elections, membership of unions and political parties, ability to file complaints

Source: R. Erikson (1993:68), 'Descriptions of inequality: the Swedish approach to welfare research', in M. Nussbaum and O. Sen (eds) *The Quality of Life*, Oxford

1968, 1974 and 1981. In those surveys, nine different components were used, as shown in Figure 7.1.

As a validation of this approach, Erikson argues that:

> To judge the level of living of an individual or a group, we have to know their resources and conditions in several respects, which are not transferable between each other. To have knowledge about, for example, economic conditions is just not enough; we also have to know about health, knowledge and skills, social relations, conditions of work, etc., in order to determine the level of living. There is no common yardstick through which the different dimensions could be compared or put on a par.   *(1993:73)*

The research approach was based on 'resources' rather than 'needs'. The researchers had to decide what were the most important resources available to people and for what purpose these could be used. The reasoning of Swedish researchers then was that 'the individual's resources, the arenas in which they are to be used, and his most essential living conditions, make up his level of living' (1993:74).

Erikson acknowledges the limitations of the approach – namely, the difficulty in composing a single indicator of inequality and the necessity of calculating each indicator separately. Also, due to the number of indicators, the complete description of the level of living becomes quite large. However, the approach has produced interesting findings, especially certain consistent patterns and correlations of variables. For example, 'a tendency was identified for problems with health, few social contacts, and a lack of leisure activities to go together', and this tendency was especially common among older people. Among other aspects of inequality, economic problems and housing problems were found to go together, especially within the working class, both in the old and the young. A low level of political activity was strongly related to a low educational level, and appeared most common among women (1993:75–6).

The Swedish approach to studies of inequality illustrates the relationship between social research and political systems. Studies of inequality are politically sensitive because any identification of inequality is also an indicator of the system of resource allocation – that is, the social policy and its underlying ideology. Erikson points out that this is why, in liberal political systems the emphasis is on studying poverty, while in social democracies the emphasis is on studying inequality. He says that 'inequality rather than poverty has been the important concept in Swedish welfare research. This follows partly from the emphasis on non-monetary aspects of welfare, given that poverty refers to economic resources. But it is also partly the consequence of an interest in variation over the whole range of conditions and not only over the poverty line'. In the political framework of social democracy's basic tenets, 'state activities are not merely a supplementary mechanism, but on a par with the market. In an institutional welfare state a redistributive model of social policy should cover the basic needs of all citizens' (1993:80).

The Swedish approach to the study of inequality aims to identify objective aspects of living that can be measured and compared. The approach also aims to identify some of the processes that lead to measurable outcomes, thus providing some explanations of any identifiable differences in outcomes. Other studies of inequality have been conducted within the conceptual framework of well-being. Such studies have raised controversies, as the concept of well-being is of necessity a normative concept that has to include subjective perceptions and judgements, including such aspects of living as choices, preferences and tastes. Other aspects that may be included are opportunity structures, which again may be perceived objectively as well as subjectively.

Studies of well-being may be conducted with a number of approaches, each focusing on measurement of a different aspect of everyday living.

However, the common feature of such studies is first the assumption that the concept of well-being has to be considered in relation to the availability of resources in society, and people's access to them; and, second, the assumption that measuring well-being by income alone is not an adequate approach to such studies. For example, Stein Ringen has proposed a typology of six approaches, considered to be relevant to well-being, which range from a narrow to a wide perspective: income, expenditure, resources, consumption, capabilities, and way of life (1995:3–15). These choices of approach should enable a comparison of well-being in more than one perspective, identifying people's choices and preferences, but without the researcher's normative evaluation. In Australia, Peter Travers and Sue Richardson (1993) conducted a study of well-being, measuring material well-being in three dimensions: distribution of wealth, of all forms of income, and specifically of earned income. Additionally, they considered social participation and inter-generational inequality. They also differentiated between material well-being and human well-being, the latter being evaluated on subjective perceptions.

Social inequality can also be studied with an emphasis on population characteristics and the spatial distribution of certain societal resources as the main variables. Each population census provides a range of data that may be analysed on a large or small scale. One such study was conducted in Sydney using data from the 1986 census, analysed at the level of local government areas (LGAs). The aim of the study was to identify differences in the distribution of human resources in families, focusing especially on families with dependent children. The researchers used 18 variables arranged in six groups: income, education, employment, family composition, overseas-born people, and employment in community services (Jamrozik and Boland 1993). In the analysis of data, the aim was to develop a 'vulnerability index' that would provide an indication of the cumulative effect of the 18 variables. A correlation of +.845 was obtained for all 18 variables, and the most significant indicators shown in the correlations were education (+.899), professional employment (+.906) and income (+.797).

An example of spatial inequalities in Australian cities is presented in Table 7.5. The data are from the 1991 census of population and give comparisons between the mean data for the total population of Australia and the highest and lowest socio-economic LGAs in two cities, Sydney and Adelaide. As shown, higher education (especially at degree level) indicates the greatest inequality, by a factor of 8.31 in Sydney (24.1/2.9) and by a factor of 12.47 in Adelaide (18.7/1.5). These differences are reflected in unemployment rates and in family income.

Table 7.5: Comparative Socio-economic Data: Selected Local Government Areas, Australia, 1991 Census of Population and Housing

Item	Australia	Sydney		Adelaide	
		Ku-ring-gai	Fairfield	Burnside	Elizabeth
Population 15 years + (000s)	*13085.65*	*79.24*	*131.59*	*31.49*	*21.96*
	%	%	%	%	%
Education					
Bachelor degree or higher	7.7	24.1	2.9	18.7	1.5
Other qualifications	19.7	20.5	15.5	19.3	14.4
Not qualified	61.1	45.1	68.4	50.9	73.8
Not stated	11.6	10.4	13.2	11.1	10.1
Labour force: men					
Participation rate	72.4	70.9	73.2	67.0	68.0
– Employed	87.6	94.5	78.8	91.9	74.3
– Unemployed	12.4	5.5	21.2	8.1	25.7
Labour force: women					
Participation rate	50.8	50.0	49.2	48.8	39.4
– Employed	89.4	95.2	76.9	93.8	78.3
– Unemployed	10.6	4.8	23.1	6.2	21.7
Income ($ p.a.):					
All families					
0–25000	27.0	10.0	25.4	19.3	45.4
25001–60000	39.2	25.8	38.6	34.6	33.9
60001 and over	13.8	43.7	10.2	30.0	3.7
Not stated, or partially stated	19.9	20.3	25.7	16.1	17.1
Parental income ($ p.a.):					
Families with offspring					
0–25000	32.9	12.5	37.7	20.7	55.4
25001–60000	41.8	27.8	33.3	35.2	30.0
60001 and over	10.9	47.6	5.0	33.5	1.7
Not stated, or partially stated	14.2	12.1	19.0	10.6	13.0

Source: ABS (1991) *Census of Population and Housing: Basic Community Profile,*
Catalogue No. 2722.0 (2,4)

The distribution of spatial inequality is not absolute – that is, the population within each LGA is not entirely homogeneous in its socio-economic characteristics. Inequality is therefore found *among* various areas as well as *within* each area. Also, manifestations of certain social problems may be found in most areas, although their frequency and/or intensity is likely to differ from one area to another. Nevertheless, studies of spatial distribution of population characteristics and the frequency of certain problems indicate that when a particular social problem is manifest in a given area, if it is a low socio-economic area then the family or individuals experiencing the problem's effects have personal socio-economic characteristics similar to those of the surrounding population, while in a high socio-economic area the personal socio-economic characteristics of any such family or individual are likely to be different from those of the surrounding population. A reverse situation is usually found in people's access to and use of certain services such as child care or higher education – that is, in low socio-economic areas, the users' personal characteristics are likely to be different from those of the surrounding population and similar in high socio-economic areas (Sweeney and Jamrozik 1984).

Structural and Institutionalised Inequality

Structural inequality in contemporary industrialised societies is part of their historical inheritance, incorporated and reinforced by the Industrial Revolution and capitalism. Ulrich Beck observes that:

> In examining the situation from a socio-historical perspective, we find that the structure of social inequality in the developed countries displays an amazing stability. Research on this clearly indicates ... the inequalities between the major social groups *have not changed* appreciably, except for some relatively minor shifts and reallocations, despite all the technological and economic transformations and in the face of the many efforts in the past two or three decades to introduce changes.   *(1992:91; emphasis in the original)*

Inequality in a class society is structural and institutionalised. It is embedded in the structure and operation of political and legal institutions – that is, in the social system itself. It is embedded also in the *Weltanschauung* of the population, so that perceptions on social issues are mediated through the class perspective. Inequality is pursued as a desirable goal and is particularly cherished and validated by those who benefit from it and who are aware that others are excluded from access to those benefits. Obtaining scarce goods, buying 'designer' clothes with the label prominently displayed, becoming a member of a club with limited membership, buying private health insurance when universal insurance is already available, being 'upgraded' to business class on an aeroplane – all such instances give the satisfaction of exclusivity.

In the allocation of resources by governments, inequality is legitimated by differential interpretations of essentially the same service and purpose. The use of different names constructs different social realities and conceals inequality. As Gusfield observes, 'aid to business in the form of tax cuts is simply called aid to general economy; aid to people at the poverty level is called "welfare" or "help" ... Subsidies to auto industry are not called "aid to dependent factories" ... Differing language frames mean differing assessments and evaluations' (1989:435). Thus, as noted in Chapter 6, child care services, heavily subsidised by public funds and used mainly by the affluent middle classes, are regarded as a legitimate entitlement of families, while intervention in the name of child welfare or child protection takes the form of surveillance and mandatory reporting of suspected cases, and is regarded as a necessary control because of parental 'pathology'. The class perspective is thus reflected in the dual role of the state: facilitative and enabling, and protective and controlling. This being the case, it may therefore be expected that inequality will be found at all three levels of social organisation – political, administrative, and operative.

The legitimation of inequality takes a number of forms. Because blunt public assertions that winners and losers are entitled to their 'just desserts' are socially and politically not quite acceptable, inequality is substantiated on other grounds. It is substantiated by the necessity for industry restructuring, by the need for greater efficiency and competitiveness, and by the 'unfortunate' necessity and corresponding outcome of 'downsizing', 'outsourcing', 'corporatising', 'privatising' – whatever kind of euphemism is in fashion for disposing of surplus labour force. Nevertheless, irrespective of the reasons advanced to justify inequality, its main form of legitimation is the belief in the rightfulness of differential distribution of qualities, attributes and abilities of individual human beings in different social classes. This belief is maintained by a variety of devices of variable scientific quality (such as intelligence tests), and is then translated into measures of classification, categorisation, and corresponding inclusion and exclusion. These are some of the methods used to legitimate inequality in policy decisions. The examples following in this chapter illustrate how the values of inequality are reflected in social research methods and in the intervention methods used by the helping professions.

Values in Inequality Research

In theory, the dimensions of social inequality may be perceived and examined as value-neutral phenomena, without ascribing to them any values or preferences, notions of goodness or badness, and desirability or undesirability. In practice, however, no study of social inequality is conducted from a value-neutral perspective because of our awareness, explicit or implicit, of the significance of inequality in the distribution of power and in advantage or disadvantage – in effect, the inequality in the 'command over resources through time'. Even in the measurement of inequality, certain conceptual and methodological approaches tend to legitimate or conceal social inequality, because they are formulated on assumptions that are rarely made explicit and can therefore be differentially interpreted.

Some concepts that guide measurements of inequality used by economists are clearly value-laden. One such concept is the distinction between 'absolute' and 'proportional' equality, which is translated into the methods of resource allocation referred to either as 'distribution' or as 'incidence'. 'Distribution', which is based on the concept of absolute equality, means that the value of an allocation to a particular section of the population is shown as the percentage of the total allocation (e.g. an education allowance of $1000 for each family with one child at school, and an allocation of $1600 for each family with two children at school). 'Incidence', on the other hand, means that the value of an allocation is expressed as the percentage of the value of the recipient's possession of the same goods before the allocation (e.g. an allowance of $1000 for the same purpose then means 10% of the recipient's income of $10 000 per year, but only 5% of a recipient's income of $20 000 per year). Measurement by the incidence method would indicate that a family with an income of $10 000 per year received an allocation twice that of a family on $20 000 per year. It follows that in using the incidence method, an allocation of, say, $100 000 to a person with a yearly income of $1 million, compared with an allocation of $10 000 to a person with an income of $50 000, would mean that the second person received twice as much as the first (20% of income for the latter as against 10% for the former). In the language of the incidence method, the allocations shown in the two examples would be called 'progressive', because the allocation would be called 'distribution downwards' – that is, from families or individuals on higher incomes to those on lower incomes. It needs to be noted that the incidence method is the method used in most economic research monographs analysing social policy (see Goodin and Le Grand 1987:6–10; Jamrozik 1991:288–92). This method, although technically 'correct' in the perspective of 'proportional equality', conceals the extent of inequality in society – for example, the greater the inequality of income distribution before the allocation, the more 'progressive' the distribution will be shown to be.

Another method of studying inequality is the study of poverty. Studies of poverty have been numerous and so we know much about the poor. Students in social work, sociology, psychology, economics and other related disciplines study poor people. Large-scale research is similar in its focus on the poor. By comparison, studies of wealth are extremely rare and tend to be anecdotal because data on wealth distribution are not collected. One of the aims of studying poverty is to determine how any people live 'below the poverty line'. The concept of the poverty line, mentioned earlier, was first adapted in Australia by R. F. Henderson in 1970 from a New York study, and became a concept guiding numerous Australian studies sponsored by the federal government. The aim of determining how many people live below the poverty line has been the subject of much debate, mainly over the issue of determining the validity of a concept that is clearly an arbitrary measure, formulated on a certain basis that might have had some rationality in 1970 but that is now rather irrelevant. The use of the concept of a poverty line, however, plays a significant social role: first, it seems to demonstrate that 'we care about the poor', and second, it removes the poor from the societal context. The 'line' plays the symbolic role of separating the poor from the rest of society. In Walter Korpi's view, the poverty line in effect 'splits the working class and tends to generate coalitions between the better-off workers and the middle class against the lower sections of the working class' (1983:193).

Studies of social issues and social problems are conducted in various social science disciplines, and the theoretical assumptions and value positions held by those disciplines lead to different areas of research interests and different methods of enquiry. For example, there are significant differences in these aspects between sociology and economics, especially 'neo-classical' economics. As Goran Therborn observes, the prevailing position in economics is to examine social issues from the perspective of the accepted theoretical and value positions of the capitalist system. Sociology, on the other hand, 'developed and became decisively established as an attempt to deal with the social, moral and cultural problems of the capitalist economic order' (1976:143). The two disciplines differ considerably in their assumptions about human nature and about society. *Homo economicus* is perceived to be 'a rational, self-interested, instrumental maximizer, with fixed preferences', while *Homo sociologicus* is a much more complex being whose actions are influenced by 'culturally given values', not solely by a 'pure (culture-bound) calculation of self-interest' (Hirsch *et al.* 1987). It can therefore be expected that studies of inequality carried out in these two disciplines are likely to come up with different findings, notwithstanding the theoretical and value orientations of particular researchers.

Inequality and the Helping Professions

In addition to the inequalities inherent in the social arrangements of a capitalist class society, there is an inherent inequality in the theories and methods of intervention employed by the helping professions. In the theories guiding these professionals' perceptions, social problems are perceived as the problems of individuals, and they are perceived and interpreted in class terms so that the same problem is differentially interpreted according to the social class of the person or class experiencing it. A second source of inequality is inherent in the professional methods of intervention. Increased sophistication of such methods, especially the ubiquitous counselling, means increased conceptualisation expressed linguistically, which increases the social-class barrier between the service provider and the service recipient. The underlying source of inequality, however, is in these professionals' focus on the individual or group taken out of the societal context. Individualisation of social problems unavoidably leads to seeking a solution in the perceived pathology of the person 'with the problem'. In commenting on certain approaches in social work practice, Lena Dominelli writes that:

> equal opportunities approaches to structural inequalities represent the individualisation of social issues and concerns. Procedures rooted in equal opportunities focus on extending access to services and positions; dealing with wrongs done to individuals and processing individual complaints. They *do not address* group deprivation and exclusion. Nor do they equalise power imbalances embedded within social relations.
>
> *(1996:157; emphasis in the original)*

Rosemary Crompton observes that 'Equality of opportunity is a powerful justification for inequality. If all have an equal opportunity to be unequal, then the unequal outcome must be regarded as justified and fair, as a reflection of "natural" inequalities of personal endowments, rather than of structural social processes' (1993:7).

Inequality as a Social Problem

Is inequality a social problem? It becomes one when it challenges the dominant values and interests and when it represents a potential threat to those values and interests. The threat is seen to be directed towards the issues of value and social morality. Extreme inequality means exclusion, one form of which is now demonstrated by the existence of the 'underclass' – which, in the opinions of some social analysts, presents a potential danger of alienation from society of an entrenched, transgenerational kind, with increasing violence within the alienated groups themselves as well as against other social groupings or classes. When inequality goes beyond a certain point, the people at each extreme lose contact with the mainstream of society: the underclass are at one end, and the powerful are at the other. The separation of the underclass from the mainstream of society tends to become entrenched by the length of separation, and by the degree of social distance from the mainstream. Social structure is then no longer stratified but polarised, with the underclass displaying certain features defined by L. J. D. Wacquant as 'advanced marginalisation' from society (1996). Outstanding among these features are: extremely transient attachment to the labour market, manifest in casual part-time employment; functional disconnection from macro-economic trends; living in poor and stigmatised suburbs; and internal social fragmentation, with little support from family, relatives or neighbours.

In our theory of residualist conversion, inequality is one of the dominant values in society, perhaps *the* dominant value. It is institutionalised in the political and legal systems, and above all, underpins the economic system; it is indeed the fundamental value of a class society. It is therefore the element universally present in all social problems. The greater the inequality, the greater the concentration and intensity of problems experienced by people at the lower levels of the class structure, and the greater the difficulty experienced by people at the top of the structure to understand the nature of the problem. The greater the inequality in a particular area of social arrangements, the greater will be the efforts of people advantaged by that inequality to explain the disadvantaged by imputing faults of character and personal pathologies. For example, in times of frequent 'downsizing' of the labour force (which can throw thousands of people out of employment), assertions that 'everyone who wants a job can get one' are not rare. Professionals in public relief agencies who earn salaries of $40 000 a year or more often make critical comments about the 'poor budgeting' of a single parent with an income of $10 000 a year.

Whether we examine the measures society adopts to deal with unemployment, poverty or child abuse – the phenomena referred to as 'social problems' that can be adequately explained by their causative links with the social structure in which they occur – we find that the dominant form of intervention focuses on the affected population, not on existing societal structural arrangements. Intervention methods may be based on the intention to help, they may be overtly coercive, or (as often happens) they may be helpful but carry an implicit (or sometimes explicit) threat of coercion and penalty. All such methods have a devaluative element in them; 'blaming the victim' takes various forms. The common element in such intervention methods is their legitimation of the rightfulness and morality of the dominant structure of power. The methods of establishing mechanisms through which its 'failures' can be helped and controlled accords the system its legitimacy, because the measures demonstrate that the system has the ability to 'take care and control' of what may be called its 'flawed or faulty parts'.

Such attitudes and values are likely to be particularly evident in societies that follow economic rationalist policies. This is because the essence of economic rationalism is the belief that human beings are driven by a basic instinct of self-interest, and the 'common good' (if it exists at all) is the cumulative outcome of individual pursuits. In its pure form, this is the basis of Adam Smith's theory of wealth creation and the essence of 'hard' liberalism. From this perspective, self-interest is a virtue, which establishes the logical and moral legitimacy of the belief and its corresponding argument that individual success is entitled to individual reward. Furthermore, the pursuit of self-interest is not only a personal virtue, but also a social virtue because the pursuit of self-interest by an aggregate of individuals, each acting independently of others, is believed to lead to common interest. The argument's logical and moral corollary is and must be that individual failure must also be seen as an individual's responsibility, and consequently deserves a corresponding negative 'reward' – namely punishment. In sum, the basic foundation of economic rationalism is the legitimation of inequality. The inequality is accepted as just, and furthermore is validated by what may be called the law of nature, in that it is also seen as being inherent in human nature. Social inequality, then, is seen to be as natural as nature itself, and the truth of this belief is regarded as self-evident. Correspondingly, as a successful person is praised and valued, an unsuccessful person is devalued and penalised.

CHAPTER 8

The Social Construction of Family Problems

The family has existed as a primary social institution since time im-
memorial and can be found in every part of the globe. As a primary
social institution, the family possesses distinct relationships with society,
the state and the market, and any concerns about the family are directly
concerned with these relationships. The family becomes a 'problem'
when it or the conditions within it present a threat to dominant values
and interests. This threat emerges when the family is no longer able to
fulfil the functions expected of it by the wider society. The pursuit of
certain interests by society and the failure of some families to participate
in the realisation of these interests result in the creation of a social
residue in the form of the 'problem family'.

This chapter provides an overview of the current socio-political response to the family, and examines the way in which both the family
per se and perceived problems within it have been interpreted and
addressed by society. A brief summary of recent changes in family
composition and organisation is provided to demonstrate the way in
which such changes have resulted in increasing concern over the ability
of families to continue their socially expected functions. The relationship between the family and the state is examined, with the family
identified as a primary site through which the state's interests in the
maintenance of social order and the facilitation of market forces are
achieved. The relationship between the family and the market is discussed with regard to effects of the consumer culture on the family,
particularly the increasing commodification of family functions. The
issue of inequality, discussed extensively in Chapter 7, is emphasised
with reference to family differences in the level of resources available to
families for the performance of their expected functions, and the
relevance of social class as a primary determinant of the way family

problems are perceived and interpreted. Finally, a summary is provided of the competing discourses on the family and the response of Australian governments to family issues, placing these in the relevant ideological and political contexts. Analyses of the pathologisation and/or politicisation of family problems complete this chapter.

The Family and Social Change

Families vary markedly in form and structure throughout the world. Their structures and functions have also changed considerably over time (Anderson 1980) and continue to change, especially in contemporary post industrial societies. Yet interpretations of these changes also differ. Within the relevant body of literature, there is certainly no consensus about the value of the family, the appropriate relationship between the family and other primary social institutions, or the future of the family. However, there are two points that are commonly agreed upon by family researchers. First is the social significance of the family within current political, social and economic arrangements, and second is the extent of change that has occurred within families in Western industrialised countries during the past century.

The higher incidence of divorce and marriage (including re-marriage), fewer births, legalised abortion, an increase in teenage pregnancies, the growing visibility of gay and lesbian relationships, and an increase in people living alone, single parents, cohabitation and new types of living arrangements, alongside continued maternal employment, all testify to change (Segal 1983:10). In addition, the development of reproductive, medical, entertainment and other forms of technology has made a significant impact on the contemporary family.

In Australia, two most noticeable changes in family structure that have occurred in recent years have been the increase in single-parent families and in people living alone. As shown in Table 8.1, in the 25 years between 1966 and 1991, single-parent families increased from 5.9 per cent of family units to 8.8 per cent, and from 10.4 per cent of families with dependent children to 16.6 per cent. Families with dependent children remained the main family unit, declining slightly over that period from 56.6 per cent to 53 per cent of all family units. In 1991, most people still lived in family settings, but the proportion of people living alone had increased since 1966 from 4.5 per cent to 6.7 per cent.

The family has certainly lost some of its stability. Most people still marry, but the marriage rate has declined and the divorce rate has increased; in 1991, there were two divorces for every five recorded marriages. Another change has been a decrease in birth rate: since

Table 8.1:   Familes, Australia, 1966 and 1991

(N = '000)

Family type	1966 N	%	1991 N	%	Change 1966–91 N	%
All families	*2772*	*100.0*	*4299*	*100.0*	*1527*	*55.1*
All families with						
dependent children	*1570*	*56.6*	*2278*	*53.0*	*708*	*45.1*
Couple families	1407	50.7	1900	44.2	493	35.0
One-parent families	163	5.9	378	8.8	215	131.9
All families without						
dependent children	*1202*	*43.4*	*2021*	*47.0*	*819*	*68.1*
Couple only	665	24.0	1319	30.7	654	98.3
Couple + other adults	341	12.3	447	10.4	106	31.1
Other (related adults)	196	5.9	255	5.9	59	30.1
Total population	*11550*	*100.0*	*16850*	*100.0*	*5300*	*45.9*
People living in families	11033	95.5	13744	81.6	2711	24.6
People living alone	517	4.5	1131	6.7	614	118.8
People in other households*	n/a	–	1975	11.7	–	–

Note: * Includes people in group households, visitors, people living in
non-private dwellings, people in non-classifiable households

Sources: ABS (1978) *Social Indicators No. 2,* Catalogue No. 4101.0
ABS (1991) *1991 Census of Population and Housing: Basic Community
Profile,* Catalogue No. 2722.0 (2,4)

1966, the fertility rate has decreased from 2.8 to 1.9 children for
each woman, meaning the birth rate is now below the population-
replacement rate.

Australian trends in the birth rate and in family formation and dissolution appear to follow patterns similar to those in the twelve
countries of the European Union, although the rates in Australia are
slightly higher. In 1988, marriage rates in those countries varied from
6.9 to 4.7 per 1000 people, divorce rates from 2.9 to 1.9 per 1000 people,
and fertility rates ranged from 2.18 to 1.43 (Lewis 1993:1–24).

Such changes have caused growing concern over their implications,
particularly over the extent to which various family types are able to
continue traditional family functions. Concerns about certain conditions directly express or infer a threat to dominant social or economic
values and interests – that is, to the power structure in society. In the
case of the family, there has been significant concern over the capacity
of contemporary families to continue traditional family functions in the

Table 8.2:   Marriage, Divorce, Births and Fertility, Australia 1966–91

Year	Marriages		Divorces		Births and fertility rates	
	N	R	N	R	N	R
1966	94000	8.3	9859	3.7	240300	2.8
1971	117637	9.1	12947	1.0	273642	2.9
1976	109973	7.8	63230	4.5	225565	2.1
1981	113905	7.6	41412	2.8	233535	1.9
1986	114913	7.2	39417	2.5	240699	1.9
1991	113869	6.6	45630	2.6	253861	1.9

Notes: R = ratio
Marriage and divorce rate = rate per 1000 population
Fertility rate = births per woman
Sources: ABS (1980, 1984) *Social Indicators No. 3 and 4*, Catalogue No. 4101.0
ABS (1994) *Focus on Families: Demographics and Family Formation*,
Catalogue No. 4420.0

light of the extensive structural and organisational changes mentioned
above. Consequently, the changes in family organisation and arrangements (often referred to as 'family decline') have at times been perceived as social problems, resulting in conflict between the values and
objectives of the 'free' market and the interests of those most in favour
of or affected by familial change. The crux of this conflict concerns the
extent to which the changing nature of families and family organisation
results in the non-performance of certain functions (i.e. care for
children, and biological, social and cultural reproduction) that are
necessary to the continuance of the existing society. In response to this
potential threat to current political, social and economic structures,
there has been growing concern over conditions occurring within the
family, which have been perceived to varying degrees as contributing to
family decline. Examples of such 'threatening' conditions have included
single parenthood, illegitimate births and homosexual relationships.

The Family and the State

The value of the family to the state is twofold. First, the family is seen as
an apparatus wherein social order can be maintained, transferred and
reproduced through family members. Second, the family provides a
venue through which market forces and expectations can be facilitated
and fulfilled. With regard to both these interests, the family is expected
and encouraged by the state to perform certain roles and functions.
When such roles and functions are performed poorly or not at all, the

state executes disciplinary and social control measures to address the problems of non-performance.

Historically, it has been the working-class family that has received the most attention in the form of regulation and social control measures by the state, a situation that continues in Western postindustrial societies today. Jacques Donzelot describes the way in which a mutual exchange occurred between the family and the state during the time of the *ancien régime* in 18th century France. Through being accountable for its members, the head of the family (usually the father) was required to 'guarantee the faithfulness to public order' of those members, for which in return the family, through its head, would receive the protection and recognition of the state (1979:49). The family head was compensated for his role by being granted a virtual discretionary power over his family members. In addition to making decisions regarding employment and marriage partners on behalf of family members, the family head could also punish those around him if they failed to fulfil their family obligations, and do this with the full support of the public authority. In this way, a clear relationship of exchange existed between the family and the state in maintaining social order, which was achieved through both the facilitation and monitoring by the state of the family's performance of its expected social roles.

A similar relationship still occurs today, whereby the family is actively promoted as an important social institution in maintaining social order, and as such is expected to perform certain roles and functions. However, the perceived increase in instances of social disorder such as rising youth homelessness, juvenile delinquency and child abuse has resulted in the view that the family is no longer able to perform its duties. When the family fails to maintain and reproduce social order – that is, when the individual pursuits of its members can no longer be controlled within the bounds of the family unit – its value to the state is diminished and this leads to a threat to the values and interests of the broader social structure. This threat of social disorder elicits responses from the state that seek to ensure the continuance and reassertion of social order in the wider society. State intervention is undertaken so as to recapitulate the value of social order and demonstrate to the rest of society the consequences of failure to fulfil this expectation. In this way, the 'problem family' is converted into a social residue and becomes a necessary and even beneficial venue through which the state is able to exercise its full authority, holding up the 'problem family' as an example and using it to provide a warning to the rest of the population. Departments of community and child welfare, as well as the juvenile justice system, provide clear examples of social control measures undertaken by the state in order to demonstrate the consequences for families who fail to perform their expected function in maintaining social order.

Another state interest in family life is in the family as an economic unit, a unit of production and consumption (especially the latter). In arguing against previous assertions regarding the natural origin of the family, Marcel Mauss and Claude Lévi-Strauss stated that the family did not possess an existence separate from organised society, but rather was a 'total social phenomenon' arising essentially from the requirements of a society of exchange (Frankfurt Institute for Social Research 1972:132). Whether its participation in the market economy be in the form of production through wage labour and the reproduction of this in the family, consumption through commodities purchased with family wages, or through the acquisition and internal transfer of capital and property, the family is considered by the state to be a crucial forum through which this participation can be facilitated and encouraged and whereby the general conditions of production can be ensured. As Zygmunt Bauman (1987:166) asserts, the market is the pivotal institution of contemporary Western society in which everything is commodified. In response, the state performs a mediating function between the market and the individual, through the family, whereby certain conditions and regulations are imposed on the market, for example in the determination of a minimum wage, to ensure the market's accessibility to the family. At the same time, the family is expected to encourage its members to participate fully in the market so as to maximise the benefits of the economic system. In this way, the family is expected to socially reproduce in its members the necessary skills and resources – educational, economic and employment-related – to make full use of the market. However, as in the case of social order, when this social and cultural reproduction does not occur in families, the state undertakes interventions intended to regulate those families who have failed to perform the functions expected of them, and also to highlight such failure and make it visible to the rest of society. In Australia, working-class families, poor families, immigrant families and Aboriginal families constitute the main clientele of the state's intervention agencies whose role is to manage at the administrative and operative levels those families who fail to fulfil the dominant social expectations. Consequently, state-sanctioned services for problem families serve a class-based clientele.

Yet the class basis of state intervention in families is not a recent phenomenon. Donzelot highlights this through a description of the influences that motivated the imposition of legal and statutory sanctions on the French family during the first part of the 19th century, saying that:

The time is passed when one could to a certain extent dispense with taking account of the lower classes and rely on the expedient of crushing them if need be when they were stirred up; now these classes think, reason, speak and act. It is undeniably much wiser and more prudent to think of taking legislative measures, some of which would be for the protection of morals and the prevention of a new wave of abandonments, while others would tend to make all these abandoned beings genuinely useful ...

(Fodéré 1825, cited by Donzelot 1979:61)

The centrality of class issues in understanding the relationship between the family and the state is also explained by the Frankfurt Institute for Social Research in their discussion of the effects of market mechanisms on the families of 19th century Europe:

That there was something not right in the society of free and just exchange showed itself first – and not accidentally – in the worker's family, whose children were pressed into the process of production as wage slaves during the period after the Industrial Revolution. Bourgeois society could only perpetuate itself by strengthening the compulsion of the principle of exchange by direct forms of dependency, and the family functioned as its agency ...

(1972:136)

As is revealed in any historical analysis of the management of poverty, the state's intervention in the lives of families, mainly working-class and poor families, has been fraught with moral imperatives and centred on the repression and control of 'problem families'. The form this social control takes in contemporary Western society is discussed later in this chapter in relation to the pathologisation of family problems.

The Family and the Market

In Western capitalist societies there is an increasing reliance on the market for the fulfilment of those functions previously performed within the family unit. Bauman's discussion of the consumer culture that has led to the current consumer society identifies the progressive loss of social skills among individuals as central to increasing market dependence. Due to their decreasing capacity and desire to enter and foster social relations, Bauman asserts, men and women are compelled to seek 'marketable goods, services and expert counsel' as a means of coping with the problems and challenges arising from their social relations (1987:164). Such dependence on market provision is particularly evident in the increasing transformation of traditional family functions into marketable commodities. These include goods and services aimed at facilitating and fostering interpersonal relationships; medical, psychiatric and legal services to address the interpersonal and practical aspects of relationships; and travel services to provide better surroundings for the solution of problems related to family or social relations, or to act as a means of escape from them. Bauman argues that, ultimately, the increasing reliance on market goods to address family problems results in the belief that for every problem there is a solution waiting at the shop. So, while participation in the processes of the market is expected of and actively encouraged through the family, it is increasingly expected that solutions to the problems and conflicts experienced within the family structure will also be sought in the market.

Certainly, the market and the consumer culture play a crucial role in the construction of and intervention in family related problems. In addition to class and power issues, the extent to which market mechanisms can compensate for and ideally benefit from increased involvement in a perceived family problem largely determines the way in which a condition is interpreted and addressed within the wider social structure. As noted earlier, the essential threat inherent in all family problems that have emerged during the past century concerns the extent to which traditional family functions will continue to be performed within changing familial arrangements. In cases where the market is able to take over some of these functions, the initial threat is diminished, and as a result the condition is often endorsed and sometimes even encouraged at the political and administrative levels. This is evident in the case of child care, which has seen the market provide care for children primarily in response to women's increased workforce participation. However, other family conditions, such as child abuse and juvenile delinquency, do not lend themselves to market intervention (or are not considered profitable), require significant state involvement, and are not endorsed as a political issue. Rather, problems of this nature are interpreted and addressed within a pathological framework, which results in increasing pressure and social stigma being directed at the 'problem families'. Because significant state involvement conflicts with the principles and objectives of the 'free' market, the causes of family problems for which large-scale state intervention is necessary must be located in forces outside the dominant structure – that is, within the population in which the problem is identified. This interpretation denies any political responsibility for the condition, thereby legitimising the existing system.

Central to the way in which family problems are constructed is the fact that some family conditions are validated for parts of the population but pathologised for others. Single parenthood provides an apt example of this differentiation. When the single parent, usually the mother, is in a position to access the economic and social resources necessary to undertake the care of her child(ren) with relative self sufficiency, the fact that she is performing this traditional family function without the assistance of a partner is seen to be of little consequence. This is partly because any 'problems' experienced by this single parent are accommodated largely through the use of resources located in the private sphere (although frequently with some forms of direct state assistance), while less-affluent single mothers are reliant on state benefits and subsidies. However, if the same single mother is unable to purchase the necessary resources from the market (such as adequate child care, house keeping, and personal or therapeutic services) and consequently requires significant state intervention, her inability to care self-sufficiently for her child(ren) is emphasised and subsequently made far more visible. The important point in these examples is the degree to which the ability to perform traditional family functions self-sufficiently, or with the assistance of the market, is a determining factor in the way changing familial arrangements and organisation are interpreted and responded to by state measures.

In an examination of single-parent families in the European Community, Roll (1991:173) raises the questions: what is it that is distinct about a lone parent, and why is it of concern? These are fundamental questions, as they are based on the recognition that single parenthood *per se* is not necessarily problematic. Rather, it is the potential conflict between dominant social goals and values and the likelihood or unlikelihood of their successful realisation that have caused such phenomena as single parenthood to be perceived as a social problem or threat. As Barrett and McIntosh (1982) assert, where conflict exists between the social and resource requirements of a certain group and the provisions allowed them by the state, the market and society in general, the disjunction that occurs is often perceived to be a social problem, but is essentially political. Put more simply, were the necessary physical, social and economic resources required by single parents available to them without stigma and social disapproval to enable them to effectively fulfil the function of caring for children in a manner comparable with the traditional two-parent family, single parenthood would not be perceived as a social problem. However, the history of single parenthood in Western industrialised countries demonstrates that this has not been the case.

The Family and Inequality

The outstanding feature of the position of families in contemporary industrialised society is inequality. As discussed in Chapter 7, the structure of inequality is multidimensional: it includes variable circumstances within which families find themselves; the differing level of resources available to families with which to perform their expected functions; and inequality of status among families, which results in differing perceptions and interpretations of family problems according to the social stratum of the family or families most affected.

As stated earlier in this chapter, there is agreement among family commentators and researchers regarding the extent of change that has occurred in family formation and structure during the past century. Many also agree that little has changed in relation to the degree of inequality among families of Western industrialised countries. For example, in describing families in the post-World War II decades, Gilding succinctly highlights the existence of family inequality during that time. 'The wealthiest still kept servants, the poorest still took in lodgers. Women with the means had a "cleaning lady", while those without the means *were* the cleaning ladies' (1991:120; emphasis in the original).

In discussing more recent family inequality, Don Edgar and Frank Maas point out that while it is necessary to recognise the increasing participation rates of women in the workforce, it is also important to remember that a high proportion of positions held by women, particularly those with dependent children, are on a casual basis (Edgar and Maas 1984, Maas 1984). It is also necessary to acknowledge that those from vulnerable groups, such as some single parents, migrants and indigenous Australians, either do not have access to employment or do not enjoy the same security or flexibility of working conditions as the rest of the population. Consequently, individuals with not many skills – particularly the young, migrants, older women and men, and families in remote or rural areas – are less able to access secure full-time employment and are less likely to secure jobs that would enable them to accommodate family responsibilities and obligations.

As far as family income is concerned, the most significant difference in income levels is between two-income and one-income families. As shown in Table 8.3, in 1994–95, the Australian Bureau of Statistics (ABS) recorded 1 991 300 'couple' families as two-earner families, close to half of all couple family units (47.4%). Of the others, 27.7 per cent of units were one-earner units, and the remaining 24.9 per cent were units with no earned income; most of these would have been pensioner units or families in which both partners were either unemployed or were not earning any income for other reasons. The difference in income between two-earner and one-earner couples was quite substantial: over one-half of the two-earner units (52.8%) recorded income over $1000 per week, while only 18.3 per cent of one-earner units recorded income in that range. The mean income of two-earner units was 46.5 per cent higher than the mean income of one-earner units.

Table 8.3: Weekly Income of Couple Income Units, Australia 1994–95
(N = '000)

Gross weekly income ($)	All couple income units		No income earner		One income earner		Two income earners	
	N	%	N	%	N	%	N	%
All income units	*4203.6*	*100.0*	*1046.2*	*100.0*	*1166.1*	*100.0*	*1991.3*	*100.0*
No income/								
negative income	47.4	1.1	12.6	1.2	12.4	1.1	22.4	1.1
1– 199	129.2	3.1	84.1	8.0	24.2	2.1	20.8	1.0
200– 399	904.9	21.5	711.6	68.0	125.7	10.8	67.6	3.4
400– 699	961.3	22.9	201.3	19.2	506.2	43.4	253.8	12.7
700– 999	881.6	21.0	21.6	2.1	283.7	24.3	576.3	28.9
1000–1499	845.7	20.1	9.8	0.9	143.8	12.3	692.1	34.8
1500 and over	433.6	10.3	5.4	0.5	70.1	6.0	358.2	18.0
Mean weekly income ($)	830	–	342	–	767	–	1124	–
Units with dependent children (%)	–	45.6	–	19.1	–	59.9	–	51.2

Source: ABS (1996) *Income Distribution, Australia 1994–95*, Catalogue No. 6523.0

It is also important to note the intergenerational transfer of inequality. In sociological literature, the family is used as the main unit of class analysis due to the fact that wealth is inherited by family members and income is the main determinant of a family's degree of access to such resources as housing, education, health care, health services and child care (Weeks and Wilson 1995:xxii). McCaughey (1987) expands on this by suggesting that families are often perceived to have similar access to resources, in the same way as they have similar needs, roles and obligations. However, as Alexander (1983) points out, families with access to wealth, education, secure employment and adequate housing can and will continue to build on these assets and transfer them from generation to generation, while for those with limited access to such resources, poverty and disadvantage are equally transferable.

Family conditions are interpreted and addressed differently on the basis of certain characteristics, related both to the condition itself and the population experiencing the condition. In this process, inequality of various kinds is firmly entrenched in the socio-political response to family problems, particularly in relation to the variable reaction of the state to the problems of families from different social strata. Weeks and Wilson effectively identify the problematic outcomes this 'inequality of response' engenders, by saying that:

On the one hand, individuals and families require economic and social resources, and yet people's access to these is ridden with inequalities related to class, gender, race and ethnicity. When the state does intervene in family life in the form of legislation, social policy and in the practice of its social services in which social workers and welfare workers are key actors, it frequently reinforces and perpetuates the inequalities and emphasises conformity to dominant norms and stereotypes.   (1995:xxiv)

This is particularly so in relation to the problems experienced by Aboriginal families, who 'on every possible social indicator ... experience a degree of social inequality far in excess of that experienced by every other social group in Australia' (Weeks and Wilson 1995:xxi). Weeks and Wilson further assert that the Aboriginal community has been the target of extensive and long-standing disregard and 'familial abuse' from the wider society and particularly the helping professions. Not only were the familial relationships and processes of Aboriginal communities either ignored or disregarded by such actors as being inferior to those of the dominant Anglo-Saxon culture, but this failure to acknowledge the importance of dense kinship networks in Aboriginal culture resulted in the widespread displacement of generations of Aboriginal children through their removal from such networks.

The issue of class as a central theme pervading all aspects of family problems and the way these are perceived and addressed within the current social structure cannot be overstated. In relation to the child care debate of the 1970s and 1980s, Sweeney and Jamrozik emphasise the unequal nature of problem identification with regard to the family. They assert that services provided by the state for children have been 'services for the poor', in that from the earliest days of Australian history 'these services have achieved little towards overcoming or countervailing the inequalities in society. At best, the services have been instrumental in maintaining law and order, but they have also re-affirmed social and economic divisions arising from the market economy' (1982:3).

In discussing the implications for the 'new poor' of the emancipation of labour from capital, Bauman points out that members of this modern proletariat are *not* consumers, by virtue of their inability to participate fully in the consumer society. This inability to fulfil the vital objective of consumerism necessitates the 'combined actions of repression, policing, authority and normative regulation' as a means of disciplining this potentially disruptive and threatening group (1987:181). Using the examples of social insurance and state-funded subsidies, Bauman argues that the intentionally divisive nature of such provisions is intended to establish recipients as second-class citizens and demonstrate to others the unsavoury consequences of losing sight of the ultimate objective of consumerism. 'Those who prove to be inappropriate objects for seduction can expect nothing but the trusty old repression,' he says (1987:183).

The way in which the 'new poor' are taught their bureaucratically assigned roles, as Bauman puts it, is particularly evident in the interpretation of and interventions in family related problems. In the conditions of the 19th century, the poor family was regarded as morally suspect and politically dangerous. Trattner comments on the activities of the New York Association for Improving the Conditions of the Poor at that time as follows:

> Entering the homes of the poor, association members quickly discovered that in the slums, where most of the needy were forced to live, all those features of poverty that middle-class citizens found most reprehensible were concentrated and intensified – filth, crime, sexual promiscuity, drunkenness, disease, improvidence, and indolence – serious obstacles to morality.
>
> *(1979:62)*

The prevalence of dangerous and damaging conditions among the poor, which were understood to be family problems, was also observed by Adolphi Blanqui, following his travels through France. In 1848 he stated that it was 'in wretched lodgings that the dissolution of the family and all its woes begin' (cited by Donzelot 1979:70).

Still, the perception persists that certain family problems such as domestic violence, youth homelessness and child abuse are located in the families of the poor and working class. While the existence of such problems within many families in the lower strata of society cannot be denied, may not the visibility of these through the surveillance and accentuation methods of the state be the only real certainty? As noted earlier, the ability of affluent families to compensate (through the facilitative apparatus of the state and the market) for changes in their capacity to perform traditional family functions is one of the primary reasons for the high visibility of 'family problems' within the lower strata of society. For example, while wealthier families may employ nannies, send their children on exclusive holiday camps, or attend private family therapists or counsellors, poor families with similar needs must rely on state-funded child care, and the youth and therapeutic services of statutory agencies.

The rationale apparent in methods of intervention in family problems is equally acrimonious for poor and working-class families. Still as evident in contemporary society as it was in 19th century France is the concern that assistance provided by the state in relation to family problems must not, and must not be seen to, either reward laziness or elicit false poverty by being too attractive (Donzelot 1979).

In addition to issues of social class, political power and market involvement, the degree of self-sufficiency present in different family types is also central to the way in which family conditions are addressed by the wider social structure. There is widespread recognition within the literature referring to Australian families that with the retreat of the welfare state the family has emerged as the obvious choice in locating responsibility for the needs of all people. In discussing the Australian Labor Government's response during the latter part of the 1980s to increasing inequality among Australian families, Lynne Davis asserts that 'Broader social equity objectives have been progressively abandoned. For all but the impoverished, families must increasingly look to their own resources and the forces of the market to meet their needs' (1991:222).

In the past 15 years, there has been growing political reinforcement of the view that groups such as youth, university students, single parents, people requiring hospital treatment, the elderly, the unemployed and migrants should look to the family to provide the social and economic resources they require. Families are expected not only to assist individuals in accessing market resources, but also to provide substitutes when market goods prove unobtainable due to cost. However, the view that the family should be self-sufficient except for reliance on the market is not peculiar to Australia (see Barrett and McIntosh 1982 for the United Kingdom perspective). Rather, this is a position common to all Western industrialised countries, which is motivated by both the goals and principles underpinning capitalist ideology and the exponents of the New Right.

As discussed in Chapter 5, there has been large-scale reduction of the public sector in Australia since the 1980s. At the same time, there has been a marked increase in the extent of class-based state intervention into family life. This increased involvement in the previously 'private affairs' of the family is evident in the recent development of political, legal and therapeutic responses to such issues as domestic violence, rape in marriage and child abuse, as well as in the growth of intervention by the helping professions in these areas. Yet the contradictory nature of this current state of affairs is clear. Decreased involvement of the state in the market economy and in areas previously managed by the public sphere is occurring in conjunction with increased though selective involvement of the state in the private sphere. Why is this the case? Is the family no longer considered private and autonomous? And how does this fit with the notion of the self-sufficient family?

Competing Discourses on the Family

The family persists as an issue of social concern due to the perceived threat inherent in its increasing loss of the capacity to perform trad- itional functions (as well as a loss of traditional functions themselves) and thus fulfil necessary social expectations. Different interest groups within society have understood and interpreted the changing functions of the family in different ways, and it is necessary to consider these interpretations in order to identify both the origins of the perceived threat and the measures taken to reduce or remove that threat.

Throughout history, the stability of the traditional family unit has been reliant on the maintenance of a balance between individualism and social responsibility – that is, between individual liberation and strong communal ties (Berger 1995). However, from the 1960s onwards, in the midst of increasing maternal employment, rising divorce rates and increasing longevity, some Leftists and radical feminists have waged war on the family, declaring that the family unit (being an instrument of repression) and its ethos were no longer viable or desirable (Ash 1973, Blankenhorn *et al.* 1990). Echoing the sentiments of Marx and Engels in their *Communist Manifesto*, there were calls for the abolition of the family[1] (Barrett and McIntosh 1982:7). An integral aspect of the growing dissatisfaction with the traditional family and increased pressure for the public recognition and endorsement of alternative family types was strongly motivated and reinforced by feminist lobbies. By the 1970s, these had succeeded in drawing public attention to the potential for oppression within the family, evident in the extent of violence against women and children that occurred in families (Pinkney 1995). Consequently, governments of almost every Western nation came under public pressure to develop 'family policies' in recognition of the extent of change occurring in families; to establish, maintain and finance supplementary and alternative structures (Berger 1995); to intervene in the mechanisms of the market so as to render it family friendly; and to provide for an increase in the number and range of intervention mechanisms available within the confines of family life.

At the same time, there occurred a resurgence of support for the 'traditional' family – that is, the two-parent family organised around a clear division of labour and caring responsibilities. Such support became apparent in a number of countries, emanating particularly from the New Right and various religious groups such as the Patriarchal Family Movement in Canada and the United States, and from similar groups in Australia such as the Festival of Light and Call to Australia (Gilding 1991). The concerns of traditional-family protagonists are based on the belief that the demise of traditional family arrangements would be threatening to wider society through the reduction of established family functions – particularly in relation to the care of children and other dependent members physically, socially and economically. Such assertions have precipitated the belief, still common today, that traditional family structures and values are declining due to the erosion of commitment within families, and a lack of support from without, resulting in a rise in social ills such as delinquency, crime, teenage pregnancy and welfare dependency (Ash 1973, Berger and Berger 1985, Blankenhorn *et al.* 1990, Bartholomew 1995, Berger 1995, Pinkney 1995). Such concerns were vigorously asserted in an alarmist statement by M. L. Cassanmagnago Cerretti in a background paper presented to the European Parliament as part of the development of a policy on the family in the 1980s. He stated that:

> It is striking that the widespread disintegration of the concept of the family as the nucleus of society, the increasing instability in family relationships reflected by the spread of cohabitation and divorces, the new position of women in society and their wish to work, the crisis in traditional moral values, the falling birth rate which is now approaching or even falling below the rate required for the population to renew itself, are trends common to all countries of Europe, even if they vary in intensity. Thus the future of the very survival of these countries is at risk.   *(cited by Barrett and McIntosh 1982:11)*

Clearly, where little or no provision is made within the social structure (such as the allocation of resources for alternative family forms), the two-parent family in which one parent undertakes paid work and one parent 'cares' is the family form most compatible with the dominant mode of economic production. Consequently, the perceived decline of the traditional family is seen as a significant threat to the successful achievement of capitalist market objectives. Other family forms are viewed as lacking the capacity to contribute to the goals of the market economy, and moreover they require increased state intervention in the form of family assistance. 'Non-traditional' families, then, become a problem or negative residue when they are unable to contribute effectively to the pursuit of such capitalist goals and objectives as market efficiency and effectiveness. The implications of this situation are clearly evident in the social and political reluctance to accept some family types.

In response to these competing perspectives on the family and its organisation in contemporary society, the socio-political responses to recent changes in familial forms and arrangements incorporate aspects of both of the positions outlined. On the one hand, certain family forms, arrangements and conditions are valued and encouraged; on the other hand, some conditions are perceived as social problems. In other cases, similar family conditions are interpreted and responded to in vastly different ways.

Australian Government Response to the Family

In order to understand these processes, it is necessary to clarify the political response to the family as a primary social institution within the Australian context. In 1976, the Fraser Coalition Government introduced the Family Allowance to replace the previous child endowment payments and tax concessions for child-related expenses. Since that time, both major parties in Australia have claimed to be the natural benefactor of the family. While both Labor and Coalition governments have asserted their commitment to the family, some clear distinctions are evident in the family policy agendas proposed by each party.

The 1980s marked the 'rediscovery' of the family in Australian politics, at a time when real disposable incomes were falling. The leader of the Labor Party, Bill Hayden, introduced the *Family Living Standards* policy during the 1980 election, which was directed at improving the conditions of disadvantaged and poor families. The policy was accompanied by strong criticism of the Coalition Government's Family Allowance – which, it was argued, increased inequalities between families with dependent children, and decreased in real value due to a lack of indexing to account for increasing inflation (Pinkney 1995). While the targeting of disadvantaged and different family types was not continued by the Coalition to the same degree, emphasis on the family as a central theme in political electioneering remained paramount in the policy proposals of both major Australian parties during the 1980s and in the following decade. The 'family budget' handed down by the-then Treasurer John Howard in 1982 highlighted the Coalition's on-going emphasis on mainstream Australian families, according increased support (through increases in Family Allowance payments and the Dependent Spouse Rebate) to the traditional two-parent, single-income family (Pinkney 1995). Although the Labor Party's proposed Family Income Supplement was adopted by the Coalition in their 1982 Budget, the pervading emphasis of Coalition family initiatives was, and remains, centred on the 'traditional' family.

In particular, the Liberal Party's 1988 *Future Directions* policy emphasised the way in which Australian families were under 'serious threat' and had failed to receive adequate support through the policies of the-then Labor Government. This emphasis on the 'plight of the Australian family' was continued by the Liberal Party headed by Andrew Peacock in the 1990 election campaign, while the Labor Government implemented its Family Assistance Package as a means of fulfilling Hawke's 1987 federal election promise that no child would be living in poverty by 1990 (Davis 1991:222).

A detailed analysis of the various family related initiatives put forward by each of the major political parties is beyond the scope of this book, but some general observations require acknowledgement. Essentially, the family related initiatives of Australian Labor governments have targeted inequality of income and opportunity and have focused on social justice strategies, the support of individual choice (particularly with regard to maternal employment), and family diversity. Alternatively, Coalition parties have maintained a strong commitment to the support and promotion of the traditional two-parent family. Examples of each party's family priorities can be seen as having some degree of consistency and continuity, from the introduction of Labor's *Living Standards* policy in 1980 through to the present time. The distinction between the parties' family policy agendas can also be clearly seen in their most-recent family packages.

The Labor Government's emphasis on supporting different family types, decreasing inequality with regard to resources and living standards, and providing services targeting the special needs of indigenous Australians, those from non-English speaking backgrounds and those with a disability, was clearly evident in their *Agenda for Families* package released in 1995. While this package placed a distinct emphasis on supporting the diversity of Australian families (in recognition of the directives for the International Year of the Family in 1994), the Coalition was critical of some of the initiatives, labelling them as discriminatory towards the traditional nuclear family. Pinkney's examination of parliamentary debates on family related legislative reform aptly highlights the parties' competing perspectives on family support, in that the level of funding accorded to the Home Child Care Allowance (for full-time carers), as compared with the Child Care Rebate, motivated the Coalition to state that 'mothers who have sacrificed an income to stay at home and care for children were the victims of extraordinary inequality' (Senator Minchin 1994, cited by Pinkney 1995:21).

The Coalition handed down their *Strengthening Families* package with the release of their 1996–97 Budget. This package demonstrated an ongoing commitment to the promotion of the self-sufficient family and the prevention of family breakdown. One of the key aspects of the Coalition's family package was the introduction of the Family Tax Initiative (FTI), which provides for an increase in the tax-free threshold (of one parent) for families with dependent children. The FTI also includes an increase in the tax-free threshold of single-income families, providing they have one child under five years old (Department of Health and Family Services 1996). This scheme gives the greatest assistance to single parents and to couples with dependent children in which one parent is a full-time carer of at least one child who is under five years old. Single parents and couples with dependent children all over five years old, where either, both or no parent is working receive less assistance. In addition to the FTI, the Coalition's 1996 *Strengthening Families* package includes financial incentives for families with dependent children who take out private health insurance; an 18 per cent rebate for individuals making superannuation contributions on behalf of spouses with low incomes (usually non-working); increased funding for the National Respite Carers Program; and increased funding for the Strengthening Families Strategy, which includes an $11.8 million funding increase for marriage and relationship education, and an additional $5 million per annum in emergency relief funding for agencies such as the Salvation Army, the Society of St Vincent de Paul and the Smith Family (Department of Health and Family Services 1996).

The *Strengthening Families* package is certainly less overt in its support of the traditional nuclear family than the Coalition's previous family policies (i.e. *Future Directions* package of 1988 and the *Things That Matter* policy statement of 1994). However, the current Government's support of a conventional division of labour with regard to work and family responsibilities, and its encouragement of one-income families and stay-at-home carers can still be seen in the FTI, in superannuation changes and in funding increases directed at the prevention of family breakdown.

In sum, even a brief analysis of the Australian governments' family related initiatives demonstrates differing perspectives regarding the role and nature of family structure and family organisation. The Labor Government's most recent family package was promoted as supporting diversity and individual choice, and criticised for neglecting the traditional two-parent family, while the Coalition's existing package is promoted as endorsing and rewarding families who recognise their traditional familial responsibilities and undertake the financial and physical care of any dependent members including children, non-working spouses, and disabled and elderly members.

The dedication of the International Year of the Family in 1994 demonstrates on a global scale the social and political significance of the family and its place in contemporary society. Twenty-one countries participated in research projects associated with the activities of the International Year, including Ethiopia, Israel, the Republic of Korea, and Slovenia (Australian Institute of Family Studies 1995). During that year, both the United Nations and the Australian National Council for the International Year of the Family (NCIYF) stressed the social benefits of family life, the latter stating that the family exists as a:

> central social network, a major site of social and economic productive activity, the provider of intimacy and emotional interdependence for spouses/ partners; for parents, grandparents and children and other relatives; the provider of care, nurture and development of children and young people, and the provider of care for other family members made vulnerable by frailty associated with old age, by disability and severe illness.   *(NCIYF 1994b:1)*

The NCIYF recommended that the Federal Government and other social organisations work in partnership with the family in an effort to complement, enhance and empower the family in recognition of its social benefits. In this way, the appropriate role of the state in family life was proposed by the NCIYF as being one that is directed at assisting and complementing the family unit and the social roles it performs, regardless of its form (NCIYF 1994a, 1994b).

While the NCIYF and the previous Labor Government strongly proclaimed their progressive commitment to assist and support the diversity of family forms in contemporary Australia, documents produced as a result of the International Year as well as the focus of family policy under the current Federal Government (particularly the FTI and the new Medicare and Austudy arrangements) clearly promote the self-sufficient family – that is, the family that undertakes the financial and physical care of any dependent members (including children, non-working spouses, and elderly or disabled members), with little or no direct state involvement. Clearly, the promotion of the self-sufficient family reflects the state's encouragement and facilitation of market participation through the socialising processes of the family.

To some extent, the pro-family platform evident in many government policies is, as Barrett and McIntosh put it, 'part of a broader political rhetoric ... a metaphor to endow the government's economic policies with a spurious "commonsense" legitimacy' (1982:12). This is to say, the rhetoric conveys a notion that the appropriate organisation of family life, particularly in terms of the division of labour, can be equated with any business or economic endeavour in which certain sacrifices must be made in order to achieve economic objectives, whether this be by the housewife, the grocer or the parliamentary treasurer.

This analogy clearly demonstrates the central concerns inherent in any response to family conditions perceived to be threatening – namely, that the functions traditionally performed by the family continue to occur, thereby decreasing any threat to dominant interests and goals, and in order to legitimate existing social arrangements. The way in which these concerns are addressed is demonstrated through the following examination of the pathologisation and politicisation of family conditions.

The Pathologisation of Family Problems

Throughout history as well as in contemporary society, the poor, working-class and marginal families of Western countries have been identified as the target for state-sanctioned intervention and social regulation, due to the potential threat they were seen to pose to dominant values and interests. Under current capitalist organisation, this threat stems from the inability of such families to actively participate in the 'free' market as a means of fulfilling or discharging their expected functions. Consequently, the unhindered pursuit of capitalist objectives has resulted in the creation of a social residue in the form of the modern proletariat family.

Rodman effectively highlights the process whereby certain social conditions have been identified as being characteristic of poor and disadvantaged families, saying that:

> The following have all been considered as characteristic of the lower class: 'promiscuous sexual relationships'; 'illegitimate' children; 'deserting' husbands and fathers; and 'unmarried' mothers. These characteristics are frequently viewed in a gross manner as, simply, problems of the lower class. My own feeling is that it makes sense to think of them as solutions of the lower class to problems that they face in the social, economic, and perhaps legal and political spheres of life ... We therefore have to stress the fact that words like 'promiscuity', 'illegitimacy' and 'desertion' are not part of the lower-class vocabulary, and that it is inaccurate to describe lower-class behaviours in this way. These words have middle-class meanings and imply middle-class judgements, and it is precisely because of this that we ought not to use them to describe lower-class behaviour – unless, of course, our intention is to judge this behaviour in a middle-class manner in order to bolster a sagging middle-class ego ...   (1959, cited by Leslie 1967:293–4)

In the process Rodman describes, the problems for which families seek public assistance are identified, defined and promoted within the political and administrative spheres as the 'problems of the working-class family'. This strategy denies any political responsibility for the problems experienced by poor families, while effectively masking the occurrence of similar problems within other strata of society. Consequently, the pathologisation of family problems occurs, whereby conditions of a distinctly political nature are translated into technical problems through a process of depoliticisation.

More recently, the process Rodman describes has persisted under the guise of different terms, but in essence there is continuity. Currently, state-sanctioned services for families are provided on a large scale and are promoted as strengthening families and preventing family dissolution through the provision of services that address a wide range of issues including parenting, parental relationships, group work and self-help programs, practical assistance in home chores, and budgeting and financial or material aid, as well as assistance for respite care, day care or out-of-school-hours care. However, with the professionalisation of family problems (which began in the early 1960s) and the emergence of 'restorative family services' in the 1980s and 1990s, public assistance to poor and marginalised families has hardly deviated from the remedial and pathologically focused support services of the 1950s and 1960s, despite professed differences of intention. Both then and now, intervention is in the name of 'help' and 'assistance' while incorporating distinct forms of surveillance and social control measures reminiscent of those employed in the 18th and 19th centuries as a means of controlling and repressing the proletariat families. The referral practices and eligibility criteria of existing programs are largely in keeping with the family support services of 30 years ago, in which families perceived to be abnormal or dysfunctional were 'treated' by professional service providers (Nocella 1996).

Leslie (1967) emphasises this notion of a social pathologisation of the working-class family by asserting the existence in English-speaking countries of a middle-class family model comprising the white, Anglo-Saxon Protestant middle-class family, which, he suggests, is a kind of prototype for the larger society. Leslie states that:

> Its patterns are the ones held up to us as models by government agencies, churches and schools. Its patterns are described in typical American novels and are displayed on movie and TV screens, and in magazines. Its patterns are 'ideal' patterns for much of the nonwhite, non-Anglo, non-Protestant, non-middle class segment of the population ...   *(Leslie 1967:256–7)*

Throughout history, the identification of certain conditions or problems within families in the lower strata has not been a mere coincidence. The depoliticisation of problems perceived to occur predominantly in working-class families and the inherent failure to recognise the political, social and structural causes of such problems has occurred in an undoubtedly conscious and planned manner. Bauman specifically highlights the intentional and in fact necessary construction of the 'problems of the working-class family' within the current social structure arguing that:

> The new poor are ... a product of the consumer market. Not of its 'mal-
> functioning' ... but of its way of existence and reproduction. Consumer
> society creates its own poor by setting the rich, the ostentatious consumer, not
> as a boss, an exploiter, a member of a different class, an enemy – but as a
> pattern-setter, an example to be followed, a target to be reached, overcome
> and left behind, as a pioneer on the road everyone must aspire to follow, and
> a confirmation that aspiring is realistic.   *(1989:186–7)*

So the problems of the working-class family accentuate the 'ideal' model of family organisation, functioning and social participation. However, as mentioned previously, they also act as an effective warning against the failure to achieve such ideals. Consequently, the construction of the problems of the working-class family incorporates certain clear and conscious objectives.

However, once constructed, the problems of the working-class family must be managed. Consequently, the translation of a given problem from the political to the technical elicits the involvement of the helping professions, thereby demonstrating a willingness on the part of the state to address problems experienced by families in the lower strata. The helping professions perform a central role within the pathologisation process as providers of technical solutions for 'problem families'. Such 'solutions' are provided in the form of therapeutic, practical and financial services, which further translate the problem (already effectively translated from the political to the technical) to one of a personal nature located in the emotional, psychological or interpersonal inability of client families to function successfully and independently. The intervention methods used by the helping professions actively reassert the causes of family problems as being located in the 'dysfunction' of client families themselves.

Donzelot identifies the feature of 'moralisation' inherent in intervention methods directed at poor and disadvantaged families, which results from the translation of the problems of the working class family from the political to the technical to the personal. He asserts that the charity societies of the *ancien régime* acted as morals police for the parish, in that requests for assistance from the charitable organisations by the 'proud poor' were strongly underpinned by certain moral criteria and imperatives. 'This is why a demand for assistance had to be accompanied by a certificate of confession signed by a priest' he says (1979:60). Donzelot also refers to the way in which the morality of families who required assistance from 19th century philanthropic societies was emphasised and called into question through a painstaking investigation upon which the provision of assistance was dependent. Through delving into the life of the poor recipient, the moral character of the client and their level of deservedness could be determined. In illustration, Donzelot says:

> a mother surrounded by children begs for your help, but do they belong to her? Has she not borrowed them for the occasion from the natural mother? An invalid entreats you, but is his infirmity real? *(1979:68)*

Donzelot states that through such methods of surveillance and penetration into the family life of poor recipients, a link was forged between morality and the economic factor. He also notes that the data collected during assessment interviews allowed for the resources of families to be recorded in conjunction with comments regarding the family's effective management of those resources. This practice is continued in family welfare agencies today.

Current methods of intervention performed at the operative level (by social welfare agencies and the helping professions) continue to encompass moral imperatives, social control and surveillance methods that recapitulate the causes of family problems for which state-sanctioned services are required, as being in the personal characteristics of service recipients. This is evident in forms of counselling and therapy, home visits, and data-collection methods practised within the 'restorative family services' (Jamrozik and Sweeney 1996, Nocella 1996). Similarly, the current practice of surveillance and public investigation to which recipients of government benefits and subsidies are subjected is evident in the degree to which their personal, social and economic circumstances are scrutinised in the determination of their eligibility (or deservedness) for assistance (Jamrozik and Sweeney 1996).

The fact that most client families of government and quasi-government family services come from the lower classes is pertinent to the way in which the problems for which they seek assistance are interpreted and addressed. Domestic violence, child abuse and juvenile delinquency to name just a few are among the primary family issues dealt with by the helping professions. They are also conditions that have continued to be perceived as problems of the working-class family. Clearly, it is largely the class status (or level of market and political resources) of the family experiencing a particular social problem that determines the measures used to address the problem at the political, administrative and operative spheres. The occurrence of the problems of the working-class family in other social classes is less visible, therefore requiring less public involvement and thereby rendering such conditions less problematic. Holman suggests that in addition to being less socially visible, when the problems of middle-class families do attract the attention of social welfare agencies, they are addressed differently from those of working-class families (cited by Jamrozik and Sweeney 1996). Jamrozik and Sweeney, using an example from a study of child abuse notifications and registrations in New South Wales, demonstrate this as follows:

> Following a notification, children from lower socio-economic families were more likely to receive a visit from welfare officers and/or be 'voluntarily' placed in care than children from higher socio-economic families who were most likely referred to another agency for assistance.   *(1996:111)*

The important legitimising function of the social pathologisation of family problems must also be acknowledged. It has already been established that the familial conditions for which state intervention is required – the problems of the working-class family – result from the creation of a social residue that emerges from the pursuit of goals and interests of the dominant social structure. Yet the management of these conditions is achieved through a systematic process whereby a condition is removed from the political domain and addressed instead in the administrative and operative spheres, where it is further translated into a pathology located in the personal characteristics of the client family. The depoliticisation and pathologisation processes effectively legitimate the existing social structure through defining the problems of the working-class family as being outside the organisation of current social and political arrangements. In addition, the significant involvement of the helping professions in conducting technical interventions into family problems at the operative level provides further legitimation, in that unproductive intervention methods and the persistence of particular family problems are seen to result from the failure of client families to make effective use of the help offered – or even more concerning, their unwillingness to be assisted at all. As the popular social-welfare adage says, 'You can't help someone who doesn't *want* to be helped.'

The Politicisation of Family Problems

As has been emphasised in this and previous chapters, the way social problems are perceived and addressed largely depends on issues of class and resultant political power. The increasing workforce participation of women in the later part of the 20th century provides an effective example of the interpretation and translation of social conditions within the politicisation process.

The issue of women's participation in the paid workforce is not solely a 20th century phenomenon. Recognition of this is essential in understanding the implications of this condition for the contemporary family.

Women have always actively participated in the labour market. The only change that has occurred in the last 50 years has been the proportion, and particularly the social class, of women embarking on paid employment. This change arose from a number of factors, including government encouragement of women's paid employment during the 1940s as a means of increasing and sustaining the war effort, and in the 1960s to meet the demands of an expanding economy (Sweeney and Jamrozik 1982:3); the rise in consciousness of women and the resultant increased visibility of the feminist movement; and technological and industrial change.

Women's participation in the workforce rose from 22 per cent in 1947 to 32 per cent in 1971 (by which time 32% of married women worked outside the home), and to 40 per cent by 1986 (Gilding 1991).

The increase in women's workforce participation had significant implications for the family. This was because the entry of such a large proportion of women into the paid workforce added an additional function to those already performed by the family. The addition of this function (increasing both the production and consumption capabilities of the family) resulted in a distinct conflict between this and the existing family (or rather women's) function of caring for children. Where this emerged as a new social problem it was perceived to demonstrate the inability of mothers to effectively perform both functions. The reduction in quality and amount of time spent by mothers in tending to their husbands and children, as well as the potential for career objectives to distract single women from marriage and childbearing, was considered extremely threatening to the stability of the family and consequently to the stability of society in general. However, unlike some other changes in family organisation, the issue of women's workforce participation remained in the political arena, thereby compelling a political response to this perceived problem.

The definition of the problem and the ensuing political response were due in large part to the number of women entering paid employment during the 1950s and 1960s, but more importantly to the predominant social class of such women. Evidence of this can be seen in the fact that growing demands were made for state support and assistance in discharging the 'traditional' family functions women had previously performed – particularly in relation to the care of children. It was only when women from the middle classes entered the labour market in force, with the backing of the increasingly vocal feminist movement, that there was public (but more importantly political) recognition of the conflict between women's participation in the labour market and the performance of 'traditional' family functions.

Table 8.4: Married Women in the Labour Force, Australia 1966–96

(N = '000)

Year/category	(1) All labour force		(2) All women			(3) Married women			
	N	%	N	%	% of (1)	N	%	% of (1)	% of (2)
1966									
Population 15 years +	*8180.3*	*100.0*	*4125.1*	*100.0*	*50.4*	*2701.9*	*100.0*	*33.0*	*65.5*
In labour force	4902.5	59.9	1497.1	36.3	30.6	782.5	29.0	16.0	50.2
All employed people	*4823.9*	*100.0*	*1458.2*	*100.0*	*30.2*	*761.2*	*100.0*	*15.8*	*52.2*
– Professional, administrative, clerical	1531.9	31.8	681.1	46.7	44.5	282.4	37.1	18.4	41.5
– Sales and personal services	793.4	16.4	444.4	30.5	56.0	265.3	34.9	33.4	59.7
– Trades, labourers etc.	2498.5	51.8	332.8	22.8	13.3	213.5	28.0	8.5	64.2
Employed in									
– Industries of material production	2222.6	46.1	397.9	27.3	17.9	248.8	32.7	11.2	62.5
– Distribution and sales	1368.9	28.4	431.5	29.6	31.5	232.3	30.5	17.0	53.8
– Management services	945.4	19.6	455.8	31.3	48.2	179.7	23.6	19.0	39.4
– Recreation, personal services	287.0	5.9	172.9	11.9	60.2	100.4	13.2	35.0	58.1
1996									
Population 15 years +	*14384.3*	*100.0*	*7303.6*	*100.0*	*50.8*	*4206.3*	*100.0*	*29.2*	*57.6*
In labour force	9090.8	63.2	3900.3	53.4	42.9	2294.6	54.6	25.2	58.8
All employed people	*8319.7*	*100.0*	*3589.4*	*100.0*	*43.1*	*2175.0*	*100.0*	*26.1*	*60.6*
– Managers, professionals, associate professionals, advanced clerical	3282.0	39.4	1511.2	42.1	46.0	1009.4	46.4	30.8	66.8
– Sales, services, other clerical	2258.3	27.1	1557.0	43.4	68.9	836.7	38.5	37.0	53.7
– Trades, labourers etc.	2779.1	33.4	521.2	14.5	18.8	328.9	15.1	11.8	63.1
Employed in									
– Industries of material production	2304.4	27.7	532.4	14.8	23.1	383.3	17.6	16.6	72.0
– Distribution and sales	2290.0	27.5	924.3	25.8	40.4	495.8	22.8	21.7	53.6
– Management services	2852.7	34.3	1677.5	46.7	58.8	1063.5	48.9	37.3	63.4
– Recreation and personal services	872.6	10.5	455.2	12.7	52.2	232.3	10.7	26.6	51.0

Sources: ABS (1986) *The Labour Force, Australia: Historical Summary 1966–1984*, Catalogue No. 6204.0
ABS (1996) *Labour Force, Australia, August 1996*, Catalogue No. 6203.0

The entry of married women into the labour force has been significant not only in numbers but also in shifts among sectors of industry
and among occupations. To mention only some of these: in 1966,
36.3 per cent of all women and 29 per cent of married women were in
the labour force. Women accounted for 30.2 per cent of all employed
people and 15.8 per cent of these were married women, being 52.2
per cent of all employed women (see Table 8.4). Of all employed
women, 46.7 per cent were employed in white-collar occupations
(professional, technical, administrative, managerial and clerical), but
only 37.1 per cent of married women were in such occupations. By 1996,
the situation had changed significantly: 53.4 per cent of women
participated in the labour force, and of these, 54.6 per cent were
married women. Women accounted for 43.1 per cent of all employed
people, and married women accounted for 26.1 per cent. Of all
employed women, 42.1 per cent were in white-collar occupations
(mainly professional, managerial and higher clerical), and 46.4 per cent
of married women were in those occupations. The increase in the
number of married women entering the labour force and the shift in
their occupations to professional and related jobs were the main factors
in the increase in two-income families among the middle classes and in
the corresponding increase in income inequality among families (see
also Table 8.3).

Prior to the federal government's introduction of child care initiatives
in the 1960s, there was no formal recognition of the conflict between
women's work and family responsibilities. Consequently, those working-
class families in which women had worked for decades were considered
the primary site, and to a significant extent the cause, for such social ills
as promiscuity, juvenile delinquency and single parenthood. Such
conditions, perceived to be the problems of working-class families, were
not attributed in the same degree to families of those middle-class
women who entered the labour market in the 1960s and 1970s. This
was due to the success of such women in effectively politicising the
'problems' of working mothers.

This is not to say there was no opposition to the large-scale entry of
(primarily middle-class) women into the workforce following World
War II. On the contrary, there was substantial opposition. Reverend
W. G. Coghlan, a pioneer of marriage guidance, asserted in the early
1950s that the wife's gainful employment was one of the symptoms of
marriage breakdown (cited by Gilding 1991:120). However, while
working mothers, divorce and broken families were among the conditions Gilding identifies as threatening the Australian family in the
1950s, he also acknowledges the politicisation of such issues, stating that
in the late 1960s these 'threats found a voice as first the "counter

culture" and then the sexual liberation movements launched a critique of the family' (1991:21).

Consequently, the political pressure exerted by those advocating the workforce participation of women resulted in a growing acknowledgement and recognition of the potential role of the market and the state in reducing the conflict of goals and functions between the family and the wider society. This recognition was demonstrated through the gradual implementation of social service and industry reforms, including increased federal involvement in the provision of child care and day care services, the introduction of flexible working hours, fractional employment and maternity leave (Sweeney and Jamrozik 1982).

As can be seen from this analysis, the identification of women's workforce participation and the consequent politicisation of that situation demonstrate the way in which some 'family problems' elicit the involvement of the market and the state as a means of reducing the initial conflict of values and interests, while other conditions do not. It is worth restating that whether or not the politicisation process occurs is determined by two factors: first, the social status of the group or social actors experiencing or participating in the condition, and second, the extent to which the continuation of the condition may, under certain circumstances, be of benefit to dominant political and economic interests. This is demonstrated by the fact that the issue was politicised only when workforce participation was seen as advantageous in enhancing the efficiency of the market (through increasing the production of the market and consumption of the family unit), and the issue found a voice in the middle class and the feminist movement.

As discussed earlier in this chapter, the flipside of this is that in other cases, family conditions that carry similar threats to the dominant social interests are interpreted outside their relevant social and economic contexts and are addressed through technical and remedial means through which causes are subsequently located in the characteristics of the population group experiencing the problem. (Such population groups usually enjoy relatively low-class status and consequently are able to exert little or no public pressure in having their interests addressed within the political and administrative spheres.) Yet in some cases, new family arrangements are accepted and accommodated at the political and administrative levels, as in the case of women's workforce participation. In both cases, conflict between the dominant goals and interests of capitalist industrialised society and its negative residue is interpreted, translated and responded to in such a way as to legitimate the existing social structure with the least amount of disruption to it.

Note

1 In any discussion of the family in feminist thought it is important to note that despite popular belief, there is no anti-family feminist consensus. Many feminists identify the family as a primary site for the oppression of women and seek to abolish it. Others argue that feminism must recognise that the majority of women are not helplessly trapped in the family but have willingly identified marriage, children and a family with their own happiness. These two views dominate history as well as current debate on feminist thought and practice, and they are of central importance in understanding the vexed position of the family in feminism. As Barrett and McIntosh enquire, 'Should feminists, recognising that women and men occupy "separate spheres" of social life, press for proper appreciation of women's work and responsibilities in the family, and for the revaluing of non-aggressive "feminine" principles? Or should they reject this artificial, socially constructed separation and press for equality *tout court* rather than for equality in difference?' (Barrett and McIntosh 1982:20).

CHAPTER 9

The Problem of Social Order

All social problems contain a threat, either potential or direct, to the dominant social order in society. The issue of social order is of fundamental concern to society, as the maintenance of social order is essential to society's functioning as a social, political and economic unit. Yet the pursuit of social order is also a source of social problems that arise out of law making and law enforcement processes. These processes are carried out by legislative bodies, the justice system, the police, the correctional system, and a plethora of agencies and occupations such as social work, psychology, psychiatry, religious bodies, and a variety of 'voluntary' organisations. In a broader perspective, however, the maintenance of social order is to a varying degree an inherent part of all social institutions.

Social order is an ever-present, evergreen social issue – an integral and essential part of social living. Correspondingly, one of the most threatening social conditions – perceived as the most serious social problem – is a condition that carries or is seen to carry the threat of the 'breakdown of social order'. At its most serious, the breakdown of social order represents a threat to security, to property (public, private, or both), and even to life itself. Extreme forms of this would be situations like those experienced in Rwanda, Somalia, Liberia and Nigeria. Another version of the breakdown of social order might be anything that is perceived as a threat to the established power structure, for example loss of respect for authority – conduct that, while not necessarily illegal, is seen to be offensive to social mores, attitudes and values, or interests. The threat to the last of these may not necessarily go any further, but it is perceived in terms of former threats, for example a peaceful demonstration against the destruction of a forest that turns violent.

In common perceptions, the term 'social order' evokes images of crime, police, courts and prisons. Certainly, social order and the related term, social control, refer to the means and methods of controlling any social conduct that deviates beyond the boundaries of accepted norms, and that therefore threatens the dominant social order. The most manifest forms of such deviant conduct are social acts that are codified by the legal system as crimes. In this chapter, we therefore include comment about crime and crime control, but our concern is much broader, addressing the issue of social order in a wider sociological/political perspective.

To consider the issues of social order from a sociological perspective is to consider Durkheim's question: what is the nature of social solidarity, what forces hold a society together, and how are these forces organised so that order is maintained? The social order may be arrived at by consensus among a society's members, or may be imposed by the force of the dominant structure of power and interests. It may also be imposed by an outside force through armed conquest or economic power. In relation to the issues discussed in this book, the question of how social order has been established in a society, and how it is maintained, is relevant to our theory of social problems, in that the kinds of social problems that occur in a particular society will be a direct outcome – a negative residue – of these processes.

Social order is essentially a political issue. The basic prerequisites for social order are some of the following: an agreement on how to establish common rules of conduct; an agreement on how to enforce the agreed-upon rules of conduct; an agreement on how to elect, nominate or appoint people to positions of power and how to remove them (e.g. appointment for a fixed term, by petition, by a change of laws etc.); an agreement on how to change any of these agreements; and an agreement on how to disagree. If such rules are not agreed upon, the problems may be immense, as the events in some African, South American or Asian countries, and also the frequent wars about access to the throne in England's early years illustrate.

The foundations of social order may be one of the following, or of a composite and cumulative kind: theocratic, nepotistic, aristocratic, liberal democratic, social democratic, socialist, fascist, or absolute totalitarian. Of interest to sociology is the outcome that any change in social organisation produces, and in the context of the issues this book examines, the question arises as to what kinds of social problems such systems tend to generate. Any system of social order reflects a certain structure of power, the structure of dominant interests – that is, it is congruent with, say, the economic system and its dominant interests, or congruent with dominant religious interests. These interests are evident in the laws prohibiting conduct that challenges the system, such as laws on blasphemy, laws on incitement to racial hatred or racial vilification, or laws on property rights. For example, the majority of recorded offences against the law in Australia and in most countries consist of offences against property, which is defined by a variety of terms such as theft, robbery, breaking and entering, fraud, embezzlement, damage to property, trespass, and so on.

The social order acts as a facilitator of the system it reflects, maintaining and legitimating that system's operation by legitimating private property, private enterprise, the ownership of the means of production, or special privileges such as those enjoyed by churches, social welfare ('charitable') organisations or certain professions. In a democratic society where there are conflicting interests, the institutions of social order act as a regulatory force. Our legislative bodies – parliament, bureaucracy, local government, professional associations, trade unions and churches – all play a role in the maintenance of a particular social order, which is the order representing the dominant interests and the values these interests reflect.

Social order is maintained and enforced by certain mechanisms of social control. These may be divided into 'informal social control mechanisms' and 'formal social control apparatus'. Informal social control mechanisms include social mores, and social institutions such as the family, schools, the Church, local communities, social class, occupational groups and peer groups. Informal social order may be seen as akin to social morality, common social values or common interests. The formal social control apparatus includes the code of law, police, courts, correctional agencies, and professions such as social work, psychiatry and teaching.

What distinguishes the formal social control apparatus is the power of violence held by its members, and given to them by the authority of the state – that is, the power in certain circumstances to apply physical coercion or disposition over people through arrest, incarceration, removal of a child from family surroundings, or bodily invasion (e.g. by medical examination or surgical procedure). In contemporary industrialised societies, the formal social control apparatus extends well beyond the traditional tripartite structure of police, courts and prisons, and is diffused among the human services, with the helping professions being prominent participants. However, as noted earlier, social control is implicit in any form of social organisation or social institution. It is inherent in social life.

Social Order in a Historical Perspective

Viewed in a historical perspective, issues of social order show some changes over time, but there is also demonstrable continuity. For example, certain social institutions such as the family and organised religions have shown themselves to be remarkably resilient in being able to adjust to changing social and economic conditions and maintaining their power, even strengthening it at times. The growth of fundamentalism in Christian and Islamic religions may be seen as an example of such adaptation or growth. On the other hand, political institutions are vulnerable to change. For example, absolute power, although not currently acceptable in prevailing world opinion, still exists in some countries and is invoked from time to time in various other places. Not so long ago, it was accepted almost universally.

There is also a discernible long-term evolutionary trend that may be identified as a tension or, at times, as an uneasy accommodation between the formally regulated social order and what may be called an 'informal (anarchical)' social order. An 'ideal model' of this trend is illustrated in Figure 9.1. This model postulates four 'ideal' societies in a historical time-perspective: two ideal 'early' societies in which social structure is simple and social conduct is uniform; and two ideal 'future' societies in which social structure and social conduct are diverse. In the early society 'O^1', social conduct is seen as uniform and guided or regulated by informal social controls such as traditions and simple religious beliefs – a society of Rousseau's 'noble savages'. In the early society 'O', uniform conduct is regulated and enforced by a monistic ideology in a totalitarian or theocratic state, perhaps best illustrated by the parable of the Garden of Eden. Society 'X' represents an ideal postmodern or future society in which conduct is diverse but is made acceptable by a libertarian 'live and let live' principle, and is not subject to any formal controls – a society in which the state has 'withered' in the Marxian vision. In society 'X^1', social conduct is diverse, but the diversity is regulated and enforced by state bureaucracy – a perfect bureaucracy in the Weberian ideal model. It is postulated in this model that, in the historical time-perspective, the movement from the early societies of simple structures and uniform social conduct to societies with complex structures and diverse conduct has progressed in two directions: the movement from regulated to unregulated social conduct has been followed by regulatory laws and executory powers to enforce them. This process may be clearly observed in contemporary industrialised societies.

Figure 9.1: Conceptual Model of Social Order

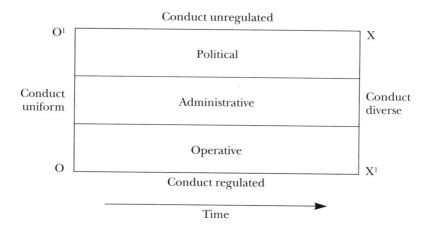

Notes: O   Monistic, totalitarian or theocratic society ('the Garden of Eden')
O[1]   Simple, unregulated society (Rousseau's 'noble savage')
X   Perfect anarchy (Marxian 'withered' state)
X[1]   Perfect bureaucracy (Weberian 'ideal' model)
O→X   Development of informal (unregulated) diversity
O[1]→X[1]   Development of formal (regulated) diversity

Social Order in Contemporary Industrialised Societies

One of the characteristics of the contemporary industrialised society
is an ever-increasing differentiation of social conduct, or action. The
differentiation occurs in social values, in attitudes to social institutions
such as the family, religion, government and the law, and in tastes in
music, dress, and cultural and recreational pursuits. The boundaries of
differentiation are usually maintained by society's informal control
mechanisms such as socialisation, customs and traditions, peer control,
or broader public approval or disapproval. However, when the differentiation exceeds certain normatively defined and accepted boundaries, informal social controls are replaced and reinforced by formal
controls and regulatory mechanisms. Foremost among these mechanisms is regulation by legislation. Each year, governments make laws
and amend existing laws as a means of bringing some of the new or
emerging forms of social activity under the political control of the state.

The extent to which laws affect, modify, control, constrain or prevent
the social activities of the public depends not only on legislation but also
on the means used to enforce such legislation at the operative level. It
also depends to a certain extent on the degree of acceptance of a given

law by society. A law may be effective in controlling people's social conduct by virtue of its existence alone. People may act or not act in a certain way simply because there is or is not 'a law against it'. In such situations, a law acquires the characteristics of informal social control, indicating that the value or values upheld by the law are accepted by the public as a guide to social conduct. If this is not the case, the law is then enforced by the rules of administrative mechanisms and applied at the operative level by appropriate personnel armed with legislative authority and specialised knowledge and skills.

In the contemporary industrialised societies there are two kinds of laws or formal rules of conduct: laws that are 'explicitly prohibitive', and laws that are 'selectively prohibitive' or 'regulatory'. Explicitly prohibitive laws are those that proscribe certain actions such as the killing of a person or appropriating a person's property without that person's permission. These laws are reflections of the dominant values of society.

However, a feature of contemporary legislation is not so much its prohibitory character but its regulatory character. Much of this legislation regulates social activities by prescribing how, when, where and by whom a certain activity may occur and the instances in which it may not occur. For example, abortion may be allowed to be practised only in certain circumstances and be performed only by certain specifically authorised persons; films with an 'R' rating may be publicly viewed only by adults; and certain medications may be taken only on the authority and prescription of a medical practitioner who is registered as such by a state law. The mechanisms of regulation extend far beyond what is normally perceived as the apparatus of social control – that is, the police, the courts and so on. Car parking inspectors, forest rangers, building inspectors for local government – all have certain state-sanctioned regulatory power.

Most of the important social control powers – regulatory powers – are vested in professions. For example, among the helping or 'caring' professions is the medical profession: it is the foremost profession vested with state authority in certain areas of society. Medical practitioners do not simply look after people's health. They have specific powers in the sphere of public health. They have the authority to determine whether a person is ill and may be legitimately absent from work, whether a person should receive compensation for injury at work, or whether a person should be treated with potentially dangerous drugs. In the branch of the medical profession called psychiatry, participation in law enforcement is especially powerful in certain situations, as the opinion of a psychiatrist may determine whether or not a person is found guilty of an offence, and whether that person is deprived of freedom by being removed from society. In countries where there is still a death penalty for a killing defined as murder (e.g. the United States), it is the psychiatrist whose opinion often means life or death for the accused.

However, the medical profession is only one of many professions that play important roles in the social control apparatus and that are endowed with special power by the state. For example, under the provisions of the *South Australian Children's Protection Act 1993*, a large number of occupations are mandatorily required to report suspicions of child abuse or neglect. These provisions include teaching staff in schools and universities. In addition to professions and occupations specifically mentioned, the Act includes 'any other person who is an employee of, or a volunteer in, a Government department, agency or instrumentality, or a local government or non-government agency, that provides health, welfare, child care or residential services wholly or partly for children, being a person who is engaged in the actual delivery of those services to children; or holds a management position in the relevant organisation'. The Act offers full protection of identity and protection from proceedings against the person who reports a suspected case, and there is a provision for a fine of $2000 for non-compliance. In conducting an investigation of reported (or suspected) child abuse, the personnel of South Australia's Department for Family and Community Services are authorised to 'enter, remain in and search (but not break into) premises or place; take photographs, films or videos; require people to provide information; require examination', and perform other related tasks. Under certain circumstances, these officers can break into premises with the authority of a magistrate's warrant, but in special circumstances they can do so without a warrant. Similar Acts are operative in all Australian states.

Social Order and Social Control as a Process

Social order is maintained by a process of interaction between the informal and formal mechanisms of social control. This process can be illustrated by identifying the activities that take place at the three levels of social organisation, illustrated in Figures 1.1, 3.1 and 9.1. The relevant activities are illustrated in Figure 9.2.

Most of us, in going about our everyday lives, engage in conduct that is determined by our socialisation and our knowledge of what is or is not acceptable in our society – that is, our knowledge and internalisation of social values and social mores. Our conduct is also regulated by our knowledge of the formal laws. We follow these laws either because we agree with them, or because we do not necessarily agree with them, but feel morally obliged to follow them or are aware of the penalties for breaking them.

Most of the time, we find ourselves in the social/political sphere (see the top section in Figure 9.1) – a state in which our conduct is regulated by the function of *indirect* social control or supervision. However, when we step into our car and go out on the road, or when we enter a public office building, other formal social institution, or any public place, we find ourselves more in the administrative sphere, where social control and supervision are more *direct*. We follow road traffic authority rules, we dress in what we consider to be appropriate attire, and we conduct ourselves in a manner we know to be acceptable in those places.

A significant change occurs in our social conduct once we engage in highly regulated activities that bring us into direct contact with authority at the operative level. This contact may be with the direct authority of the state, a 'delegated' authority of the state, or the authority of a legitimate business that conducts business activities with the legal approval of the state laws. The contact may be face to face, by telephone, or by written communication. For example, we make such contact when renewing our driver's licence, applying for a passport, filling out our income tax return, or being stopped on the road by police and requested to take a breathalyser test. We are in such contact, although it is rather one-directional, when we are in a public place and under the scrutiny of television cameras monitored from a chamber that may be far away. The ultimate direct, mostly one-directional contact with authority at the operative level is that which occurs in a total institution, such as the experience of detention in a prison where contact with authority is complete 24-hour surveillance carried out with the assistance of electronic technology – a perfect Bentham's panopticon (Goffman 1961, Foucault 1977). In this situation, one's behaviour is not only under constant surveillance but is also constrained by rigid rules and penalties for breaking them.

Complete surveillance, which places individuals under the authorities' 'gaze', now also takes a different form. People in receipt of income support from the public purse forfeit much of the freedom that the rest of society takes for granted. In addition to requirements for compulsory frequent reporting and form-filling, and disclosure of some quite intimate personal details to the authorities, income-support recipients also surrender details of their financial affairs, such as bank accounts and taxation returns. Their personal activities can also come under scrutiny through official visitation to their homes by the authorities, and questions about their personal relationships. Furthermore, the public is frequently encouraged to report to authorities any instance of suspected cheating or fraud. In effect, the income-support recipients not only surrender some rights of citizenship that the rest of society jealously guards, but each recipient's personal morality and integrity are seen and felt to be under suspicion and subject to the possibility of ongoing surveillance (see Chapter 8). Thus, unlike the lives of most of the public, whose daily activities take place mostly in the social/political sphere and in the administrative sphere (but only occasionally in the operative sphere), the lives of people who are confined in total institutions or who receive income support from the public purse take place either totally or predominantly in the operative sphere. The control apparatus of the state enters their private domain and exerts surveillance and control over their daily activities. Thus it appears that the more the field of public sector service provision is reduced and the market takes over the affairs of the affluent population, the more the state enters the private domain of the poor. The distance between the social world of the 'seduced' and the social world of the 'repressed' (discussed later in this chapter) grows wider (Bauman 1987).

Social order is maintained at all three levels of social organisation and may be strengthened or relaxed at any of the three levels or at all three levels. These processes are presented schematically in Figure 9.2. The three levels are arbitrarily divided as shown in Figure 9.2 into the regulated area of social conduct (area A) and unregulated area (area B). A greater area of regulated conduct can be achieved by legislation designed to bring under control a particular area of social conduct that has been previously unregulated. As the legislation is being

Figure 9.2: Methods of Regulating Modes of Conduct

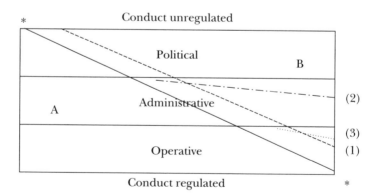

Notes: A   Regulated area
        B   Unregulated area
        (1) Increase of regulation by legislation
        (2) Increase of regulation by administrative change
        (3) Increase of regulation by operative change
        *   Division between regulated and unregulated areas

implemented, it increases the regulated area at all three levels of social organisation (line (1)). Examples of such action can be seen in the legislation that requires the wearing of seatbelts in cars, or the requirement of health warning signs to be printed on all tobacco products. Some expansion in regulation of conduct may be achieved by administrative measures, without changing legislation (line (2)). Most legislation provides for an area of administrative interpretation, regulation and discretion, which facilitates the conversion of the political decision into a technical task or problem. Regulations by public administration are frequently made, effectively expanding the regulated area of social conduct at the operative level as well, while the legislation itself (which provides the legal basis for the regulation of the given activity) remains unchanged. A typical example would be a decision restricting traffic in certain areas of the city, a requirement for additional details when applying for a permit to hold a public meeting, or an increase in the frequency of health inspections in certain business premises. Finally, an expansion in the regulated area may be effected solely at the operative level (line (3)). This may be done by administrative direction or by individual decisions of people working at the operative level, such as police officers, social workers or health inspectors. Police may decide to increase their surveillance of certain parts of the city, social workers may visit a single-parent family more often than is usually expected, and health inspectors may decide to be more thorough in their inspection of certain premises.

Certainly, as the extent of the regulation of social conduct may be increased in scope or intensity, it may also be lessened by the same forms of action. However, reduction in the areas of regulated activity takes place more frequently by administrative or operative decisions than by legislative acts. Changing or repealing legislation is a cumbersome task, and governments as well as administrators often prefer a piece of legislation to remain in force 'just in case it may be needed', but they may cease to enforce it, or enforce it with less intensity. Also, legislation that is 'on the books' but is not necessarily enforced serves as a reminder to the public, for example, that such and such conduct is illegal and that the law may be enforced at any time. Such legislation may also serve as a guide to social conduct.

Social Order and Social Control Over Time

The issues of social order, law making, law breaking and law enforcement have always been problematic. Living in society always means establishing certain rules, which are necessary sometimes for the sheer survival of the society. Rule making means establishing boundaries of acceptable social conduct. Once these boundaries are established, the question arises: what is to be done when someone breaks the rules – that is, when someone's social conduct goes beyond the established boundaries? Throughout history and even now, societies have used a variety of methods to maintain social order and social control. Rule breakers have been punished by various means such as torture, incarceration, banishment, branding, ridicule, forms of expropriation, or death (Foucault 1977). This issue is of particular significance in Australia because the English conquest of this country took place for the purpose of establishing a prison colony: European society in Australia began as a prison. This seems to have affected people's thinking on such things as law and order, and particularly punishment, which to this day has some features of being in the proverbial time warp. Reminders of convict times are part of the landscape: tourist attractions in other countries are medieval castles or ancient temples, while comparable tourist attractions in Australia are 19th century convicts' prisons.

A question often asked in relation to social control and law enforcement is: 'Has there been progress in this area?' If by progress we mean changes for the 'better' – that is, more humane, effective or suchlike – then there is no easy answer. We no longer execute law breakers, although demands for a death penalty are again increasing. The rope still has its advocates, as do whipping and other similar measures. The simplistic belief that 'tough measures' will be effective in maintaining social order tends to be promoted and has considerable public appeal: it also seems to win elections. What is meant by 'effective' is not made clear, either. We need to see current measures of punishment in the context of the time, in the same way that we have to look at law breaking in the context of the time. For this reason, the notion of 'progress' is not a very useful one by which to arrive at a definitive answer.

The perennial question of utmost relevance to social order, and one that should always be kept in mind while examining the issues of social order and social control, is the old Roman question: *'Quis custodiet ipsos custodes?'* – 'Who guards these guardians?' As a means of understanding the working of the system of social order – its manifest purpose, compared to the purpose and interests of the guardians who operate it – an approach such as that demonstrated earlier is essential. It is also important to note, as discussed in Chapters 3 and 4, that at each level of social organisation the manifest purpose is not always the same as the assumed purpose, or real (extant) purpose of activities, whether such purposes consist of legislation, administration or direct service delivery. Legislators make laws: administrators enforce them. In the process of law enforcement, the administrators also in effect make policy by adapting the laws to established bureaucratic procedures and then interpreting and applying them at the operative level. This also means that the intent of the law, as perceived by legislators, is accommodated, or converted, to the values and norms of the administrative organisation. The intent is then further converted to the intervention methods and values of the people working at the operative level. The conversion process and its effects are of particular significance in the area of social order, as attitudes towards social order and the values underpinning these attitudes tend traditionally to be more rigidly held by many people than attitudes and values in other areas of social concern.

We also need to keep in mind the nature of social phenomena – that is, the lack of separation between their existence and the perception of the observer. In issues of social order and social control it is the interpretation and application of the manifest purpose of the apparatus of social control that needs to be the focus of study. The reason for this is that *perceptions and interpretations of social phenomena in the system of social control are authoritative perceptions and interpretations performed, and acted upon, with the sanction of the law.* They are social constructs, but they have direct and concrete consequences for individuals and groups who become the subjects, or rather objects, of the system's activities.

Social Order in a Class Society

A system of social order and social control always reflects the power structure in society and the interests and values embedded in that structure. As there is no known society that exhibits complete equality, there is no social order that treats all people equally. In a class society such as Australia, and in other industrialised societies, the social order favours the affluent, the educated and the powerful. Equality before the law is upheld as a principle but in practice things are quite different. Our system of social order and social control is certainly class based. For a sociological analysis of these issues, maintaining the perspective on the distribution of power in the social structure is essential. For example, in earlier times a male child of the aristocracy who misbehaved was punished by being made to watch a boy from the village being whipped for the aristocrat's own misbehaviour, the memory of this practice being retained in the term 'whipping boy'. (We must assume that girls in aristocratic families never did anything wrong.) It is therefore appropriate to ask whether social order and social control in the contemporary class society are administered and enforced on a class basis – that is, are the poor punished for the offences of the affluent. This question may appear strange at first, but it is quite plausible. Whether we look at data on family violence, child abuse, crime, youth offenders or unemployment, the common factor in all these problems of social order is the low social class of the affected population. Indeed, social problems are perceived, analysed, interpreted and intervened in in class terms, not as social phenomena pertaining to the whole of society, but as phenomena related to the specific, implicitly inferior characteristics of the affected populations. In the concerns expressed about the poor, biological determinism and Social Darwinism do not seem to be out of place. Occasionally, it is suggested that some of these problems occur across all social strata, but this is not upheld by the evidence.

The class nature of social order is most clearly evident in the fields of crime and criminal justice. In Australia, the majority of people in prisons were unemployed at the time of their arrest. Indeed, the most consistent common social characteristics of people in prisons are unemployment at the time of arrest, being an indigenous Australian, and prior imprisonment. In the prison census conducted in 1991, close to two-thirds (64.6%) of all prisoners were unemployed at the time of arrest, and 56.9 per cent had been in prison before. Prisoners from an indigenous Aboriginal background accounted for 14.9 per cent, although the indigenous population accounts for less than two per cent of the total population of Australia (Walker 1992). In the law enforcement apparatus, as unemployed people are processed from apprehension through courts and then to prison, their numbers as a proportion of all people undergoing this process increase with each step of the process. For example, official statistics for 1992–93 in South Australia show that the percentage of unemployed people who were before the courts, having been charged with offences, rose from 50.9 per cent in Magistrates' courts, to 58.3 per cent in Supreme and District courts, and to 61.9 per cent of commitments to prisons (Attorney-General's Department 1994). In reports prepared in correctional agencies (such as pre-sentence reports), comments about 'irregular work history' are frequently made, unwittingly conveying an impression that unemployment goes hand in hand with the tendency towards criminality. The association between 'poor work history' and conflict with the law starts early in adolescence, as is shown by the data from juvenile courts, where the most consistent and frequent characteristic of young people charged with offences is their early school leaving and unemployment. Unemployed young people account for one-third to one-half of all young people appearing in courts (Nocella 1994).

The class nature of the social order and social control is also evident in the spatial distribution of certain characteristics of the population. Unemployment, low income and high frequency of family dislocation are paralleled with the incidence of law breaking. Examining these associations in the characteristics of the population in Adelaide's metropolitan area, Gail Smith found a significant correlation (Spearman

Rho +.918) between the rates of unemployment and the rates of appearance in courts of summary jurisdiction. Low household income was another telling indicator (1995:46–51). These data are not surprising, as spatially located clusters of high levels of problems of social order are a world-wide phenomenon. Loic Wacquant writes that:

> In nearly every major First World metropolis, a particular urban district or township has 'made a name for itself' as that place where disorder, dereliction, and danger are said to be the normal order of the day. The South Bronx and Brownsville in New York City, Les Minguettes and Vaux-en-Velin near Lyons, London's Brixton and East End, Gutleutviertel in Hamburg, Rinkeby on the outskirts of Stockholm, and Neue West in Rotterdam – the list gets longer by the year.   *(1996:125)*

The ineffectiveness of social control measures in such areas is well known. In Australia, extreme forms of social disorder in low socio-economic areas are probably not as high in level as in the cities mentioned by Wacquant, but nevertheless there are clusters of disorder in every large city. Also, the prevailing belief is that the disorder is becoming progressively worse and that law enforcement agencies do not appear to be effective in arresting this trend. A solution has been sought in increasing penalties on those individuals who are brought to court and found guilty of offences of violence or offences against property. As a result, since the early 1980s, an unprecedented number of new prisons have been built in Australia, and the prison population has significantly increased during the past decade.

The increase in the prison population has not occurred solely because of the increase in the recorded incidence of law breaking; in relation to the country's population, the number of serious recorded offences (homicide, robbery, burglary, assault, fraud, etc.) increased from 1983–84 to 1993–94 by 30.4 per cent (Australian Institute of Criminology 1996). The courts seem to be more inclined to impose prison sentences, and these are longer prison sentences than in past decades. Such concepts as 'the truth in sentencing' means that remissions in the imposed length of imprisonment (e.g. for good behaviour) are being progressively eliminated, further increasing the number of people in prison.

Another significant factor in the operation of the legal system, which accentuates class inequality, is the adversarial system of justice administration. It is a well-known fact that good legal representation in court lessens the accused person's likelihood of being found guilty, or, if the person is found guilty, it lessens the likelihood of their imprisonment. However, legal representation is expensive, and legal aid is not always available (and when it is available, often produces a rather simple, ritualistic defence). In the majority of cases dealing with offences against property (e.g. stealing and burglary), which are the most frequent offences dealt with in criminal jurisdiction, the accused person pleads guilty to the offence.

The operation of the adversarial system pervades Australian social and political institutions and their operation. It also influences people's social attitudes towards one another. The dichotomous nature of this system and of the attitudes the system generates is particularly problematic in a society of great ethnic and cultural diversity. Functions and attitudes are reduced to 'either/or' dichotomous alternatives and to 'winners and losers'. Even in the Family Court, where the 'no fault' principle has been introduced in divorce proceedings, adversarial attitudes are clearly evident in the disputes about property settlement and the custody of children.

As economic and social inequality increases, law enforcement follows suit. Pressures develop for imposing increasingly severe penalties for law breaking, and interesting concepts are introduced into the language of criminal justice, such as 'truth in sentencing' or 'three strikes and you're out' (or rather 'in', because it means incarceration). Prisons are now profit-making activities in the private sector. In the field of child and family welfare the focus of problem identification is narrowed to the family. Concern with domestic violence and child abuse revolves solely around internal family relationships, focusing almost exclusively on poor working-class areas and distracting attention from an ever-increasing impoverishment of the social and economic environment, as well as the natural environment, in which these families live.

In considering the issues of social order in a broad societal perspective, it is evident that the problem of social order in a class society is essentially the problem of unequal distribution of power in the social structure. In addressing this issue, Eva Etzioni-Halevy puts forward what she calls some of the 'elementary assumptions pertaining to power and elites'. She says: 'power is based on the control of, or having at one's disposal, resources on which others are dependent, of which they have a need, or which may otherwise affect their lives ... Elites are simply those people or groups of people who hold power and influence, i.e. have disproportionate control of resources in a given sociopolitical system' (1990:208). As she further explains:

> For any orderly, contemporary, state controls the main means or resources of coercion, which in turn lends it the ability to control a great variety of other resources, whether or not it exercises this control in actual practice. No less important is the fact that the state and its elites also command resources of 'pure' power. Such power is backed up by coercion when all else fails ... coercion 'constitutes the final court of appeal' in human affairs. But this

'pure' power is not straightforward coercion. More immediately, it is based on the control of structures engaged in regulatory and co-ordinatory activities, such as policy making, legislation, adjudication, administration and defence.

(1990:208–9)

Closely related to the power of coercion, Etzioni-Halevy argues, the contemporary Western state controls major economic or material resources, and the economic power based on these resources is also ultimately backed up by coercion. This power gives the state the ability to absorb discontent and protest, so that the state does not have to resort to overt coercion except in certain extreme circumstances. For example, symbolic resources (such as the need for public safety) may be used negatively to denigrate, discredit or delegitimate a protest movement.

Social Order and Postmodernity

The class structure of the industrialised 'free' market societies has not disappeared with the emergence of postmodern perspectives and the corresponding plurality or division of interests. In the perspective and interpretation of the postmodern trends, some sociologists have identified a new dichotomous social structure of the 'seduced' and the 'repressed'. Seduced populations are those who are intensively courted by the market, which aims to ensure from them a high, sustained level of consumption. The repressed are those who 'cannot be regulated by the mechanism of seduction' because they do not possess the means to consume market products. Instead, the repressed become the object of 'law and order' bureaucracies. Hence, the typical postmodern society is a society of 'two nations'. Zygmunt Bauman writes that:

> 'The two nations, mark two' society is constituted by the opposition between 'seduction' and 'repression' as means of social control, integration and reproduction of domination. The first is grounded in 'market dependency': replacement of old life-skills by the new ones, which cannot be effectively employed without the mediation of the market . . . The second is grounded in a normative regulation pushed to the extreme, penetration of the 'private' sphere to an ever growing degree, disempowering of the objects of normative regulation as autonomous agents. *(1992:112)*

Social order and social control in the 'seduced' social classes are thus exerted by the market: consumption of goods and services becomes a necessity for ensuring the lifestyle of the class collectivity. It becomes an obligation of class solidarity. The credit card opens doors in society, and its use pleases the bank manager. To the repressed class, the social world is the world of state bureaucracies and non-government agencies, which provide the necessities of life and sometimes give friendly advice, while impressing the view on recipients that any aspirations towards reaching that other world are unfounded because of the limitations inherent in the recipients' personal attributes.

It needs to be acknowledged that the policies of economic rationalism have been demonstrably successful in terms of maintaining material well-being for the majority of the population. This is evident in the high rate of consumption, but such success is achieved at the price of creating a growing surplus population – a 'human residue'. This logical outcome of capitalism is acknowledged (although not always explicitly) by the disciples of economic rationalism, yet they justify it as an unavoidable 'small price' to pay for the benefits enjoyed by the majority. It is the residue's extent, or numerical size, that they see as a 'problem', for two reasons. First, this human residue has to be maintained at a certain minimum standard of living, lest its presence becomes too obvious. This means some cost but also some benefits for the economy, as the recipients of benefits and pensions act as 'middlepeople' of economic transactions, in that they keep the money only for a few days and feed it back into the economy. The regularity of their consumption of goods and services is an important stabilising factor in economic activity. Second, concern over the human residue is political. It is politically very important to ensure that marginalised sections of the population do not become entirely cut off from the mainstream. Such separation is politically dangerous, as may be seen by the riots that occur now and again in the United States, in England and in other countries of the industrialised world. In Australia, marginalised sections of the population have so far not become a big problem (as a collectivity) in the maintenance of social order; however, their numbers in courts and in prisons indicate that their marginalisation has been converted into individual pathologies.

The Helping Professions in Social Control

The increasing complexity of the postmodern society means an increasing diversity of social conduct, but also an increasing range of mechanisms of formal social control. Anne Edwards (1988) points out that social control can be exercised by a variety of methods and under various labels. Such control may be physical, psychological, economic, moral, ideological or political. In contemporary industrialised societies, formal social control is exercised mainly by social institutions located in three systems: legal-judicial, medical-psychiatric, and welfare. Each of the three systems is manifestly concerned with a specific area of social order, but the areas they aim to control are closely interrelated. What in the perspective of the legal-judicial system is seen as crime may be seen as illness in the medical-psychiatric system, and as dependency in the welfare system. We need to accept, Edwards says, that 'whenever we use such terms as persuade, restrain, discipline, coerce, penalise, reward, direct, manage or regulate to describe aspects of the activities of individuals, groups, organisations or society, we are talking about the exercise of social control over people's bodies, minds and behaviour' (1988:1).

In this wide range of concepts and corresponding intervention methods, the helping professions play an increasingly important role. Psychiatrists, psychologists, specialist teachers, social workers and social researchers have become an integral part of the formal social control apparatus. As Stanley Cohen observes:

> Professionals in systems such as mental health, crime control or social work are locked into a network of bureaucratic and corporate interests. They are 'mind bureaucrats' – a new class of whose interests range from universities, foundations, professional associations, corporate legal firms, pharmaceutical companies, crime-technology manufacturers and central or local bureaucracies. *(1985:163)*

Cohen observes that in the tasks these professions perform in the field of social control they exercise considerable power over the subjects of their attention, but that this power tends to be 'anarchic and unpredictable. There is no firm knowledge base, no technology, nor even any agreed criteria of success or failure' (1985:165). The significant part of social control is exercised not so much by the visible police on the street as by 'eternal case conferences, diagnostic and allocation board or pre-sentence investigation unit' (1985:185).

The most significant effect of the helping professions' involvement in the formal structure of social control is the legitimation of the dominant power structure. Psychiatrists and psychologists seek explanations exclusively in the pathology of the person they examine, test and attempt to 'cure'; the intervention methods used by social workers are also focused on the person regarded as the 'client'. The conversion of problems of social order into problems of personal pathologies achieves completion in the intervention methods practised by these professions. Indeed, the extent to which social workers especially have been drawn into the apparatus of social control is remarkable. It is not surprising that social work, as a profession, has become such an instrument of the dominant power structure and its policies of economic rationalism; social work, like any other profession whose specialised knowledge and professional authority is sanctioned by the state, has become part of the dominant power structure. What is remarkable is social workers' constantly expressed belief that the work they do helps the poor and the disadvantaged, and so is instrumental in lessening the inequalities of the system (which social workers, in effect, serve to legitimate). Undoubtedly, this belief is genuine, but it is intellectually blinkered, and maintained by professional socialisation.

It is to be expected that prevailing ideologies, theories, professional attitudes and political movements will always reflect what may be called the 'temper of the times'. The dominant ideology of the world in the 1990s is the ideology of the 'free' market, and this ideology, underpinned by economic and political power, pervades most public activities. Along with other professions, social work has not remained unscathed, although it has adjusted to the dominant ideology in an interesting way. The profession projects some noble ideas in its rhetoric, like self-determination, concern for the disadvantaged, social justice and 'empowerment'. However, in social work practice, three features are clearly identifiable: the disappearance of social perspective on social problems; an increasing and apparently willing acceptance of the role of social control along class lines; and the legitimation of the profession's activities, not by the application of the rich mine of available knowledge in the social sciences (especially in sociology), but rather by the use of what would best be described as 'self-validating practice wisdom'. This apparent contradiction is not confined to the social work profession, although it is particularly problematic in social work because of that profession's repeatedly expressed commitment to social justice. The acknowledgement of this contradiction and the inherent dilemma of value-incompatibility is the essential first step towards the possibility of change.

CHAPTER 10

The Theory of Residualist Conversion: Does it Meet the Test?

In this book, we have sought to provide one complete theoretical framework within which social problems can be analysed. This perspective perceives social problems as social phenomena that emerge in society as a form of threat to the values and interests dominant in that society, and that evoke certain methods of intervention designed to attenuate, control or solve such problems. In the sociological literature concerned with social problems, there has been a division between studies that focus on identification and explanation of social problems, and studies that focus on methods of intervention (the latter studies being more frequent in literature emanating from the helping professions, especially social work). We have attempted to bring these two aspects and two disciplines (theoretical and the applied) together as we consider that studies of social problems are a form of intervention, often the first form of intervention. Also, most sociological theories of social problems that have been formulated over the past century have taken as their main focus various forms of social deviance, with such deviance being perceived as a threat to the social order. While we acknowledge the importance of such perspectives, because a threat to social order is perhaps the most serious threat a society might encounter, we have aimed to focus our attention on the kinds of social problems that occur in society in the course of that society's 'normal' activities and pursuits, especially the pursuits of the dominant social strata and social classes. From this perspective, we formulated the theory that we call the theory of residualist conversion of social problems. Stated in a form of a broad hypothesis, the theory reads:

> Social problems are social conditions arising out of structural and cultural arrangements in society that cause social and economic malfunctioning of those arrangements and that are perceived to be in some way a threat to the

established order and power structure. These 'negative conditions' are by-products of the values and goals that a society, especially its dominant power structure, seeks to pursue and maintain: they constitute a logical 'negative residue' of the activities directed at the pursuit of such dominant values, interests and corresponding goals.   *(See Chapters 1 and 5.)*

We consider that our assertion in this hypothesis – that social problems emerge logically, not from some kind of deviant behaviour, but as a 'negative residue' from the pursuit of dominant values and interests – constitutes a radical but logical departure from the conventional theories of social problems, in which social problems are perceived as forms of deviance or pathology. This shift in theoretical perspective brings into focus, and presents an intellectual as well as ethical challenge for, the currently prevailing theories and methods of intervention in social problems.

The aim of this chapter is to validate the perspective advanced earlier that was illustrated by the examination of various areas of societal arrangements and activities through which dominant goals are pursued and social problems are predictably created. By restating our main proposition about the nature of social problems and elaborating on the arguments advanced earlier, we aim to identify with greater clarity some of the questions and implications our theory raises for sociology and for the professions whose members are involved in the various fields of social problems. In relation to sociology, our argument is that sociology, as a living social science, needs to focus more intensively and systematically on the analyses of 'intervening variables' through which societal issues, many of which are political in nature, are converted into the problems of individuals and interpreted in terms of the personal or group characteristics of those people. In relation to the helping professions whose members are actively engaged in these conversion processes, our aim is to demonstrate the social/political significance of their activities – namely, that the act of such 'helping' also entails the removal of social problems from the political sphere and converts them into the personal problems of those in affected populations, with the added stigma of personal pathology.

With the benefit of the study of a number of social problems, we need to add the following observations:

If the negative effects of a social problem are experienced mainly or exclusively by the lower and socially marginalised social classes, such social problems are likely to be converted first from problems with a political status into technical problems requiring action at an administrative level. They are then subject to further conversion into individual problems of personal pathology of the population experiencing the problem, and will be dealt with as such at the operative level. However, if the problem produces negative effects on the politically influential middle classes, the response is likely to take the form of a re-conversion of the problem into a political issue, and the solution to the problem will be sought at the political level of social organisation.

The direction that a response to a problem is likely to take depends on a number of factors: the power of the affected population to demonstrate successfully that the problem is indeed a political issue and to exert pressure on the government to accept responsibility for the problem's solution; the claimants' ability to substantiate their demands through arguments based on articulated needs and rights, as well as the common good; and the claimants' ability to successfully maintain the perception of the problem as a 'collective' problem that impedes that collectivity's performance of their legitimate social roles. The success or failure of the affected population in achieving a social construction of the problem incorporating these three factors will determine the outcome. The problem will either be acknowledged as a political issue and will be solved by a political decision, or will remain in the political arena for further contestation; or it will be converted into personal problems of the affected population and will be treated as personal pathology. We examined these processes in Chapters 3 and 6, and illustrated them schematically in Figures 3.1 and 6.1.

The social problems we have used in this book as examples of analyses from the perspective of our theory of residualist conversion fall broadly into three categories: problems that are converted into problems of the populations experiencing them and that are treated as personal pathologies; problems that are successfully demonstrated to be social problems – that is, they are shown to be political issues and their solution is placed, or forced, into the hands of the government; and problems that remain in the contested sphere. We need to note, however, that social problems do not always fall neatly into one category or another. Some problems remain partly in one category and partly in another; others can move over time in one direction and then in another, influenced by a changing political climate, changing economic conditions or the fluctuating success of political lobbying. Using those examples of social problems examined in previous chapters (and with the addition of some others), the various categories may be classified as follows:

Problems Accepted and Solved at a Political Level

Examples of these are equal pay for both sexes, the sole parent pension, child care, and the issue of homosexual behaviour between consenting partners. The political legitimacy of all these demands was eventually accepted, against opposition, after long struggles. The demands were substantiated on the grounds of needs and rights, on the grounds of social justice, and on the grounds of economic gains for society. We cannot go into a detailed analysis of those struggles, however it is appropriate to note that in each case, legitimacy of the claims was obtained by a construction, or a re-construction, of the public's perspective on the issue. For example, acceptance of the sole parent pension was reached after a series of conversions. The first advance was achieved when it was accepted that an unmarried mother and other categories of women with dependent children (such as women separated or divorced, deserted wives, widows, and women whose husbands were in gaol) all had one common attribute – namely, they were *supporting mothers*. On recognition of this, the previously used 'public relief' (which was a discretionary payment) became a 'supporting mother's benefit'; then, on the recognition that some men were also supporting parents, the payment became a 'supporting parent's benefit', and finally the 'sole parent pension'. In Australia, this series of re-constructions also entailed a shift of responsibility from state governments to the federal government. Child care, and equal pay for both sexes both had a long story of political action – as did homosexuality, which was not only a crime but was regarded as a mental illness and was treated as such, often under the authority of a court order.

Problems Converted into Personal Problems

Examples of these are poverty, unemployment, child welfare, and gambling addiction. The source of these problems can be identified in the pursuit of certain values and goals, and in the corresponding allocation of resources. The underlying common factor in the first three problems is inequality, and the source of the fourth is in a state-conducted and state-promoted activity. The common factor in all four problems is the methods of intervention at the operative level, which are based on perceptions of certain personal pathologies in those experiencing these problems. Methods employed entail a range of personal services of a counselling and therapeutic nature, reinforced by surveillance and an implicit (and sometimes explicit) threat of withdrawal of income support, or other punitive sanctions. Even when there is some acknowlegement of structural or external causes of the problem, intervention remains in these cases at the operative level, substantiated at times by the argument that 'this is the best one can do'.

Problems in Contestation

In Australia, examples of social problems that continue to be contested would be issues of multiculturalism and the issue of land rights for the indigenous Australian population. Contestation in these two areas takes place at two levels of social organisation: in the context of Australian society as a whole, and in the context of government policy. In both areas of contestation, attitudes towards the legitimacy of claims change from time to time. Multiculturalism was accepted formally in the federal sphere, within certain conditions and parameters that were formulated in the *Agenda for a Multicultural Australia* in 1989, and operationalised by (or converted into) an 'Access and Equity' administrative implementation program. As discussed in Chapter 6, the implementation of the National Agenda program in the public sector was only partly successful, and since Australia's change of government in 1996, the policy of multiculturalism has been effectively abandoned. The term 'multiculturalism' itself has been withdrawn from the official vocabulary of the federal government and replaced by 'cultural diversity' or 'ethnic diversity'. As noted by Paul Kelly (1997), multiculturalism has become a 'curse word', being perceived as applying only to ethnic minorities but not to the Anglo-Australian population, and therefore as a threat to social cohesion. The federal government has also established a new advisory body, the National Multicultural Advisory Council, which is expected to formulate a new agenda for policy on ethnic diversity.

Similarly, the struggle of Aboriginal people to regain at least some parts of the land taken from them by conquest has been a long one, with limited success and with growing uncertainly about the outcome. Each new claim predictably meets with resistance and antagonism, and even when the High Court decides on the legitimacy of a claim, the government introduces legislation to countervail the Court's decision.

Three other problems examined in this book may be regarded as falling into a contested category: degradation of the natural environment, reduction of the public sphere, and the demise of the welfare state. The nature of each of these problems is contested in the public arena, but all three are linked to the same currently dominant goal endorsed by government policy – namely, the belief in the primacy of private interest and effort over public effort, and the pursuit of private profit. Degradation of the environment constitutes a threat to the very survival of the planet as a 'living thing', but the threat does not seem to be taken seriously enough by governments and dominant economic interests, as from their perspectives the magnitude of the threat does not outweigh immediate economic gains. The public sphere is decreasing in size because of the reduction of economic and social activities in the public services sector, and because of a corresponding change in perceptions of the value of the common good. The public sector's reduction, ostensibly for reasons of efficiency, is also in line with the ideological perspective of those in power; whenever it is demonstrated that a service in the public sector performs efficiently, an argument is raised that 'the state should not be in the business of conducting business'. As to the demise of the welfare state, it is clear that the state plays an important role in providing the infrastructure of social and material services, including income support for a significant proportion of the population. However, it is arguable whether these services are now provided primarily for their value as a support for the citizenry, or for their beneficial effect on the economic activity in the private sector. At this stage of development in this area, the most appropriate term to use would seem to be the 'post-welfare state'.

The conclusion from our analysis is clear – namely, if (as we argue) social problems arise at a societal level out of certain values and the corresponding pursuit of goals that are embodied in the dominant power structure, they can be solved only by changes in those values and goals. Such a solution would necessarily entail a change in the structure of power. However, more often than not, the dominant structure of power is preserved by organisational mechanisms that enable social problems to be converted from problems in the public sphere into a 'residue' in the form of personal problems of negatively affected populations. The 'residue' is then controlled by intervention methods that assist the affected population to adjust to their situation. The compliance of the affected population in turn legitimates the power structure, by demonstrating that the structure and its organisational apparatus have the means and methods to control the 'negative residue' without undue disturbance to the dominant social order.

Management of Human Resources

Methods of intervention in social problems are a form of management and control of society's human resources. The development and management of human resources is one of the key issues in the management of the economy, and also in addressing problems related to the labour market and unemployment. Historically, Australia's record in the human resources area has been rather poor, the inadequacy being evident mainly in its lack of development of these resources through education. In colonial days and in the early years of federation, education did not rank highly on state governments' lists of priorities. The federal government did not enter the field of education until the late 1950s, first offering assistance to private schools and then accepting partial responsibility for tertiary education.

The federal government did not accept full responsibility for tertiary education until 1972. Now, in the late 1990s, when the maintenance and further extension of tertiary education is of prime importance in the development of the economy in its transition to high-technology production, government commitment to maintaining responsibility for tertiary education is again under threat. At a time when it is demonstrably clear that post-secondary and particularly tertiary education is the main qualification for obtaining employment, one-half of the labour force in Australia still does not have any post-secondary qualifications, and the majority of unemployed people are in this category. A re-assessment of post-secondary and tertiary education and training curricula, coupled with increased investment in education and related research, would undoubtedly create a labour force that would provide the basis for technological advance and the establishment of new, high-technology industries with corresponding new employment opportunities.

The most comprehensive and promising program, designed to reduce unemployment and particularly bring back the long-term unemployed into the labour market, was the *Working Nation* program introduced in 1994 by the-then Labor Government (Keating 1994). However constructive the program might have been, it also had an element of compulsion built into the conditions that governed participation. The compulsory aspect of the program was based on the belief that long-term unemployment creates a severe negative effect, aggravating the perceived problem of an 'unwillingness to work'. The program aimed to overcome this expected difficulty by including certain conditions – namely, in addition to providing the unemployed with personal 'case managers' who were paid by results, there was also a clear warning, which was:

> penalties for failure to accept a job offer or attend an interview or a training course will be increased in line with the increased assistance being provided by the government. Penalties will increase with the duration of unemployment. They will increase if obligations are breached more than once.
>
> *(Keating 1994:126)*

The *Working Nation* program was reduced in scope after the change of government in 1996, and now there are no programs of any significance to attenuate the problem of unemployment, which has been acknowledged as a problem of utmost severity since the mid-1970s. Statements emanating from government sources promise an improvement in this situation, but such statements have been made now for many years without any tangible results. There is clearly a need for new perspectives, because it is extremely doubtful whether the 'big' problems like unemployment can be solved within the current political and economic paradigm. Levels of unemployment on the national scale ranging from seven to eleven per cent are probably the best that can be expected under current perspectives on the labour market, and in some schools of thought unemployment on that scale is close to what may be regarded as 'full employment'. Unemployment can be explained by many factors, but debates on this issue follow the same pattern – namely, that unemployment is expected to decrease if the gross domestic product (GDP) exceeds a certain rate of growth. No other measures of significance have been mooted. The organisational structure of the labour market has been very stable for some years, except for a mean reduction in hours worked per person through the introduction of part-time and casual work. However, unemployment would feasibly be reduced by structural change in the labour market. One such measure, for example, could be a re-assessment of the division between paid and unpaid work.

The existing division between paid and unpaid work is not based on any unchallengeable rational grounds: it is based on tradition, convention, interests and social values. In some instances, paid and unpaid work consist of the same activities; indeed, in many organisations and services, paid and unpaid work take place side by side. This is a common occurrence in health services, welfare or education, and especially in the broad field referred to as 'community work'. There are also interesting differences and paradoxes – for example, taking dogs for a walk is now frequently a paid occupation in some affluent areas of our cities, but taking an elderly person for a walk is performed by volunteers. Child care at home is unpaid, but child care in community-based centres is paid and is partly or entirely subsidised by public funds. While there will always be a place for voluntary labour, there is no valid economic or other reason why many such services should not be provided by paid labour. This is not a matter of economic priorities; it is a matter of politics and a matter of human values.

Figure 10.1 illustrates the various ways in which human resources are employed in society. Some of the activities listed constitute paid work, others indicate non-paid (voluntary) work. There is no intrinsically valid reason for maintaining the existing division. As an illustration, in addition to re-assessment of the division between paid and unpaid work, many other possibilities have been advanced from time to time, such as:

1 Shared work, in a variety of forms (e.g. working every other week)
2 Invention of new social needs to translate into wants so that goods and services can be produced to meet them

Figure 10.1: A Typology of the Use of Human Resources in Industrial Societies

| | Informal/formal division | |
	Informal	Formal
Type of Organisation — Primary groups	Domestic economy Family Friends Relatives Self-help groups	Family business (e.g. 'the corner shop') Co-operative skills exchange
Commercial	The 'black' labour market Drug trafficking 'Black' economy generally	Private sector labour market Private corporations Public corporations Self-employment Small business
Non-commercial	Local welfare organisations Cultural, educational, recreational activities Pressure groups (informal)	Pressure groups (formal) Formal welfare organisations Community service organisations (e.g. RSL, Rotary) Research 'think tanks' Educational, research, health organisations, etc.
Government	Lobby activities Informal advisory bodies and individuals	Commonwealth departments State departments Local departments Statutory bodies

Source: A. Jamrozik and C. Boland (1993), *Human Resources in Community Services: Conceptual Issues and Empirical Evidences*, Kensington NSW

3 Commodification of activities currently in the domestic economy
4 Redefinition of unemployment
5 Redefinition of paid and unpaid work
6 Reduction in market production for profit and increase in social production (e.g. production of long-term value, such as reforestation)
7 Redefinition of the relationship between markets and social life to make the markets fit into social life demands

Social Problems and Class Theory

In our analysis of social problems, we asserted that capitalist 'free' market societies are, by definition, class societies, and that class division remains the basic social division in such societies and is the main factor in social inequality. Our definition of social class uses Richard Titmuss's concept of differential 'command over resources through time'. While this definition might not be regarded as fitting neatly into either the Marxian or the Weberian concept of social class, it conveys clearly the structure of inequality in contemporary industrialised capitalist societies. 'Command over resources' is certainly highly differentiated in those societies, but it may be argued that differential access to resources is not necessarily a sufficient criterion for identification of class division. One might ask whether there are identifiable collectivities in contemporary industrialised societies that act as a 'class' – that is, collectivities that not only possess common characteristics such as occupation, income, education and so on, but that express collective values and interests. Do they see their interests to be in conflict with those of other classes, and do they engage in struggles to maintain or enhance their class position?

Such questions are frequently raised in sociological literature, as researchers attempt to discover to what extent and in which direction changes have occurred in the structure of labour markets, in family composition, in patterns of consumption, and in the formulation of social policies, and how these changes have affected the previous divisions in the social structures of those societies. For example, Stefan Svallfors has examined these issues in the context of Swedish society, taking into account the views and explanations of various theorists such as Ulrich Beck with his observations about 'risk societies' (1992), and Esping-Andersen with his comparative studies of welfare states in capitalist societies (1990). Svallfors notes that class theory has been challenged by postmodern concepts, by gender conflicts and by the growth of individualism. He notes particularly that 'in feminist discourse, it is implicitly argued that gender will, or has already become, an important social division crosscutting class demarcations' (1995:55). It is true, Svallfors acknowledges, that women are more directly involved in the welfare state, both as employees and as clients. However, it is exactly these two roles that constitute class divisions among women. Furthermore, if consumption is taken into consideration as a factor, then the division in that aspect of activity is certainly on class lines. Svallfors states that:

> The stability found in the cleavage structure is a finding that goes against much of the debate on recent changes. Neither those convinced that political differences between men and women will come to the foreground in times of welfare crisis, nor those believing that new consumption groups will replace class as constituting the most important social cleavage received much support from the analysis.   *(1995:69)*

Svallfors concludes by saying that 'social research would perhaps be better served by putting more effort into explaining the "remarkable persistence of class-linked inequalities and of class-differentiated patterns of social action, even within periods of rapid economic change at the level of economic structure, social institutions, and political conjunctures" than by searching for new structural cleavages or envisaging the end of class politics' (1995:71).

There are two points to note on this issue. First, gender conflict is a conflict *within* class or *about* class, and not a conflict *between* classes (Przeworski 1977). Second, social class is the outcome of the cumulative effect of complementary attributes. Furthermore, it is of relevance that the majority of people now in the helping professions are women, and that in intervention methods, class division between service providers and service recipients is quite clear. Social problems are clearly perceived in a class perspective, and this perspective can easily be observed in the interpretations of social problems by the helping professions and also in their methods of intervention – an observation recorded by such social analysts (writing mainly in the context of British society) as Julian Le Grand (1984), Fiona Williams (1989) and Rosemary Crompton (1993). Also in Britain, Gordon Marshall and Adam Swift have examined the argument and data of class inequality versus meritocracy and conclude that 'survey data suggesting that the effect of class origins on class destinations is only partially mediated by educational achievement. Class privilege can compensate for educational failure' (1993:187).

In Australia, a belief in classlessness and egalitarianism as the features of Australian society is a cherished myth, inherited from the colonial days and cultivated by the affluent. Now, the members of the affluent new middle class also deny the advantage of their class position. In that, they take the same attitude that wealthy people have displayed through the ages – namely, asserting that they are not really very wealthy and that money does not bring happiness anyway. Class division is a reality of Australian social life. For example, voting at elections in Australia is clearly on class lines. There might have been some changes in this pattern in the 1996 elections because of the influence of the arguments on multiculturalism, attitudes towards the indigenous population, and attitudes towards immigration from the neighbouring Asian countries, but the electoral map has remained largely undisturbed. Allowing for some fluctuations in voting patterns (due perhaps to specific local issues or personalities of the candidates), the broad pattern of voting has been fairly consistent, and it correlates closely with the social class of the electorate, as identified by income, occupation and education. An additional factor is ethnicity, as the majority of the immigrant population resides in relatively low-income areas. Western and inner-southern areas of Sydney always elect Labor candidates, and so do the north-western areas of Adelaide and the western suburbs of Melbourne. The opposite is true for the northern areas of Sydney, and for the eastern areas of Adelaide and Melbourne.

The denial of the significance of social class in Australia is cultivated by the new middle class of affluent professionals. Verity Burgmann and Andrew Milner, writing about 'New social movements in the class structure', make the following observation:

> The preponderance of intellectually trained people within the new social movements is precisely what has enabled and even required them to construct movement identities in increasingly overt opposition to class-based identity. These movements are organised and led, not by a random sample of all women, or all homosexuals, but precisely by a layer of intellectuals whose unrepresentative status actually follows a very clear pattern. That unrepresentativeness is most easily legitimated, both internally to the new social movements and externally to the outside world, if its significance – which is precisely the significance of class – is systematically denied. Femocrats have much less in common with female welfare recipients, gay studies academics with working class homosexuals, ethnic affairs advisers with unemployed immigrants, than the new social movements proclaim. The denial of class, initially faltering but gaining increased momentum, has articulated both the general class interests and concerns of those most active within the new social movements and the particular self-interests of new social movement leaders as alternative political elites. *Ironically, the theoretical retreat from class has expressed precisely the class interests of those advocating that retreat.*
>
> (1996:122; emphasis in the original)

Burgmann and Milner further comment that 'the logics of class soon overtook the new social movements, operating as they were within a capitalist system', and their class interests as socio-economically advantaged 'proved much more attractive and much more readily attainable than the kind of structural changes which might eliminate, or ameliorate, the inequalities suffered by the majority of the imagined community, and, notwithstanding any claims to the contrary, the new social movements have clearly not challenged the fundamentally class-divided nature of societies such as ours' (1996:122).

Social Problems and Postmodern Theories

How does our theory of social problems fit into, and be reconciled with, the various postmodernist theories? Or, if the tenability of our theory has been demonstrated, is it perhaps more appropriate to ask whether the perspective poses a test for those theories? Are the theories of postmodernity overstated by those enthusiasts who promote new ideas but eschew critique on the grounds that no such critique is possible because of the relativity of values and pursuits, as Rosenau (1992) has asked? A further question may be whether the notion of postmodernity appeals to the new middle classes because it serves to validate their various pursuits, and because it claims not only the rationality of those pursuits but also the support of the community, both legal as well as financial.

Mike Featherstone argues that 'to speak of modernity is to suggest an epochal shift or break from modernity involving the emergence of a new social totality with its own distinct organising principles' (1988:198). However, he points to the limitations of the concept by saying that:

> For those who welcome postmodernism as a mode of critical analysis which opens up ironies, inter-textuality and paradoxes, attempts to devise a theory of postmodern society or postmodernity, or delineate the role of postmodernism within the social order, are essentially flawed efforts to totalise or systemise. In effect they are authoritarian grand narratives which are ripe for playful deconstruction.
> *(1988:204–5)*

Featherstone further asserts that postmodernism 'is of interest to a wide range of artistic practices and social science and humanities disciplines because it directs our attention to changes taking place in contemporary culture' (1988:207–8). This orientation has been brought into the centre of social science disciplines, especially into sociology. Featherstone also adds that there is nothing that may be regarded as a unified 'postmodern social theory'. Rather, one is struck by the diversities between theories often lumped together as 'postmodern'. In reading various critics' contributions, one is also struck by the 'inadequate and undertheorised notion of the "postmodern" in various social theories which call themselves "postmodern", or are identified in such terms' (Kellner 1988:241). Habermas, for example, rejects the claims that postmodernism constitutes a break with history. Rather, he sees it as a neo-conservative ideology (1993:99–109). Kellner notes that 'It remains an open question for radical social and cultural theory today as to whether the alleged rupture in history asserted by postmodernists is itself ideological and reactionary' (Kellner 1988:266).

In social problems, the conservative nature of postmodernism is evident in the way such perspectives view social problems. Nowhere is the power structure challenged, and the fragmented arguments about inequalities among various group interests tend to revolve around inequalities 'within the class' that serve to reinforce class division because such 'internal struggles' enlarge the class membership and class advantage. This is certainly the case in the new middle class, which has grown in numbers, is highly differentiated and tension-ridden in its composition, and yet is conscious of its common interests and actively defends its advantage (Jamrozik 1991).

Among the helping professions, especially in social work, much is said about the need for social justice, but in the perspective of modernism, pursuit of social justice means pursuit of competition, pursuit of inequality. What is really meant by 'social justice'? Among the helping professions, mainly social workers, it is usually a concern about a particular population group, such as children, women, young people, the aged, immigrants or indigenous Australians. Concern about any such group is substantiated by defining the group as being in some ways 'disadvantaged'. If one follows the argument, in due course one finds that *any* group may be defined as disadvantaged in some way. Who then is 'advantaged'? The outcome of this approach is a form of competition, not unlike the competition in the 'free' market economy. First, for politicians this is very useful because they can align themselves with a group whose members are electorally important to them. This shows that disadvantage may be demonstrated on a number of dimensions. The choice of one dimension over another can show disadvantage. Second, all such groupings are stratified in terms of a socio-economic dimension. Inequality is multidimensional, and this means that inequality based on class structure is still fundamental in our society.

The Focus of the Helping Professions

The helping professions employed in human services claim their commitment is to the welfare of the people with whom they work – their 'clients'. In social work, one of the cherished beliefs is the belief in the value of clients' self-determination. The social reality is rather different. As Lena Dominelli observes, 'the "choice" "clients" are given is illusory; its proponents do not encourage challenges to a system which contributes to "client" distress' (1996:157). Social division between 'us' and 'them' in social workers' consciousness is clearly evident. The awareness of a conflict of interests and a corresponding antagonism is firmly in social workers' minds. Welfare agencies' offices are now provided with built-in security precautions not unlike those used in banks. Social workers' desks have panic buttons in case of personal attacks by clients. The conflict of interests is clear.

It is perhaps also ironic, but predictable, that the professionalisation of human services has served to reduce the effectiveness of those services – if 'effectiveness' means a higher level of social functioning among the recipient population. Because in their individualised intervention methods the helping professions focus almost entirely on the person, seeking an explanation of pathology and a 'cure' for the person, they no longer look to other community resources, formal or informal, that may be used to great effect. The shift in this direction has also strengthened the social control aspect of human service organisations.

Non-professionals, lacking therapeutic expertise, focus out of necessity on 'practical' remedies, which may indeed be more effective. A better use of the knowledge available in the social sciences, especially in sociology, would widen social workers' perspectives on social phenomena, thus enabling them to develop more effective intervention methods in direct service, and enabling them to participate in the analysis of (and thus influence) social and economic policy. It would enable them to better identify the sources of the problems their clients encounter, and communicate this knowledge to society through reports, literature and public debate.

CHAPTER 11

Conclusions and Implications

In writing this book, we have presented a theoretical perspective on social problems, which we think offers a framework for potentially fruitful sociological analyses of social problems, as well as a framework for more effective methods of intervention in social problems. This concluding chapter addresses some wider issues arising out of the causal relationship between society's pursuit of certain values and desirable goals, and the negative outcomes in the form of social problems that arise from such pursuits. We also attempt to identify from this causal relationship some implications for governments and for their policies of resource allocation, and to emphasise the benefits and corresponding costs of the promotion of certain values and corresponding goals. In pointing out that social problems constitute logical residual outcomes of the pursuit of certain values, interests and corresponding goals, our conclusion also indicates the need for the introduction of policies and methods of intervention that would be logically linked to the causative factors in social problems.

Times of Transition to the Unknown

Postindustrialism, post-Fordism, poststructuralism, postmodernism – all these terms suggest the end of a period, the exhaustion of ideas, and a transition to an unknown future. The extent of the unknown is so great that we have not yet found a name for it. It is a period of uncertainty, a period of unease.

The response in the social organisation of industrialised countries to this uncertainty is not so much a form of 'back to the future', but rather 'forward to the past'. The theory, or rather the dogma referred to as economic rationalism, as neo-classical economics, or as the ideology of the New Right, is nothing but the old idea of *laissez faire, laissez passer* that failed so badly early this century. Now, this theory, and the values it represents, are more powerful because since the demise of socialism there is no theoretical or ideological challenge to it, and it is also implemented with the backing of economic and political power, being supported internally in various states by governments and globally by transnational finance and trade arrangements.

These are also times of increasing coercion, descending in some aspects of social control into barbarism. The greatest democracy in the world, the United States, has reverted in some of its states to using capital punishment, which only a decade or so ago was declared by the Supreme Court of that country as a 'cruel and unusual punishment' and therefore unconstitutional. Like any system that lacks a defensible moral foundation, the excesses of the 'winners' are legitimated by increasingly punitive attitudes and policies towards the 'losers'.

These are also times of increasing distance between the majority of the population, who enjoy the good life that the market-dominated, consumption-oriented society can offer, and the growing minority of the increasingly marginalised 'underclass'. How successful is the market economy when in an affluent country like Australia over a quarter of the population must rely on public income support as its main source of income (see Chapter 7)? How large is this distance likely to become if the trend continues, considering that 30 years ago in the 1960s, only ten per cent of the population relied on public income support as their main source of income?

In considering the kinds of social problems generated by the contemporary industrialised 'free' market society, we need to be conscious that the market is indeed the dominant force. As Zygmunt Bauman observes:

> The role of the state is reduced to the employment of political means in the service of perpetuating the conditions for the domination of the market. The state is, first and foremost, an instrument of re-commodification ... the market becomes ... the principal mechanism of social integration. This role of the market promotes radical individualisation of the members of society; they are constituted as individuals by the market-generated translation of systemic need into private consumption.   *(1987:188–9)*

The market demonstrates success by ever-greater and more diverse consumption, while at the same time an increasing number of people become excluded from the market because of their inability to pay. It is this 'human residue' of the market economy that the state expects the helping professions to control through specialised knowledge and skill. This prevents the residue from becoming too troublesome, and

minimises the need for open coercion. A social worker, a friendly
counsellor, a helpful medical practitioner; these professions are prefer-
able to the police, but now the police are also trained in human
relations and counselling skills.

In the coming years, if the present trends in world politics and
economy continue, the pressures on the helping professions to play a
controlling, remedial and legitimating role will increase. With the likely
continued increase in social inequalities, social workers and suchlike will
be expected to contain the resentment of the 'surplus population' – the
'human residue', or 'underclass' – and act as instruments of social
control through their methods of 'helpful intervention' and surveillance, thus lessening the need for more overt methods of control.

In Australia, the policies of economic rationalism are narrowing
the national and international perspectives to the one dimension of
money and markets. There is an ongoing erosion of the public service
structure, systematically pursued by restricting public expenditure and
by conversion of public utilities into private for-profit activities. And
paralleled with this trend, there is a growing 'population surplus' of
long-term unemployed who see their chances of re-entering the labour
market fast diminishing. It is this 'human residue' that provides the field
of the helping professions, especially social work, with the task of
maintaining a compliant state.

The issues examined in this book raise some important questions for
researchers and teachers in the social sciences generally, and for
sociologists particularly. The issues also raise important corresponding
questions for the members of the professions working in human services
at all levels of the organisational hierarchy in social organisation. We
have demonstrated how social problems that arise out of dominant
values in society create a human residue that then has to be taken care
of by intervention methods that might have more features in common
with coercion and punishment than with care. However, we have also
demonstrated that problems experienced by individuals can also be
converted into political problems demanding political solutions. The
direction a response to a problem takes is determined by the ability of
the affected population to act collectively in maintaining political
pressure on governments to accept responsibility for the solution of the
problem.

The Role of Sociology

This knowledge turns our attention to the choices a sociologist may have
and may be willing to exercise in setting out to investigate a social problem. What approach will be taken, who will be the subject of the enquiry,

what questions will be pursued, how will the data be analysed and how will the results be disseminated? In a nutshell, the question is: how can sociology be a committed social science and simultaneously retain its intellectual objectivity? It is clear that society expects its social scientists not only to explain how certain social problems arise, but also how they can be solved, attenuated or controlled. It may be argued that any analysis that shows clearly the nature of social problems and their causative links to certain societal arrangements and/or pursuits will also point to the remedies, these being, as it were, embedded in the premises of the explanation. Whether society would accept the validity of any such explanation is another matter. If social problems arise as a logical outcome of cherished pursuits and dominant goals and values in society, then the abandonment of such goals and pursuits is unlikely without a profound change in the structure of power and corresponding pursuits and values.

A very important issue in sociology, identified by Gouldner in 1971, is the absence of the knowledge among sociologists of themselves, of what they are doing, why they are doing it, and with what effects. Gouldner argued that self-reflection in sociology, as in all social sciences, was needed urgently so that the gap between the theorists and researchers and the people 'out there' could be removed. He argued that:

> A systematic and dogged insistence upon seeing ourselves as we would see others would ... transform not only our view of ourselves but also our view of others. We would increasingly recognise the depth of our kinship with those whom we study. They would no longer be viewable as alien others or as mere objects for our superior technique and insight; they could, instead, be seen as brother sociologists, each attempting with his varying degree of skill, energy, and talent to understand social reality.   *(1971:490)*

It is true that social scientists tend to study 'the others' rather than studying 'ourselves'. There is a multitude of studies of 'deviance', of 'the poor' or of 'the disadvantaged', but relatively few systematically conducted studies of the affluent and of the powerful. Class division begins with the theoretical and value assumptions of the researchers.

The Role of the Helping Professions

Gouldner's argument certainly applies to all social actors in the studies of and interventions in social problems, and especially to the latter. Intervention methods are carried out with a dual authority – the authority of the profession and its specialised knowledge, sanctioned by the state; and the authority of the state itself expressed in statutory acts and the state power delegated to or vested in the professions to exercise it on the state's behalf.

A close relationship between sociology and social work is certainly indicated as a prerequisite. In some ways, this would mean a return to the early days of both disciplines when sociology and social work were drawing on the same source of ideas, both being driven by the desire to make society a better place in which to live (Heraud 1970). Each discipline has something to offer the other discipline, and both would be better for it if they exercised this reciprocity.

At present, the input of sociology into the curricula on social policy, social administration and social work is minimal. It is treated as a marginal input of some interest but without the possibility of systematic application and operationalisation in practice. This situation persists because of the narrow perspectives and lack of vision in both disciplines. Sociologists fear that addressing 'practical' issues would demean the value of the discipline as a social science, and social workers continue to focus their endeavours almost entirely on their version of the medical model, while questioning that model in their rhetoric. The situation carries a dose of irony, as this 'modelling' continues in social work while the medical profession seeks to widen its methods of operation and addresses issues of health at the level of policy and administration of public health.

The task for the professionals in human services must be to reassess the theoretical bases of their methods of intervention and develop effective means of operationalising such theories in their methods of intervention. Professionals (and the services they provide and/or use) need to abandon the remedial mode and focus on the maintenance and enhancement of societal informal structures. This paradigm shift would first require a shift at the level of theorising and corresponding teaching in professional courses.

Social work and related occupations are of particular importance here. For social workers to effectively implement the values they have claimed to pursue, they would have to 'bring back the social' into their intervention methods, in the full meaning of the term. Social workers have never managed to achieve this aim very far beyond the rhetoric, but this does not mean that such achievement is not possible in the future.

This is the challenge that the helping professions, especially social workers, have to face. To meet this challenge, these professions will need to re-assess their role in the social sciences, especially in sociology, both as the users of knowledge generated in these sciences and even more as contributors to the knowledge in these sciences. The helping professions' (especially social workers') contribution of knowledge to the social sciences has considerable potential to enhance the scientific base of sociology, as well as establish its value base, which will then enable sociology to contribute more effectively to society's well-being. This was the role the founding fathers and mothers of sociology and social work envisaged for these disciplines, and this is the role to which these disciplines need to return. In the currently dominant political and economic climate a return to this role will not be easy, but such a climate will not remain dominant forever because the human cost it generates will in the foreseeable future become too great for society to bear.

Sociologists and the helping professions must speed up the process of change. Greater sociological input into the educational curricula of the helping professions, especially social work and closely related occupations, has great potential to enhance the development of intervention methods that have much greater effectiveness than the current individualistic methods. On this issue, Znaniecki wrote that 'The ultimate test of social theory ... will be its application in practice, and thus its generalisations will also be subject in the last resort to the check of a possible failure. However, practical application is not experimentation' (1969:105). On the integrity of research, Bjorn Wittrock's comment is apposite, when he says:

> In an age in which the call for involvement sounds more demanding and persistent than ever and in which the reasons for engagement may be greater than ever and aloofness and disengagement may often be just another word for cynicism, some scholars must still remain true to the need for critical distance and speak truth, whether power is listening or not.   *(1985:107)*

We cannot think of a better and more appropriate message to communicate to our readers than this expression of courage and integrity.

Bibliography

Abbott, T. (1990) 'The real issue is the changing face of our society', *The Australian*, 31 May

Albrow, M. (1996) *The Global Age: State and Society Beyond Modernity*, Cambridge: Polity Press

Alexander, J. (1983) *Services to Families: With Many a Slip*, Melbourne: Institute of Family Studies

Alexander, J. C. (1995) *Fin de Siécle, Social Theory: Relativism, Reduction and the Problem of Reason*, London: Verso

Alexander, J. C. and Sztompka, P. (eds) (1990) *Rethinking Progress: Movements, Forces and Ideas at the End of the 20th Century*, London: Unwin Hyman

Anderson, M. (1980) *Approaches to the History of the Western Family 1500–1914*, London: Macmillan

Angus, G. and Wilkinson, S. (1993) *Child Abuse and Neglect, Australia 1990–91*, Canberra: Australian Institute of Health and Welfare

Angus, G. and Woodward, S. (1995) *Child Abuse and Neglect, Australia 1993–94*, Canberra: Australian Institute of Health and Welfare

Archard, D. (1993) *Children: Rights and Childhood*, London: Routledge

Aristotle (1962) *The Politics*, translated by T. A. Sinclair, Harmondsworth: Penguin

Aronowitz, S. (1992) *The Politics of Identity: Class, Culture, Social Movements*, New York: Routledge

Ash, R. (1973) *Talking About the Family*, London: Wayland

Attorney-General's Department (1994) *Crime and Justice in South Australia 1993*, Adelaide: with authors

Australian Broadcasting Corporation (1997) *Frontier*, Television Documentary, 2, 9, 16 March

Australian Bureau of Statistics (1978, 1980, 1984) *Social Indicators No. 2, 3, 4*, Catalogue No. 4101.0

(1986) *The Labour Force Australia, Historical Summary, 1966–1984*, Catalogue No. 6204.0

(1991) *Census of Population and Housing: Basic Community Profile*, Catalogue No. 2722.0

(1994) *Child Care Australia, June 1993*, Catalogue No. 4402.0

(1994) *Focus on Families: Demographic and Family Formation*, Catalogue No. 4420.0

(1996) *The Labour Force Australia, August 1996*, Catalogue No. 6203.0

(1996) *Transition from Education to Work*, May 1996, Australia, Catalogue No. 6227.0

(1996) *Income Distribution Australia 1994–95*, Catalogue No. 6523.0

Australian Institute of Criminology (1996) *Australian Criminal Justice Statistics – at a glance*, Canberra: with authors

Australian Institute of Family Studies (1995) *International Directory of IYF Research Activities*, Melbourne: Australian Institute of Family Studies

Barrett, M. and McIntosh, M. (1982) *The Anti-social Family*, London: Verso

Bartholomew, J. (1995) 'How misguided politicians are obliterating the family', *Daily Mail*, June 10: 12.2–4, London

Baudrillard, J. (1983) *In the Shadow of the Silent Majorities*, New York: Semiotext

Bauman, Z. (1987) *Legislators and Interpreters: on Modernity, Post-modernity and Intellectuals*, Cambridge: Polity Press

(1989) 'Sociological responses to postmodernity', *Thesis Eleven*, 23: 35–63

(1992) *Intimations of Postmodernity*, London: Routledge

(1995) *Life in Fragments: Essays in Postmodern Morality*, Oxford: Basil Blackwell

Beck, U. (1989) 'On the way to the industrial risk-society? Outline of an argument', *Thesis Eleven*, 23: 86–103

(1992) *Risk Society: Towards a New Modernity*, London: Sage

Becker, H. S. (1963) *Outsiders: Studies in the Sociology of Deviance*, New York: Free Press

(1967) 'Whose side are we on?' *Social Problems*, 14 (3): 239–47

Beckett, K. (1996) 'Culture and the politics of signification: the case of child sexual abuse', *Social Problems*, 43 (1) February: 57–76

Berger, B. (1995) *The Social Roots of Prosperity: Twelfth Annual John Bonython Lecture*, Sydney: The Centre for Independent Studies

Berger, B. and Berger, P. L. (1985) *The War Over the Family*, New York: Basic Books

Berger, P. L. and Luckmann, T. (1966) *The Social Construction of Reality: a Treatise in the Sociology of Knowledge*, Harmondsworth: Penguin

Best, J. (ed.) (1989) *Images of Issues: Typifying Contemporary Social Problems*, New York: Aldine de Gruyter

Blankenhorn, D., Bayme, S. and Elshtain, J. B. (1990) (eds) *Rebuilding the Nest: a New Commitment to the American Family*, Wisconsin: Family Services America

Blumer, H. (1971) 'Social problems as collective behaviour', *Social Problems*, 18: 298–306

Boland, C. and Jamrozik, A. (1989) *Young People and Health: An Overview of Current Research*, Report to the National Youth Affairs Research Scheme, Hobart: National Clearing House for Youth Studies

Boreham, T. (1997) 'Going for broke', *The Australian*, 7 March

Brennan, D. (1994) *The Politics of Australian Child Care: From Philanthropy to Feminism*, Cambridge: Cambridge University Press

Burgmann, V. and Milner, A. (1996) 'Intellectuals and the new social movements', in R. Kuhn and T. O'Lincoln (eds) *Class and Class Conflict in Australia*, Melbourne: Longman

Burton, J. (1979) *Deviance, Terrorism and War: The Process of Solving Unsolved Social and Political Problems*, Canberra: Australian National University Press

Butler, T. and Savage, M. (eds) (1995) *Social Change and the Middle Classes*, London: UCL Press
Cicourel, A. V. (1968) *The Social Organisation of Juvenile Justice*, London: Heinemann
Clement, W. and Myles, J. (1994) *Relations of Ruling: Class and Gender in Post-industrial Societies*, Montreal: McGill-Queen's University Press
Cloward, R. A. and Ohlin, L. E. (1960) *Delinquency and Opportunity*, New York: Free Press
Cohen, S. (1985) *Visions of Social Control: Crime, Punishment and Classification*, Oxford: Polity Press and Blackwell
Coleman, J. S. (1991) 'Prologue: constructed social organisation', in P. Bourdieu and J. S. Coleman (eds) *Social Theory for a Changing Society*, New York: Russell Sage
      (1993) 'The rational reconstruction of society', *American Sociological Review*, 58, February: 1–15
Commission of Inquiry into Poverty (1975) *Poverty in Australia*, First Main Report, Canberra: Australian Government Publishing Service
Commonwealth Government (1996) *Budget Statements, Paper No. 1*, Canberra: Australian Government Publishing Service
Connelly, M. and Kennedy, P. (1994) 'Must it be the rest against the West?', *The Atlantic Monthly*, December: 61–90
Crompton, R. (1993) *Class and Stratification: An Introduction to Current Debates*, Cambridge: Polity Press
Daniel, A. (1990) *Medicine and the State: Professional Autonomy and Public Accountability*, Sydney: Allen and Unwin
Davis, L. (1991) 'Inequality and family policy' in R. Sharp (ed.) *Inequality in Australia: The Social Justice Collective*, Melbourne: William Heinemann
De Graffenried, C. (1896–97) 'Some social economic problems', *American Journal of Sociology*, 2 (2), July 1896–May 1897:190–201
Department for Community Welfare (1978) *Annual Report for the Year 1977–78*, Adelaide: Government Printer
Department for Family and Community Services (1994, 1996) *Annual Reports 1993–1994, 1995–1996*, Adelaide: Family and Community Services
Department of Health and Family Services (1996) *Strengthening Families*, statement by Judi Moylan, Minister for Family Services, Canberra: Commonwealth Government Publishing Service
Department of Immigration and Multicultural Affairs (1996) *Access and Equity: Annual Report 1996*, Canberra: Australian Government Publishing Service
Department of Social Security (1975, 1991) *Annual Reports 1974–75, 1990–91*, Canberra: Australian Government Publishing Service
Docherty, T. (ed.) *Postmodernism: A Reader*, New York: Harvester Wheatsheaf
Dominelli, L. (1996) 'De-professionalising social work: anti-oppressive practice, competencies and postmodernism', *British Journal of Social Work*, 26 (2): 153–75
Donnison, D. and Chapman, V. (1965) *Social Policy and Administration*, London: Allen and Unwin
Donzelot, J. (1979) *The Policing of Families: Welfare Versus the State*, translated by R. Hurley, London: Hutchinson
Dore, C. (1997) 'MP's basic wage soars 70pc in decade', *Australian*, 8–9 March
Edgar, D. and Maas, F. (1984) 'Adolescent competence, leaving home and changing family patterns', in The Australian Institute of Family Studies (1984) *XXth International CFR Seminar on Social Change and Family Policies: Key Papers (Part 2)*, Melbourne

Edwards, A. (1988) *Regulation and Repression*, Sydney: Allen and Unwin
Eldridge, J. (1986) 'Facets of "relevance" in sociological research', in F. Heller (ed.) *op. cit.*, 171–83
Encel, D. (1989) *Unemployment in Australia: An Annotated Bibliography, 1983–1988*, SWRC Research Resource Series, No. 6, Kensington: University of New South Wales
Encel, S. (1970) *Equality and Authority: A Study of Class, Status and Power in Australia*, Melbourne: Cheshire
Erikson, R. (1993) 'Descriptions of inequality: the Swedish approach to welfare research', in M. Nussbaum and O. Sen (eds) *op. cit.*, 67–83
Esping-Andersen, G. (1990) *The Three Worlds of Welfare Capitalism*, Cambridge: Polity Press
Etzioni-Halevy, E. (1990) 'The relative autonomy of èlites: the absorption of protest and social progress in western democracies', in J. C. Alexander and P. Sztompka (eds) *op. cit.*
Featherstone, M. (1988) 'In the pursuit of postmodern: an introduction', *Theory, Culture and Society*, 5 (2–3), June: 195–215
Fook, J. (1993) *Radical Casework: A Theory of Practice*, Sydney: Allen and Unwin
Forbes, C. (1997) 'Scant figures hide dark side of chance', *The Australian*, 28 January
Foucault, M. (1977) *Discipline and Punish: The Birth of the Prison*, Harmondsworth: Penguin
Frankfurt Institute for Social Research (1972) *Aspects of Sociology*, Boston: Beacon Books
Freidson, E. (1986) *Professional Powers: A Study of the Institutionalisation of Formal Knowledge*, Chicago: University of Chicago Press
Fuller, R. C. and Myers, R. R. (1941a) 'Some aspects of a theory of social problems', *American Sociological Review*, 6, February, 24–32
(1941b) 'The natural history of a social problem', *American Sociological Review*, 6, June: 320–8
Galbraith, J. K. (1958) *The Affluent Society*, London: Hamish Hamilton
Gallie, D. (1994) 'Are the unemployed an underclass? Some evidence from the social change and economic life initiative', *Sociology*, 28 (3):737–57
Gil, D. (1976) *The Challenge of Social Equality: Essays on Social Policy, Social Development and Political Practice*, Cambridge, Mass: Schenkman
Gilbert, N. (1995) *Welfare Justice: Restoring Social Equity*, New Haven: Yale University Press
Gilding, M. (1991) *The Making and Breaking of the Australian Family*, St Leonards: Allen and Unwin
Gittins, D. (1985) *The Family in Question: Changing Households and Familiar Ideologies*, London: Macmillan
Goffman, E. (1961) *Asylums: Essays on the Social Situation of Mental Patients and other Inmates*, Harmondsworth: Penguin
Goodin, R. E. and Le Grand, J. (1987) *Not Only the Poor: The Middle Classes and the Welfare State*, London: Allen and Unwin
Gouldner, A. W. (1971) *The Coming Crisis of Western Sociology*, London: Heinemann
(1975) *For Sociology: Renewal and Critique in Sociology Today*, Harmondsworth: Penguin
Government of South Australia (1993) *Children's Protection Act 1993*, Adelaide: Government Printer
Graycar, A. and Jamrozik, A. (1993) *How Australians Live: Social Policy in Theory and Practice*, Second Edition, Melbourne: Macmillan

Gregory, R. G. (1993) 'Would reducing wages of the low paid restore full employment to Australia?' in P. Saunders and S. Shaver (eds) *Theory and Practice in Australian Social Policy: Rethinking the Fundamentals*, SPRC Reports and Proceedings No. 111, Sydney: University of New South Wales, 93–108

Gusfield, J. R. (1989) 'Constructing the ownership of social problems: fun and profit in the welfare state', *Social Problems*, 36 (5) December: 431–41

Gutting, G. (ed.) (1994) *The Cambridge Companion to Foucault*, Cambridge: Cambridge University Press

Habermas, J. (1989) *The Structural Transformation of the Public Sphere: An Inquiry into a Category of Bourgeois Society*, Cambridge, Mass: MIT Press
(1993) 'Modernity – an incomplete project', in T. Docherty (ed.) *op. cit.*, 99–109

Haferkamp, H. (ed.) (1989) *Social Structure and Culture*, Berlin: de Gruyter

Hallberg, M. and Rigne, E. M. (1994) 'Child sexual abuse – a study of controversy and construction', *Acta Sociologica*, 37: 141–63

Hassan, R. and Jamrozik, A. (1996) *An Open Door or Fortress Australia: Policy Choices for Australia in the 21st Century*, Discussion Paper No. 352, Centre for Economic Policy Research, Canberra: Australian National University

Heller, F. (ed.) (1986) *The Use and Abuse of Social Science*, London: Sage Publications

Henderson, R. F., Harcourt, A. and Harper, R. J. A. (1970) *People in Poverty: A Melbourne Study*, Melbourne: Cheshire

Heraud, B. (1970) *Sociology and Social Work: Perspectives and Problems*, Oxford: Pergamon

Hirsch, F. (1977) *Social Limits to Growth*, London: Routledge & Kegan Paul

Hirsch, P., Michaels, S. and Friedman, R. (1987) ' "Dirty hands" versus "clean models": is sociology in danger of being seduced by economics?', *Theory and Society*, 16: 317–36

Hood, M. (1997) *The Social Construction of Child Abuse: In Australia and South Australia*, unpublished PhD Thesis, Adelaide: University of South Australia

Howe, D. (1992) 'Child abuse and the bureaucratisation of social work', *Sociological Review*, 40 (3): 491–508

Ife, J. (1991) 'Social policy and the Green movement', *Australian Quarterly*, 63 (3) Spring: 336–46
(1995) *Community Development: Creating Community Alternatives – Vision, Analysis and Practice*, Melbourne: Longman
(1997) *Rethinking Social Work: Towards Critical Practice*, Melbourne: Longman

Ironmonger, D. (ed.) (1989) *Households Work: Productive Activities, Women and Income in the Household Economy*, Sydney: Allen and Unwin

Jamrozik, A. (1989) 'The household economy and social class', in D. Ironmonger, *op. cit.*, 64–78
(1991) *Class, Inequality and the State: Social Change, Social Policy and the New Middle Class*, Melbourne: Macmillan
(1992) 'Managing the policy process: issues for the '90s', *Australian Journal of Public Administration*, 51 (1) March: 1–9

Jamrozik, A. and Boland, C. (1993) *Human Resources in Community Services: Conceptual Issues and Empirical Evidence*, SPRC Reports and Proceedings No. 104, Kensington: University of New South Wales

Jamrozik, A., Boland, C. and Urquhart, R. (1995) *Social Change and Cultural Transformation in Australia*, Cambridge: Cambridge University Press

Jamrozik, A. and Sweeney, T. (1996) *Children and Society: The Family, the State and Social Parenthood*, Melbourne: Macmillan

Johnson, T. J. (1972) *Professions and Power*, London: Macmillan

Keating, P. (1994) *Working Nation: The White Paper on Employment and Growth*, Canberra: Australian Government Publishing Service

Keating, P., Baldwin, P. and Crowley, R. (1995) *An Agenda for Families*, Canberra: Australian Government Publishing Service

Kellner, D. (1988) 'Postmodernism as social theory: some challenges and problems', *Theory, Culture and Society*, 5 (2–3) June: 240–69

Kelly, P. (1997) 'The curse of the M-Word', *The Australian*, 30–31 August

Kempe, C. H., Silverman, F., Steele, B., Droegemueller, W. and Silver, H. (1961) 'The battered child syndrome', *Journal of the American Medical Association*, 181 (11): 17–24

Korpi, W. (1983) *The Democratic Class Struggle*, London: Routledge & Kegan Paul

Kumar, K. (1995) *From Post-industrial to Post-modern Society: New Theories of the Contemporary World*, Oxford: Blackwell

Kymlicka, W. (1995) *Multicultural Citizenship*, Oxford: Clarendon Press

Lauer, R. H. (1976) 'Defining social problems: public and professional perspectives', *Social Problems*, 24 (1) October: 122–30

Le Grand, J. (1984) 'The future of the welfare state', *New Society*, 7 June: 385–86

Legge, K. (1996) 'Jackpot society', *The Weekend Australian*, 6–7 April, Review 1–2

Leslie, G. (1967) *The Family in Social Context*, New York: Oxford University Press

Lewis, J. (ed.) (1993) *Women and Social Policies in Europe: Work, the Family and the State*, Vermont: Edward Elgar

Lindenfeld, F. (ed.) (1973) *Radical Perspectives on Social Problems*, Second Edition, New York: Macmillan

Lyotard, J. (1984) *The Postmodern Condition: A Report on Knowledge*, Minneapolis: University of Minnesota Press
(1993) 'Answering the question: what is postmodernism?', in T. Docherty (ed.) *op. cit.*, 38–46

McCaughey, J. (1987) *A Bit of a Struggle: Coping with Family Life in Australia*, Fitzroy: McPhee Gribble/Penguin Books

McCrann, T. (1996) 'Why the wages of sin is a GST', *The Weekend Australian*, 30–31 March: 28
(1997) 'Lloyd's big gamble', *The Australian*, 8–9 March

McMichael, A. J. (1993) *Planetary Overload: Global Environmental Change and the Health of the Human Species*, Cambridge: Cambridge University Press

Maas, F. (1984) *Should Families be a Focus for Policies?* Melbourne: Institute of Family Studies

Macleay, J. (1997) 'It's the Economy, stupid', *The Australian*, 10 April

Manis, J. G. (1976) *Analysing Social Problems*, New York: Praeger

Marshall, G. and Swift, A. (1993) 'Social class and social justice', *British Journal of Sociology*, 44 (2): 187–211

Marshall, T. H. (1981) *The Right to Welfare and Other Essays*, London: Heinemann

Martin, L. and Kettner, P. M. (1996) *Measuring the Performance of Human Services*, Thousand Oaks, California: Sage

Matza, D. (1969) *Becoming Deviant*, Englewood Cliffs: Prentice-Hall

May, T. (1996) *Situating Social Theory*, Buckingham UK: Open University Press

Merton, R. K. (1957) *Social Theory and Social Structure*, Revised and Enlarged Edition, New York: Free Press

(1976) 'Introduction: The Sociology of Social Problems', in R. K. Merton and R. Nisbet (eds) *op. cit.*

Merton, R. K. and Nisbet, R. (eds) (1976) *Contemporary Social Problems*, Fourth Edition, New York: Harcourt Brace Jovanovich

Miller, D. and Walzer, M. (eds) (1995) *Pluralism, Justice and Equality*, New York: Oxford University Press

Miller, S. M. (1976) 'The political economy of social problems: from the sixties to the seventies', Social Problems, 24 (1): 131–41

Mills, C. Wright (1943) 'The professional ideology of social pathologies', *American Journal of Sociology*, 49 (2): 165–80

(1959, 1970) *The Sociological Imagination*, Harmondsworth: Penguin

Milner, A. (1991) *Contemporary Cultural Theory: An Introduction*, Sydney: Allen and Unwin

Mongardini, C. (1990) 'The decadence of modernity: the delusion of progress and the search for historical conciousness', in J. C. Alexander and P. Sztompka (eds) *op. cit.*

Morris, L. (1995) *Social Divisions: Economic Decline and Social Structural Change*, London: University College London

Mowrer, E. R. (1941) 'Methodological problems in social disorganisation', *American Sociological Review*, 6 (6) December: 839–52

Murray, C. (1984) *Losing Ground: American Social Policy, 1950–1980*, New York: Basic Books

National Council for the International Year of the Family (1994a) *The Heart of the Matter*, Canberra: Australian Government Publishing Service

(1994b) *Creating the Links: Families and Social Responsibility*, Canberra: Australian Government Publishing Service

National Multicultural Advisory Council (1995) *Multicultural Australia: The Next Steps Towards and Beyond 2000*, Volume 2, Canberra: Australian Government Publishing Service

Nocella, L. (1994) *The Changing Nature of Juvenile Justice in South Australia: Is There a Place for Social Work?*, unpublished BSW Honours Thesis: University of South Australia

(1996) *Restorative Family Services: A New Approach to Family Assistance or Mutton Dressed up as Lamb?*, paper presented at the Fifth Australian Family Research Conference, Australian Institute of Family Studies, Brisbane, 1996

Nussbaum, M. C. and Sen, O. (eds) (1993) *The Quality of Life*, Oxford: Oxford University Press

O'Connor, J. (1973) *The Fiscal Crisis of the State*, London: St James Press

Offe, C. (1984) *Contradictions of the Welfare State*, London: Hutchinson

(1985) *Disorganised Capitalism: Contemporary Transformations of Work and Politics*, Cambridge, Mass: MIT Press

Office of Multicultural Affairs (1989) *National Agenda for a Multicultural Australia . . . Sharing our Future*, Canberra: Australian Government Publishing Service

O'Neill, J. (1996) 'These million-dollar executives: are they worth it?', *Independent Monthly*, June: 24–33

Organisation for Economic Co-operation and Development (1981) *The Welfare State in Crisis*, Paris: OECD

Park, R. E., Burgess, E. W. and McKenzie, R. D. (1967/1925) *The City*, with an introduction by M. Janowitz, Chicago: University of Chicago Press

Parliament of the Commonwealth of Australia (1994) *Australia's 'Carrying Capacity': One Nation – Two Ecologies*, Canberra: Australian Government Publishing Service

Pinkney, S. (1995) 'Fights over "family": competing discourses in the two decades before the International Year of the Family', *Just Policy*, 2: 17–25

Przeworski, A. (1977) 'Proletariat into a class: the process of class formation from Karl Kautsky's "The Class Struggle" to recent controversies', *Politics and Society*, 7: 343–401

Pusey, M. (1991) *Economic Rationalism in Canberra: A Nation Building State Changes its Mind*, Cambridge: Cambridge University Press

Queen, S. A. (1941) 'The concepts social disorganisation and social participation', *American Sociological Review*, 6 (3) June: 307–16

Quinney, R. (1977) *Class, State and Crime*, Second Edition, New York: Longman

Randall, C. D. (1896) 'The Michigan system of child saving', *American Journal of Sociology*, 1 (5): 710–24

Raskall, P. (1994) *Perks of the Job: The Distribution of Non-cash Income in Australia in the 1980s*, Study of Social and Economic Inequalities, SSEI Monograph No. 5, Sydney: University of New South Wales

Rees, S. (1991) *Achieving Power: Practice and Policy in Social Welfare*, Sydney: Allen and Unwin

Rein, M. (1970) *Social Policy: Issues of Choice and Change*, New York: Random House

(1976) *Social Science and Public Policy*, Harmondsworth: Penguin

(1983) *From Policy To Practice*, London: Macmillan

Ringen, S. (1995) 'Well-being, measurement and preferences', *Acta Sociologica*, 38: 3–15

Roll, J. (1991) 'One in ten: lone parent families in the European community', *Social Policy Review*, 1990–91

Rosenau, P. M. (1992) *Post-modernism and the Social Sciences: Insights, Inroads and Intrusions*, Princeton New Jersey: Princeton University Press

Rouse, J. (1994) 'Power/knowledge' in G. Gutting (ed.), *op. cit.*, 92–114

Rubington, E. and Weinberg, M. S. (eds) (1995) *The Study of Social Problems: Seven Perspectives*, Fifth Edition, New York: Oxford University Press

Santiago, A. S. (1993) 'Comments from the special collection editor: global perspectives on social problems – current issues and debates', *Social Problems*, 40 (2) May: 207–11

Segal, L. (1983) (ed.) *What is to be Done About the Family: Crisis in the Eighties*, Ringwood: Penguin Books

Sheppard, M. (1995) 'Social work, social science and practice wisdom', *British Journal of Social Work*, 25 (3) June: 265-93

Small, A. W. (1898) 'The methodology of the social problem: Division 1. The sources and uses of material', *American Journal of Sociology*, 4 (1): 113–14

Smart, B. (1992) *Modern Conditions, Postmodern Controversies*, London: Routledge

Smith, G. (1995) *Unemployment and Social Control: The Role of Social Work in the Judicial Process*, unpublished BSW Honours Thesis: University of South Australia

Spector, M. and Kitsuse, J. I. (1987) Constructing Social Problems, New York: de Gruyter

Spicker, P. (1995) *Social Policy: Themes and Approaches*, London: Prentice Hall-Harvester Wheatsheaf

Sutherland, E. H. and Cressey, D. R. (1978) *Principles of Criminology*, Fourth Edition, Philadelphia: J. B. Lippincott

Svallfors, S. (1995) 'The end of class politics? Cleavages and attitudes to Swedish welfare policies', *Acta Sociologica*, 38: 53–74

Sweeney, T. (1989) 'Inequalities in our provisions for young children' in R. Kennedy (ed.) *Australian Welfare: Historical Sociology*, Melbourne: Macmillan, 304–328

Sweeney, T. and Jamrozik, A. (1982) *Services to Young Children: Welfare Service or Social Parenthood*, SWRC Reports and Proceedings, No. 19, Kensington: University of New South Wales

  (1984) *Perspectives in Child Care: Experiences of Parents and Service Providers*, SWRC Reports and Proceedings, No. 44, Kensington: University of New South Wales

Swift, A. (1995) 'The sociology of complex equality', in D. Miller and M. Walzer (eds) *op. cit.*

Theobald, R. (1965) *Free Men and Free Markets*, New York: Doubleday

Theory, Culture and Society (1988) Postmodernism, Special Issue, 5 (2–3) June

Therborn, G. (1976) *Science, Class and Society: On the formulation of Sociology and Historical Materialism*, London: New Left Books

Townsend, P. (1979) *Poverty in the United Kingdom: A Survey of Household Resources and Standards of Living*, Harmondsworth: Penguin

Trattner, W. I. (1979) *From Poor Law to Welfare State: A History of Social Welfare in Australia*, Second Edition, New York: Free Press

Travers, P. and Richardson S. (1993) *Living Decently: Material Well-being in Australia*, Melbourne: Oxford University Press

Turner, B. S. (1986) *Equality*, Chichester: Ellis Harwood

Vidich, A. J. (ed.) (1995) *The New Middle Classes: Life-styles, Status Claims and Political Orientations*, London: Macmillan

Wacquant, L. J. D. (1996) 'The rise of advanced marginality: notes on its nature and implications', *Acta Sociologica*, 39 (2): 121–39

Walker, J. (1992) *Australian Prisoners 1991*, Canberra: Australian Institute of Criminology

Walzer, M. (1983) *Spheres of Justice: A Defence of Pluralism and Equality*, Oxford: Basil Blackwell

Weeks, W. and Wilson, J. (1995) (eds) *Issues Facing Australian Families: Human Services Respond*, Melbourne: Longman

Weiss, C. H. (1986) 'Research and policy-making: a limited partnership', in F. Heller (ed.) *op. cit.*, 214–35

White, S. K. (1991) *Political Theory and Postmodernism*, Cambridge: Cambridge University Press

Whitlam, G. (1985) *The Whitlam Government 1972–1975*, Ringwood: Viking

Whitmore, R. (1984) 'Modelling the policy/implementation distinction: the case of child abuse', *Policy and Politics*, 12 (3) July: 241–67

Wilensky, H. L. and Lebeaux, C. N. (1958) *Industrial Society and Social Welfare*, New York: Russell Sage Publications

Williams, F. (1989) *Social Policy: An Introduction: Issues of Race, Gender and Class*, Cambridge: Polity Press

Wittrock, B. (1985) 'Knowledge and policy: eight models of interaction', in H. Nowotny and J. Lambiri-Dimaki (eds) *The Difficult Dialogue Between Producers and Users of Social Science Research*, Vienna: European Centre for Social Welfare Training and Research

Woodroofe, K. (1962) *From Charity to Social Work in England and America*, London: Routledge & Kegan Paul

Young, L., Baker, J. and Monnone, J. (1989) *Poverty and Child Abuse in the Sydney Metropolitan Area*, Child Abuse and Neglect Programme Paper No. 6, Sydney: Department of Family and Children's Services

Znaniecki, F. (1969) *On Humanistic Sociology*, Selected Papers, edited by R. Bierstedt, Chicago: University of Chicago Press

Zolberg, A. R. (1989) 'The next wave: migration theory for a changing world', *International Migration Review*, 23, Fall: 403–30

—— (1991) 'Bounded states in a global market: the uses of international labour migration', in P. Bourdieu and J. S. Coleman (eds) *Social Theory for a Changing Society*, New York: Russell Sage

Index

Abbott, T. 111–12
Aboriginal people 110, 155, 161, 192, 203;
  see also culture; indigenous;
  populations
abortion 151, 185; views on 67
abstraction, level of 9, 29
academics 68–71, 96
access 38, 124
Access and Equity program 113–14, 203
actions 1, 11, 66
activities: mainstream 5; regulated 187;
  social 26; state-promoted 8; *see also*
  three-level activity
Adams, Phillip 72
adjustments, marginal 6
administration 46, 49, 185, 189;
  administrators 11; *see also* three-level
  structure; intervention
adolescence 192
adversarial legal system 36, 193–4
advisory services 121
affected populations 4, 6, 14, 39, 44, 46,
  47, 49, 50, 58, 62, 104, 106, 148, 192,
  200–1, 204; compliance of 204
African-Americans 25
age 4, 5, 131
Age, The 72
Agenda for a Multicultural Australia 203
Agenda for Families 167
Albrow, M. 81
Alexander, Jeffrey 33, 160
American bias in social sciences 2, 78
American Declaration of Independence
  130
American Dream, the 27
American Society for the Study of Social
  Problems 13, 29, 69, 72

American Sociological Association 69
analysis, sociological 2
ancien régime 154, 172
Anderson, M. 151
Anglo-Australians 12, 21, 203
Angus, G. 116, 117–18
anomie: social 77; theory 2, 26–7
Aquinas, Thomas 130
Archard, D. 119–20
Aristotle 130, 131
Aronowitz, S. 111
arrangements: societal 1, 4, 128; structural
  6, 27, 31
arrest 182, 192
Ash, R. 164, 165
Asia 12, 209; 'Asianisation' 21
assumptions, *see* theory
Athenian city-state 130
attitudes 1, 194
Attorney-General's Department 192
Australian, The 72
Australian Association of Social Workers
  (AASW) 63
Australian Broadcasting Corporation
  (ABC) 72, 111
Australian Bureau of Statistics (ABS) 100,
  134, 159
Australian Family Law Court 36
Australian High Court 112
Australian Institute of Criminology 193
Australian Institute of Family Studies 168
Australian Medical Association (AMA) 63
authority: professional 55, 73–4; public 154

barbarism 215
Barrett, M. 158, 163, 164, 165, 169, 179n
Bartholomew, J. 165